# ESTATE PLANNING

THE NEW GOLDEN OPPORTUNITIES

# ESTATE PLANNING

## THE NEW GOLDEN OPPORTUNITIES

**ROBERT S. HOLZMAN, Ph.D.**

**BOARDROOM® BOOKS**
500 Fifth Avenue, New York, New York 10110

Fourth Printing

Boardroom Books publishes the advice of expert authorities in many fields. But the use of a book is not a
substitute for legal, accounting, or other professional services. Consult a competent professional for answers to
your specific questions.


**Library of Congress Cataloging in Publication Data**
Holzman, Robert S.
    Estate planning.

    Includes index.
    1. Estate planning—United States.
2. Inheritance and transfer tax—Law and
legislation—United States. 3. Gifts—
Taxation—Law and legislation—United States.
I. Title.
KF750.H588     1982     343.7305′3     82-12942
ISBN 0-932648-31-2     347.30353


Printed in the United States of America

# THEME OF THIS BOOK

For many years, most estate planners thought that the name of the game was taxation. Now that the Federal estate tax is virtually passing into extinction, planners have the *opportunity* to devote themselves, without the distraction of the estate tax, to the real objective of estate planning.

# CONTENTS

# ESTATE PLANNING

## THE NEW GOLDEN OPPORTUNITIES

# 1

## ESTATE PLANNING IS STILL VERY MUCH ALIVE

With the phased-in dismemberment of the Federal estate tax, which by 1987 will exempt an estimated 96 to 98 percent of all estates from liability, most people have come to believe that estate planning no longer is of compelling or practical importance. It is the purpose of this chapter to demonstrate how mistaken and dangerous that belief is. It will be shown that emasculation of the Federal estate tax that we have known since 1916 most decidedly does not mean the end of estate planning. The Economic Recovery Tax Act of 1981 merely changes the nature of estate planning.

Until now, an estate plan had been regarded universally as a means of avoiding or reducing estate taxes, so that as much as possible of a person's wealth after taxes could be transmitted to his beneficiaries. But the saving of taxes should be regarded as merely one of the objectives of estate planning. It is important but is by no means the chief consideration of the decedent-to-be. As will be shown here, an estate plan designed chiefly for the purpose of saving taxes is apt to ignore a person's real objectives or to defeat what he actually wants to do. Until now, that unfortunately has been the situation where an estate plan was designed by an individual or firm that had a brilliant understanding of the estate tax law but that ignored every consideration aside from tax savings.

Consider first what an estate plan really is. The United States Tax Court, which has reviewed more of such plans than has any other tribunal in the land, provided the following definition, which is not theoretical but utterly relevant. Three sources cited are, respectively, a professor at the Harvard University School of Law, the author of this book, and an outstanding New York City attorney who specializes in estate planning:

> A complete analysis of an estate involves more than a consideration of tax consequences: in fact it is basically concerned with transferring the client's property to the persons he wishes to re-

1

ceive it. The client's financial condition, the nature of his property, the extent to which he wants various persons to share in his estate, the needs and capacity of each intended beneficiary, the details of State law, and the need for flexibility are among the multitude of factors, which are considered in establishing a plan to dispose of a client's wealth. Casner, Estate Planning, Ch. 1 (3d ed., 1961); Holzman, Estate Planning, Ch. 1 (1967); Trachtman, Estate Planning, Ch. 1 (rev'd ed., 1968).[1]

Few tax specialists admit that their field of expertise is not the stuff of which an estate plan primarily is to be built. But here is what two practitioners have written on what an estate plan really should be:

> [Tax] planning, important as it may be, is not the most important part of estate planning. The overriding concern is the welfare and security of the individuals involved and how they may be protected by wills and trusts and other tools of the estate planner.[2]

Estate planning, then, is the procedure by which a person arranges to transmit his property to persons of his own choice in order to effectuate his wishes and objectives in the most appropriate manner. The saving of taxes rarely is his chief objective. Higher priorities should be given to considerations of the consequences of acting with only the tax savings in mind.

☐ Giving or willing property to your spouse may save taxes because of factors such as the marital deduction. But it may provide the recipient with more wealth than he or she needs or wants or has the capacity or time to handle. It may shut out other persons for whom you want to provide.

☐ Transfer of property or income to your children can result in lowered taxes. But it may be far more important to you to reserve your bounty until a later time when the needs, aspirations, and character of the children are better known to you.

☐ By disposing of property to relatives, friends, or charitable organizations, you may be saving taxes. But that could put you in an intolerable position in later years if inflation, failure of investments, or health problems eat up your remaining resources.

☐ By acquiring or holding property in joint ownership with your spouse or someone else, it is possible to save taxes. But a divorce or a financially irresponsible co-owner can create dangerous and incalculable problems.

☐ Giving away property, especially income-producing assets, to the subject of one's affection can save taxes. But you should consider whether the recipient will be as knowledgeable about the uses and the potential of

---

[1] Sidney Merrians et al., 60 T.C. 187 (1973).

[2] Sidney Kess and Bertil Westlin, *CCH Estate Planning Guide* (Chicago: Commerce Clearing House, 1977), p. vii.

this property as you are. If you are thinking of putting the gift in the form of a trust, you might consider whether any trust officer can manage investments as well as you can. Such considerations might lead you to decide to retain control over the property in order to have it managed to your own satisfaction.

☐ A person's most valuable asset may be stock in a closely-held corporation. In order to protect this property for his beneficiaries against loss through a malpractice verdict against him or a claim by an injured party that exceeds liability insurance coverage or the like, he transfers the property to an irrevocable trust for the benefit of his beneficiaries. His ability to continue holding his job, to control the amount of his salary and "perks," and to name his own managerial successor depends upon retention of voting rights over the stock, which represents control. That is more important to him and perhaps to his beneficiaries than the Federal estate tax liability that will result from his possession of voting power for as long as he lives.

☐ The annual gift tax exclusion can be doubled if husband and wife consent to the making of joint gifts. For example, if some of the husband's property is given to third parties and the wife consents, this is a joint gift. But the wife now has gift tax liability should her husband fail to pay the tax. And he may gladly forego the tax saving where a jointly submitted gift tax return enables his spouse to find out the names of all persons to whom he had made gifts.

With the phasing out of the Federal estate tax, estate planning in the future will be concerned with such matters as the following. They are important in deciding how to implement a person's wishes, which is the true goal of estate planning.

☐ In what form should property be transmitted to a beneficiary? This calls for a consideration of trusts, custodianships, forms of ownership.

☐ What plans for disposition of stock in a closely-held corporation should be made? Possibilities include buy-sell agreements, business continuation trusts, recapitalizations, mergers.

☐ What means are available to a person to have his wishes implemented in the light of circumstances that take place after his death? If he wants his executor or executrix to be his spouse or other close relative or friend, but that person lacks expertise in this area, what steps can be taken at this time in order to protect the designated party from oversights or the consequences of them?

Certainly it is a minority point of view to say at this time that estate planning did not die with the enactment of the Economic Recovery Tax Act of 1981. But consider the following:

1. There are many reasons for estate planning other than avoidance of the estate tax. Some of them have just been mentioned.

2. The phasing in of higher exemption levels will not reach its peak of $600,000 until 1987. Can you be certain that your estate tax return will not have to be filed before that time? It may be prudent to continue playing by the old rules until 1987 or at least until some earlier year when the exemption point is higher than it is now.

3. Many persons are, or at the time of death will be, far wealthier than they now believe. Inflation, more liberal employer benefit plans such as group insurance, astronomical jury awards in the case of wrongful death claims and other matters, and one's own mounting success can place a person's estate on that plateau where it is subject to tax.

4. Most states have some form of death tax. People generally have not considered the reduction in value of property passing to beneficiaries by reason of state death taxes because in the past these taxes have not been much of a burden. The reason has always been that computation of the Federal estate tax allowed a credit for state death taxes, which usually were so structured that the amount of the state tax would be a credit against Federal tax. Without a Federal estate tax, state death taxes no longer will be a credit against anything and will be an expense to be borne.

5. The record-keeping requirements, inventories of assets owned by the decedent, and information critical for its valuation still are needed. Beneficiaries who inherit property will require information as to the value at the time of death in order to compute Federal income taxes when that property subsequently is sold. Much of the material that good estate planning formerly had made available for the estate tax return continues to be needed.

6. One of the most valuable benefits of estate planning—one that rarely is mentioned—still exists as definitely as ever: *peace of mind.* This refers both to the person whose estate is being planned and his beneficiaries. It is a priceless asset to know that whatever happens and when, careful and unhurried consideration already has been given to meeting the changing circumstances in accordance with a person's true objectives. Substantial dismemberment of the Federal estate tax by the Economic Recovery Tax Act of 1981 has not eliminated the need for estate planning. The new law merely has presented in dramatic form the need to rethink one's real priorities.

# 2

## NON-ESTATE-TAX OBJECTIVES OF ESTATE PLANNING

It is declared in the House Ways and Means Committee Report that accompanied the Economic Recovery Tax Bill of 1981, "The committee believes that the tax laws should be neutral and that tax consequences should not control an individual's disposition of property." Here is a clear statement that from now on, "tax consequences" should not be regarded as the principal objective of estate planning. So plans based upon the avoidance of Federal estate tax—the old concept of estate planning—are being replaced now by an entirely new concept: transmission of one's wealth in a manner which best will carry out his desires in the light of the aspirations and capabilities of his beneficiaries.

Plans designed to implement one's wishes and obligations are too numerous and too varied to catalog in their entirety. They depend upon what one has or expects to have, the degree of control which he wants to retain over his property or his beneficiaries, the amount of flexibility he would preserve under changing circumstances and imponderables. What follows, however, is a sampling of half a hundred estate plans where the term "estate tax" does not appear. A person's complete estate plan may consist of one or two or a dozen of the terms that follow. The priority or relative importance of a particular plan depends upon what you regard as most appropriate in *your* case.

1. Transmission of property or income now, or over a period of years, or upon the occurrence of some event, or at death to designated persons, or classes of persons (such as grandchildren), or institutions.

2. Choice of the form in which beneficiaries will receive their interests in such property as you designate. A trust or custodianship may provide professional or other expert management of properties or income until a particular beneficiary has attained a specified age or financial capacity. A trust may continue for a beneficiary's entire life if desired.

3. Decision as to how your estate will be carved up. Usually a will or other testamentary disposition makes dollar provisions for the beneficiaries, with a designated remainderman to get whatever is left. (*Remainderman* is the term used for the person who gets whatever is left

after all beneficiaries receive their individual entitlements.) But because of inflation or the impossibility of estimating the size of your estate at a future and generally unknown time, it may be better to specify what *percentage* of your net assets will go to each beneficiary.

4. Consideration of the degree of control you wish to retain over property or income earmarked for beneficiaries. You could set up a trust for the benefit of specified persons or classes of persons, reserving the right to say what proportion of principal or income will go each year to any designated party. You could give the trustee(s) the authority to exercise discretion here, absolutely or in accordance with your own instructions or guidelines. The trustee, if a close friend or relative, might be instructed to make distributions and allocations in accordance with what he believes you would have done had the property remained in your control.

5. You may wish to have your property and/or income distributed during your lifetime or afterwards to your children or grandchildren, in certain proportions. But you fear that your prejudices, biases, or perhaps some unfortunate interpersonal friction will prevent you from viewing your distributions objectively and dispassionately. Arrangements can be made, as through a power of appointment, for dispositions to be made to beneficiaries with a third party's detachment.

6. A person wants to leave assets to parties of his own choice. But a beneficiary may die before his benefactor. Or the beneficiary, for reasons of his own, may not want that property or may refuse to accept anything from the intending beneficiary. So that your property will be distributed according to *your* wishes, make certain in your will, trust instrument, or other document that contingent beneficiaries be named, so that regardless of what happens to a beneficiary or how he reacts to the bequest, the property still will go to a party of your choice, even if it happens to be your second or third preference.

7. Your estate should be handled by a person, persons, or an institution of your choice. So that the executor or executrix will be someone you have selected, provide for contingent, alternate, or successor executors of your own choice. Your original nominee may die. He may refuse to serve. He may be "unavailable." For many reasons, it is highly undesirable to have a court name an administrator or administratrix to handle your estate for lack of a person of your own choice.

8. Your intention may be to leave all of your wealth, or a substantial portion of it, to your spouse. But what if he or she dies with you in a common disaster? State simultaneous death laws provide for what will happen to jointly-held property, survivorship insurance, and other matters if it cannot be established which spouse had died first. Find out what the law of your state says on this subject. If you do not like that arrangement, you can make other provisions under a "reverse simultaneous death" clause.

9. Often a husband wants to leave all or a substantial portion of his wealth to his wife. The wife would like to make a comparable provision for

the husband in her will. But each may fear, with some reason, that upon the death of the surviving spouse, the remaining property of the first to die all will go to the relatives or friends of the second spouse, with relatives of the first getting none of what had been the first spouse's property. This is what frequently happens in the case of children by an earlier marriage. Joint wills or a mutual will can spell out how the intended beneficiaries of each spouse will be provided for when the second spouse dies.

10. A person's present annual income is more than he requires at this time, with the result that he is paying higher income taxes than his way of life requires. But in later years, when he retires, or prefers to slow down, or is unable to earn so much, he would again like to receive the annual income that he finds unnecessary (and unnecessarily taxed to him) at this time. To plan for this, he could transfer securities or other income-producing securities to individuals or to charities of his choice, thus reducing his income taxes. He can do it in such a way that he will get back the properties in later years when, predictably, he will need them. If he dies before then, the properties will go under the terms of his will to beneficiaries he names.

11. A person often sets up a trust in order to protect beneficiaries from the consequences of financial errors or misjudgment of character. Similarly, he may protect himself from his own lapses of business acumen, carelessness, and inability to evaluate problems and people that so often surface when an individual gets older. He may accomplish this by setting up an *inter vivos* trust that will function during his lifetime.

12. An individual may provide himself with an income in later life that he cannot outlive. He can do this without family loss of any of his wealth should he die shortly after making such an arrangement. Arrangements can be made so that even when he dies at a much later date, his property will not be lost to the family.

13. When a person's dependents die off or become financially self-sufficient, he may look forward to converting his life insurance policies into annuities to ensure a better economic future for himself.

14. One can transfer all or a substantial part of his property for the benefit of his spouse or other designated party, such as a daughter, in such a manner that he need not fear that she will be the object of attention of fortune hunters, attracted by the fact that she now is the possessor of wealth.

15. If a person wants to see how competent his beneficiaries-to-be are in the handling of money, property, or business interests, modest amounts or proportions can be given as gifts at this time, so that an evaluation can be made on a pilot-plant basis. On the evaluation of each person's performance, final plans can be formalized as to the manner in which bequests are to be made.

16. An individual wishes to make dispositions of property *in strict confidence* to other parties when he dies. A will is open to interested or in-

quisitive eyes at the place where it is filed, such as a hall of records or a courthouse. One's property dispositions can be made in such a way that the world does not learn about them through probate proceedings.

17. Steps should be taken to keep one's affairs secret from even close relatives or trusted business associates. A person's wealth can be eroded considerably by tax informants who "leak" information to the Internal Revenue Service. An individual is in a particularly vulnerable posture when he no longer is alive to explain what he has done or to produce supporting evidence to justify his actions, even if all of the accusations have been completely without foundation.

18. You want to leave your wealth to your designated nominees without erosion by unnecessary Federal income taxes. But after your death, your Federal income tax returns for the past three years (or even more under certain circumstances) are very likely to be examined by Revenue Agents. If you are not here to explain deductions or credits that you have taken, to answer questions, or to present documentary back-up for items on the tax returns, substantial additional income taxes may be assessed. To these may be added penalties because no "reasonable cause" for what you have done can be offered. There are steps that can be taken now to mitigate this risk, such as having fully documented records in the possession of a certified public accountant or other person who is knowledgeable about your affairs.

19. Consideration should be given to closing out any transactions that might bring problems to beneficiaries with which they would be unable or unwilling to cope. For example, a person might have invested in a questionable tax shelter. He may be confident of his ability to establish that his shelter is not what the Internal Revenue Service and the courts characterize as "abusive," a charge with very disagreeable consequences. But his beneficiaries may not be so knowledgeable as he in this area, and they may be far less comfortable about coping with assessments and court proceedings. Your beneficiaries could be far less disposed to fight back. Ponder well whether you wish to expose them to risks and unpleasantness with which you yourself are prepared to cope.

20. An estate that is left to one's beneficiaries can be far larger if the executor knows where all assets are located, the extent of your interest in jointly-held property, where the records are to be found, and the best market for certain assets. For example, a certain business may have been trying to buy your real estate in order to enlarge its plant, or a distant collector may have expressed great interest in something you own should you ever decide to sell it. Without a lead from you, the executor may be unable to get the highest prices for your assets.

21. Ensure that none of your assets is lost to your beneficiaries because of steps you had taken to conceal it from creditors or a disenchanted spouse or ex-spouse. For example, confide in someone you trust about a numbered Swiss bank account or funds you had on deposit in another name, perhaps in a distant city.

22. An individual may take steps to safeguard his property or particular assets, such as stock in his business, for his family against the consequences of a malpractice suit or other claim. In this day of high jury awards the amount could exceed the insurance reimbursement, if any.

23. In many states, a person can protect wealth that he has earmarked for a beneficiary against the financial extravagances and wasteful habits of that person, such as gambling debts. Check with local counsel about the validity of a spendthrift trust.

24. It is possible to insulate property intended for grandchildren against financial excesses of your own offspring's spouse.

25. Provision may be made for a high degree of lifetime care for a disadvantaged child or other relative, with the assurance that he will continue to be cared for in the same manner after your death or in the event you should have financial reverses during your lifetime.

26. An individual may be concerned about the mismanagement or hasty liquidation of his business after he dies. The carefully chosen executor who is knowledgeable about one's personal affairs and aspirations could be without expertise in this particular business. There is a choice of steps that can be taken to prevent this.

27. A person might deem it advisable to make plans for ways for his family or executor to find a buyer for his shares in a closely-held corporation for which there is no apparent market. As he grows older or becomes seriously ill, he could try to merge the company into a better-known corporation, so that the shares that he receives in return will be more marketable. If he ever has received "feelers" from another corporation, he should keep this correspondence readily accessible as an aid to his family's ultimate marketing of his shares.

28. A businessperson can make provisions for what will happen to his interest upon the death of a partner or another stockholder in a closely-held corporation. Without advance planning, he may find that he has a new associate with whom it is utterly impossible to continue the business. Or the decedent's executor or family may force a disadvantageous liquidation of the going business in order to pay debts or to implement bequests.

29. An individual may sincerely believe that he is more knowledgeable about investments or other properties that he transfers to a trust for the benefit of his family than is any professional trustee. But he wants to use a trust because of the insulation of the property from his own creditors, to assure continuity of management, and the like. He can create a trust and also retain administrative or veto rights over portfolio investments without owning the property.

30. You may be disturbed by the real possibility that your principal beneficiaries will squabble over your estate when you die. This could shatter family ties and even besmirch your memory. But you can plan at this time to minimize such a possibility.

31. A person can take steps to reduce the possibility of multiple state death taxes when he dies.

32. An individual may have to consider the possibilty that his properties will be worth far less in the hands of his beneficiaries when he dies because of *fragmentation*. Steps can be taken at this time so that parcels of real estate, collections of antiques, and the like are not sold piecemeal by beneficiaries with a resultant lower aggregate price when the whole actually is worth far more than the sum of its parts.

33. The value of an estate that passes to beneficiaries can be dissipated if the executor has to sell assets at the wrong time (too quickly) in order to obtain cash for taxes and other expenses. Insurance on the decedent's life could be earmarked for the executor's use so that estate assets are not jettisoned in order to implement bequests or to satisfy creditors.

34. A person can plan so that his present contributions to charitable, religious, or educational organizations are continued annually after his death. Funds can be earmarked for regular payments into a building fund until the target goal is attained.

35. An individual's desire to have his name live on after his death may be achieved by gifts or bequests that will perpetuate his name or that of a parent or relative. Examples are a gift of a new wing at a hospital, an endowed professorship at a university, fellowships or research grants.

36. You can plan so that your ownership of a family corporation can go to your beneficiaries in forms most appropriate to their capabilities and needs for protection. For example, a recapitalization from the present one-class stock into voting common and nonvoting preferred shares will enable you to give or to leave the relative security and stable income of preferred stock to persons who will not participate in the management of the business, while active participants will get the common stock with its greater risks, earnings potential, and incentive.

37. If a marital rift appears likely, plans can be taken to insulate a person's business and his most vital assets from the reach or knowledge of a disenchanted spouse.

38. It may be highly important to a person's peace of mind that his property go to his beneficiaries free and clear of any indebtedness or liabilities. Declining-value term insurance may be obtained to pay off major items such as the home mortgage. Specialized types of policies can take care of credit-card or other indebtedness.

39. It could be desirable to an individual that his estate be as highly liquid as possible upon his death, so that his beneficiaries can receive the kind of property they are most likely to understand: money. There are some forms of investment that can become instant cash upon one's death. Some government certificates of deposit cannot be converted into cash without substantial forfeitures—except in the case of death of the owner. There are bonds in the private sector that sell at a discount but that are redeemable at par upon the owner's death.

40. A person may be worried about whether the proper settlement options will be elected by the beneficiary of his life insurance on the basis of facts as they exist at that time. An insurance trust is one way of making as certain as possible that an experienced professional person will make the decisions.

41. Plans should be made so that the incentive stock options authorized by the Economic Recovery Tax Act of 1981, or other options and elections, are not wasted or allowed to lapse because neither the executor nor the beneficiaries know about them.

42. Arrangements frequently can be made in executive salary negotiations so that after a person's death, compensation continuance or profit participation coverage will provide for his surviving spouse or other nominee.

43. In order to keep out of the higher income tax brackets and thus prevent erosion of one's estate, it may be possible to negotiate with your employer for a deferred compensation arrangement. Contracts could provide that royalty, fee, or other forms of income are payable only over a stipulated period of years.

44. Take steps to anticipate the effects of your death upon the operation of a business. For example, if you now operate as a proprietorship, any unmatured installment obligations will represent taxable income when you die. Incorporation avoids this. Would your death cause the cancellation of a valuable franchise, as where General Motors Corporation can terminate a dealership upon the death of a principal? Endeavor to see that a competent, experienced person can step into your shoes in order to persuade the franchisor to continue the arrangement. Would your death, or that of one of your partners, terminate the partnership automatically? Steps can be taken to prevent this.

45. One can provide for the economic consequences of illness, accident, or other catastrophe through disability, health, income maintenance, and certain forms of use and occupancy insurance. Failure to make plans for such major misfortunes could wipe out what otherwise could be a goodly estate for your beneficiaries.

46. Plans can be made so that upon a person's death, designated assets will go immediately to the beneficiaries without serious loss of time by reason of timid executors or a lengthy probate process.

47. An estate plan can make provisions so that your ultimate wealth-splitting among your children will be equalized when you die. For example, bequests or life insurance proceeds can make up to some children for the fact that they had been treated less generously than others whose entry into business, a profession, or an artistic career had been handsomely financed or whose debts had been paid at the expense of an equal wealth-sharing plan for all of the children.

48. Make plans for the Federal income tax treatment that your beneficiaries will have when they sell properties received from you. A bene-

ficiary's basis (tax cost) for inherited property will be fair market value at the date of death or six months later, if the executor elects to value at this alternate date. A donee's basis for sale of property acquired by gift is what the donor had paid. Make it easy or at least possible fopr him to learn what that was. In the absence of proof of what you had paid, the donee may have a zero basis, and his full realization wil be taxable.

49. Plans are possible so that a person can control the disposition of what had been his properties and income from the grave, in the light of circumstances unknown to him when he died. Examples are powers of appointment, discretionary trusts, contingent beneficiaries.

50. If you wish to increase your life insurance coverage but find that at your age the premiums are too costly to start, or if you have become uninsurable, explore the possibilities of group insurance. Such coverage is available through many professional societies or associations. Many employers have "cafeteria" plans, where each year an employee may decide which of the available fringe benefits he will select; frequently, additional company-provided insurance is an option. If your insurance needs are great, consider accepting employment with a corporation that has a generous group insurance program.

There is almost no limit to the number of estate plans that may be appropriate to your own objectives. In fact, you already have an estate plan, unless you choose to do something about it. If you do not have a valid will at the time of your death, state laws of intestacy determine how your property will be divided. If you don't like the state's pecking order, make your own plan, such as a valid will.

# 3

## THE ECONOMIC RECOVERY TAX ACT OF 1981: WHAT IT HAS DONE AND WHAT IT WILL DO

The Economic Recovery Tax Act of 1981 will virtually eviscerate the Federal gift and estate tax structure by 1987. As will be shown in this chapter, potential impact of the estate tax gets less or may even disappear by 1987. Here is what the 1981 law has done to exempt cumulative transfers from gift and estate taxes:

| Year | Amount Exempted |
|---|---|
| 1981 | $175,625 |
| 1982 | 225,000 |
| 1983 | 275,000 |
| 1984 | 325,000 |
| 1985 | 400,000 |
| 1986 | 500,000 |
| 1987 and subsequent years | 600,000 |

By that time, it is estimated that only 2 to 4 percent of all estates will be subject to tax. Meanwhile, take good care of yourself.

The maximum Federal gift and estate tax rates, which had been 70 percent through 1981, will decline as follows:

| Year Decedent Dies or Gift Is Made | Maximum Tax Rate |
|---|---|
| 1982 | 65% |
| 1983 | 60 |
| 1984 | 55 |
| 1985 and later years | 50 |

The maximum rate applied to transfers in excess of $5,000,000 in 1981. That figure decreases as follows:

| Year | Amount |
|------|--------|
| 1982 | $4,000,000 |
| 1983 | 3,500,000 |
| 1984 | 3,000,000 |
| 1985 and later years | 2,500,000 |

If gifts reach the point where they will be taxable, it might appear to be practical to defer transfers until the unified credit, according to existing law, reaches its highest point in 1987. On the other hand, if it is anticipated that inflation will continue to spiral, from a tax point of view there is reason to make gifts that are taxable at this time, in order to freeze present values for transfer taxes. The mathematical consequences of *now* and *then* should be evaluated.

## OVERVIEW

The changes made in Federal gift and estate tax laws by the 1981 legislation will reduce vulnerability to those taxes very considerably. In the old-fashioned sense that estate planning is the reduction or elimination of estate taxes, estate planning may appear to be becoming obsolete.

But that is a shortsighted way to regard the matter. Except for the increase in cumulative transfers exempt from tax and the lowering of maximum tax rates, most of the tax boons are far from automatic and may not even be desirable in many instances. Complacency, frequently nurtured by oversimplified explanations of these changes, can be a dangerous trap.

For example, "unlimited marital deductions" are far from unlimited. Many questions must still be asked. What is being transferred and how? What command can the transferor retain over the ultimate disposition of the property transferred? How do state laws as to the marriage, previous marriage, and previous divorce of the spouses affect the marital deduction? (Brief answer to the last question: *considerably.*)

In the case of gifts, spousal and otherwise, how complete was the so-called gift? What do state laws say about the requirements for transfers of such items as real estate or securities?

On the other side of the coin, a decedent's estate may be considerably in excess of the apparent safeharbor of the permissible cumulative transfers exempt from tax. Stock in a closely-held corporation may be valued by the Internal Revenue Service well above current estimates. Gross estate may include many forms of retained interests, insurance proceeds on the decedent's life where significant incidents of ownership were held by him at the date of death, reversionary or remainder interests that had not been taken into account, property subject to a general power of appointment, prior transfers for insufficient consideration, gifts that were incomplete under state law. . . . The list of properties or interests that may be thrown into gross estate is almost limitless. (All of these subjects will be discussed in appropriate chapters of this book.)

## UNLIMITED MARITAL DEDUCTION

In the case of gifts made and persons dying in 1981, there was a limited marital deduction in arriving at taxable transfers from one spouse to another. Transfers of community property in the eight states recognizing this system and terminable interests did not qualify for the marital deduction. Transfers between spouses of community property now are eligible for the marital deduction.

Terminable interests generally are created where an interest in property passes to the spouse and another interest passes from the donor or decedent by means other than a sale at full value. (In the interest of simplicity, the donor or the decedent is referred to here as the husband; the donee or beneficiary is referred to as the wife. The terms could just as easily be reversed.) For example, the gift of an income interest by a husband to his wife did not qualify for the marital deduction where the remainder interest was transferred by him to a third party. Starting in 1982, a *qualifying terminable interest* is eligible for the marital deduction.The nature and ground rules for this will be presented in Chapter 8, which discusses fully the marital deduction.

## CHARITABLE SPLIT-GIFTS

Previously, if an individual (here called the husband) transferred a life income interest in property to his spouse, the remainder to go to a designated approved charitable organization upon her death, this was regarded as a terminable interest not qualifying for the marital deduction. In the case of transfers of qualified income interests after December 31, 1981, the disallowance rule for terminable interests does not apply if he creates a qualified charitable remainder annuity trust or unitrust, and the only noncharitable beneficiaries are himself and his wife. So he will receive a charitable deduction for the amount of the remainder interest and a marital deduction for the value of the annuity or unitrust.

## CONTRIBUTIONS OF COPYRIGHTS

Where there is a contribution to an approved charitable organization of less than an entire interest in property, no deduction ordinarily is allowed. Exceptions are where the remainder interest is (1) in certain highly specialized and technical forms, such as a charitable annuity trust or unitrust or a pooled income fund or (2) in a personal residence or farm. In the case of gifts made or decedent's dying after December 31, 1981, where a donor or decedent makes a contribution of a copyrightable work of art to an approved charitable organization, a charitable deduction generally will be allowed whether or not the copyright is simultaneously transferred to the organization.

## JOINTLY-HELD PROPERTY

Prior to 1982, a decedent's gross estate included the entire value of property held jointly at the time of his death by him and his wife with right of survivorship, except that portion of the property that had been acquired by her for full consideration or by bequest or gift from a third party. There were special rules in cases where the spouses had taken ownership of real property as joint tenants. In the case of persons dying after December 31, 1981, each spouse is considered to own one-half of property jointly-held with right of survivorship, regardless of which party had furnished the original consideration.

This keeps out of the gross estate of the first spouse to die any amount that is more than one-half of the value of jointly-held property, even though there is no evidence or record of how much each spouse had paid for the interest.

## SPECIAL-USE VALUATION

Ordinarily, property owned by a decedent is valued for estate tax purposes according to its highest and best use, regardless of how it actually happens to be used. But when an estate consists in substantial measure of a farm or of closely-held business assets, since 1976 the value could be computed according to its current use if prescribed requirements could be met. These requirements were very complicated, and they still are, although they have been liberalized in the case of persons dying after December 31, 1981. In some instances, these changes have been made retroactive to apply to persons dying after December 31, 1976. This subject will be considered in Chapter 5, which discusses special-use valuation.

Even if all of the requirements were met, the amount by which the fair market value of qualified property could be reduced was $500,000. This has been increased as follows:

| Year of Decedent's Death | Amount of Reduction |
|---|---|
| 1981 | $600,000 |
| 1982 | 700,000 |
| 1983 and thereafter | 750,000 |

## ANNUAL GIFT TAX EXCLUSION

In the case of gifts after December 31, 1981, the annual exclusion for gifts subject to tax has been increased from $3,000 to $10,000 per donee. As previously, the exclusion in effect can be doubled where both spouses consent to the making of a gift.

In addition to the exclusion(s), there may be excluded from taxable gifts made after December 31, 1981, any amounts paid on behalf of any individual (1) as tuition to certain educational organizations for his education and training and (2) for payment to any provider of medical care. This exclusion is available without regard to the relationship between the donor and the donee.

## GIFT TAX MARITAL DEDUCTION

Unlimited amounts of property (other than certain terminable interests) now can be transferred without gift tax. Transfers to the spouse, however, may be more beneficial if made as bequests rather than as gifts; for although the marital deduction treatment is similar, deathtime transfers of appreciated-value property give the recipient a higher tax basis for future sale.

## GIFTS WITHIN THREE YEARS OF DEATH

In the past, the value of gifts made within three years of the death of a decedent automatically had been included in his gross estate. In the case of persons who die after December 31, 1981, the only gifts within that time that are includible in his gross estate are gifts of (1) life insurance and (2) interests in property that are regarded as incomplete, such as transfers with a retained life interest or those subject to the donor's power to alter, to amend, or to terminate an arrangement.

So-called deathbed transfers now are possible. But if appreciated-value property is transferred, Federal income tax liability may be generated for the donor.

## ORPHANS' DEDUCTION

The Economic Recovery Tax Act of 1981 has stricken one former exclusion from gross estate. The deduction for specified amounts passing to minor children without a known surviving parent has been terminated in the case of decedents dying after December 31, 1981.

# 4

# WHERE ESTATE PLANNING STARTS: THE VALUATION OF ASSETS

If a person does not have a fair idea of the dollar size of his estate, present and future, he cannot make intelligent plans for what to do with it. It is possible that because of inflation or because he has not kept up with present-day values, an individual's plans may not take into account the full extent of his wealth. Consequently, when he makes bequests in his will, his planned dispositions are likely to be far less than his estate. The result will be that the chief beneficiary of this incomplete planning will be the remainderman, who gets what is left after each named person gets his specified entitlement. The remainderman is apt to be a person or an institution that was not the decedent's most preferred beneficiary.

On the other hand, if his lifetime and deathtime transfers "transmit" more to his beneficiaries than his executor can deliver, someone (or many persons) will be shortchanged. Relatives and friends who had been assured that they would receive their "expectancies" may find that despite the decedent's oft-repeated promises and intentions, living and perhaps business commitments cannot be met. Predictably, there will be acrimony, and disappointed "heirs" whom you thought you had been providing for may bring suit to break your will on the ground that you lacked mental capacity at the time you made it.

The valuation of assets that will comprise one's estate must be considered at the outset for a variety of reasons:

1. An individual's plan is based on how much he wishes to make available to his beneficiaries, and when; or how much income-producing property he is prepared to rechannel from himself in order to avoid income taxes. This includes outright bequests, income to be paid during a beneficiary's lifetime or some portion of it, money to be set aside for future educational or other requirements of relatives, retirement of a mortgage, fulfillment of an alimony obligation, and the like. If the objectives of a person cannot be met with the dollar amount available, it may be necessary to increase the size of the estate, such as by taking out additional life insurance. Or it may be necessary to revise his objectives downwards.

2. An understanding of valuation will help to decide whether a proposed gift exceeds what may be given away tax-free and to determine the tax where it is required. Where a person does not know the value of property which he is giving away, there may be unsuspected gift tax liability. In addition, there could be a penalty for failure to file a gift tax return. More realistically, that penalty will be for failure to find out the value of the property.

3. Often it seems desirable to leave an estate with sufficient liquidity so that the executor will have money for immediate needs: taking care of beneficiaries until bequests can be passed along, paying bills and claims, and the like. In the case of very large estates, there may be Federal transfer taxes to be paid. This liquidity can be attained by having cash or the equivalent available, or life insurance payable to the estate or to the executor. If it appears certain that estate taxes will be payable, investment in "flower bonds" may be advantageous, a subject that will be discussed in Chapter 20. In order to provide liquidity, valuations must be made in order to forecast what will be required.

4. Under special circumstances, corporate stock can be redeemed for the purpose of paying death taxes and administration expenses without dividend implications. This is available only where the decedent's shares in the corporation amounted to more than 35 percent of the value of the adjusted gross estate. To make plans to take advantage of this technique, the ratio between the value of the shares and the value of the adjusted gross estate must be reviewed periodically. The subject will be discussed in Chapter 16.

5. Special-use valuation of certain farms and other real property can result in significantly lower Federal estate taxes. Utilization of this procedure is possible only where the value of specified closely-held assets exceeds 35 percent of adjusted gross estate. The subject will be discussed in Chapter 5.

For all of these reasons, a person cannot adequately make estate plans without knowing the value of his present or future estate. The remainder of this chapter will consider how this can be determined.

## FAIR MARKET VALUE

The term "value" as used in the Federal taxing statutes means "fair market value." For tax and other purposes, fair market value has been defined by the courts as *the price at which property would change hands in a transaction between a willing buyer and a willing seller, neither being under compulsion to buy or to sell and both being informed as to the relevant facts.* To this standard definition there might be added these words, *with a reasonable time afforded the people to get together on the terms and conditions.* That is, the concept presupposes that the figure is arrived at after negotiations.

The value must be considered at the highest and best use of the property. But an important exception is made in the case of certain property that had not been used at the highest and best manner when the decedent died. This will be the subject of Chapter 5.

Sales made under peculiar and unusual circumstances may signify neither a fair market price nor a value. The unusual circumstances could include sales of small lots, forced sales, sales in a restricted market or a transaction between husband and wife made under the emotion and tension of divorce proceedings. Transactions between parties who are related, or corporations under common control, ordinarily do not establish fair market value.

Fair market value depends on the market, not on some intrinsic worth of the property. Book value is not synonymous with fair market value, for the former represents original cost in most instances. Good will, patents, and the like may be carried on the books at only nominal value. Stated capital is not equivalent to fair market value. Appraised value for state or local propert taxes is not acceptable as fair market value.

Only in rare and extraordinary cases can it be said that property has *no* fair market value.

The taxpayer has the burden of proof in establishing fair market value. Stated differently, fair market value is whatever the Internal Revenue says it is, unless the taxpayer can prove another figure in court.

## ACTUAL SALES

The price at which property actually is bought and sold in an arm's length transaction generally is held to be the best evidence of the fair market value on that date, in the absence of exceptional circumstances. The best evidence of value for a traded security is an actual transaction, provided there is an active market in the issue. Treasury regulations stipulate fair market value as the mean between the highest and lowest quoted selling prices on the valuation date.

But even where there are actual sales between unrelated parties dealing at arm's length, the figures can be disregarded for valuation purposes if there were important factors bearing on value that were unknown to the general public, the transactions of which determined market prices.

Actual New York Stock Exchange sales on the valuation date were ignored by one court in setting the value of shares in favor of convincing proof of the fair "real" value of this stock because the shares had been acquired at the peak of a stock inflation.

High value was imputed to stock because some sales were made at that price to unsophisticated buyers willing to speculate on a cheap, unlisted stock without regard to the underlying financial structure. The court disregarded those sales in setting a valuation.

A prominent "movie mogul" vainly argued that the value of the shares of his cinema corporation on the New York Stock Exchange was not set by actual trading because the investing public could not know what a depressing effect the outbreak of worldwide war would have on the company's earnings.

Actual sales of stock do not always set a valuation. A corporation that buys out the shares of a troublesome minority shareholder, paying him more than the stock was worth just to get rid of him, does not thereby set the value of the stock. Price does not determine value either when the buyer really is trying to get more than the shares themselves, for example, where purchasers of corporate stock believe that, as major shareholders, they could have themselves hired as president and as counsel. And value was not set by a hurried sale of shares by an individual who wished to unload before a government agency began an investigation into the corporation's stockholders.

Sale of a small quantity of shares or commodities does not set a fair market price for larger amounts. Here, the seller, such as a bank that was disposing of the collateral for an unpaid loan, may not have expended the effort to obtain the highest possible price because there was not enough money involved. An Internal Revenue Service sale of property seized for unpaid taxes may have been made at whatever figure would compensate the government for what was owing, without any attempt to realize a larger amount, which the government could not have retained anyway.

## BLOCKAGE

Listed or actively traded over-the-counter shares may be valued at less than the prevailing market prices because of *blockage*. The term is used to characterize the depressing effect on the market price of a stock caused by a sale of a quantity substantially in excess of the normal level of trading. Stock may be valued for less than actual sales or quotations on a regular market if it can be demonstrated that because of the large size of the block held by the decedent or the number of shares given by the donor, the market could not have absorbed that quantity without "breaking" and producing a lower figure. But a court is not likely to arrive at a lower-than-market figure for valuation if an executor could have peddled out a larger block to numerous small buyers in the near future under approximately the same market conditions.

Lower-than-market values have been approved by courts where knowledgeable brokers testified that the ways of selling off unusually large quantities of a stock were limited. They could be sold through secondary markets, through wholesale houses, or by special offerings. Any of these procedures would have resulted in lower prices or in substantial selling expenses that would have resulted in reduced net prices.

Treasury regulations provide that a large block of stock may be valued by reference to the amount for which it could be sold to an underwriter for secondary distribution. Values are set in terms of what the brokers or specialists received or had expected to receive, less the additional costs of marketing the securities by secondary distributions or otherwise.

Customarily, a beneficiary has as his basis (tax cost) when he sells property the value at which it had been included on the decedent's estate tax return. But where the estate shows a reduced value because the blockage rule was used, the beneficiary can show the higher value *before* application of the blockage discount.

> The blockage rule was applied to an estate for valuation purposes. A beneficiary who ordinarily would take the value used on the estate tax return as his cost basis for a bequest was permitted to use the *full value* as his *basis for tax purposes*.

The existence of a large block of shares actually may *increase* the per-share value under certain circumstances. For example, where there is friction between two shareholder groups, a decedent's stock, a small minority interest, might represent control for whichever large group that could acquire it. The resultant spirited bidding could increase the stock's value, perhaps to an exorbitant extent.

The blockage theory can be applied to property other than securities. Perhaps the most dramatic examples have occurred when the chief value of an estate is a large number of paintings or other works art created by the decedent. Most of the time, a convincing argument can be made that the works cannot be sold without breaking the market. One court agreed with this thinking in the case of musical scores written by the decedent, who was a prominent composer.

## RESTRICTIVE AGREEMENTS

Property that is subject to a restriction is valued at a lower figure than is property without such a restriction. When there is an absolute prohibition against the transfer of property with no income or other advantages (other than mere possession), the ascertainment of fair market value may be impossible.

Even if property cannot be sold publicly because of a restriction (such as restricted stock that had not been registered under the Securities Act of 1933), the stock could be sold privately, for example, to an employee's pension fund. Or it could be given away, used to pay debts, put up as collateral, or used to create a deductible charitable contribution. So the property certainly has value.

The holder of investment letter stock cannot sell it on the open market for a stipulated period. He may be obliged to warrant to the seller that he is acquiring the shares for personal investment, without any intention of selling or otherwise distributing them. Such stock may be entitled to a discount in setting its value.

In one case, where shares without the restriction were selling at 11, the court valued the investment letter shares at 7.

Where sale of stock was completely barred for one year by a restrictive agreement and the corporation was an unproven new one of a speculative nature, no ascertainable value was found.

It is up to the executor to establish that property subject to a restrictive agreement has no alternative valuable use. That may not be simple, even where the assets are negligible. There are parties who are interested in many situations if the price is right. The following advertisement appeared in the *Wall Street Journal* of December 5, 1972: "We want to purchase restricted legended or investment stock in NYSE or AMEX companies. Please respond to..."

## STOCK REDEMPTION AGREEMENTS

Sometimes a corporation has a stock redemption agreement with shareholders that provides that open the death of a stockholder, the corporation will buy up his shares at a stipulated or, more commonly, at a formula price.

Or the shareholders themselves may have an agreement to buy up the shares of a stockholder who dies. The existence at the date of death of a valid, enforceable agreement or option that compels the executor to sell the decedent's shares at a stipulated price fixes their value at that figure for tax purposes, even if fair market value is a higher figure.

On occasion, shareholders have the right to purchase stock at the figure an outsider offers. Most outsiders hesitate to go to the expense involved in investigating the facts essential to making an offer. This would restrict marketability, and hence the valuation of these shares.

## STOCK OF CLOSELY-HELD CORPORATIONS

Closely-held corporations are corporations the shares of which are owned by a relatively limited number of shareholders, often by the members of a single family. As a result, little, if any, trading in the shares takes place. There is, therefore, no established market for the stock, and such sales as occur at widely irregular intervals seldom reflect all the elements of a representative transaction as implied by the term "fair market value."

In order to set the value of closely-held stock in accordance with an actual sale, the taxpayer must demonstrate that the sale was an arm's length transaction in the normal course of business. The sale, for example, may have taken place because a member of the family was ill and desperately required money, which might have been supplied without regard to what the shares actually were worth. Or some particularly disagreeable family member may have been bought out in order to get rid of his participation and presence at a price that included a sizeable element of nuisance value.

The premium paid in such cases is likely to be disregarded in establishing value for tax purposes.

Accordingly, shares of closely-held corporations usually are valued according to special guidelines. Sometimes valuations under two or more of the following methods are determined and then averaged in order to arrive at a result that satisfies the court:

1. *The various ratios on the balance sheet and earnings statement.* A prudent investor, searching for a basis for a reasonable estimate of the future, does not depend upon averages alone. He searches for significant trends, and his use of data that measure past performance must be governed by all those considerations that enter into managerial projections of sales and earnings.

2. *The earnings capacity.* For this guideline, a determination is made concerning the capitalization rate of return at which an investor is willing to invest his funds, assuming the corporation is capitalized at the going

rates for this type of company, taking into account the rate of a "riskless" investment and adding in an allowance for the risk involved in the investment being contemplated. In contrast, the average rate of return on capital is simply the yearly income of an enterprise divided by the capital invested in the corporation. For example, comparable corporations in the same industry may have annual income equivalent to 10 percent on invested capital. This 10 percent is adjusted up or down because of the relative risk or uncertainty of the company being valued. Then it is a matter of arithmetic. What is the dollar amount at which this company's earnings, capitalized at, say, 11 percent will produce the earnings reported?

Valuation is not always appropriate on the basis of earnings. A particular corporation may have been run for long-range appreciation rather than for current earnings and dividends.

Earnings as a factor are given greater weight when valuing stocks of companies that sell products or services to the public. In an investment type of company, the greatest weight may be given to assets underlying the security.

3. *The value of the underlying assets.* Liquidating value might be used to value stock in the case of a shareholder large enough to compel liquidation of the corporation. But the liquidating value of a corporation's stock is not an appropriate test in the case of a minority interest, for the holder of such an interest could not compel liquidation in order to get at the assets. In one case, a court held that stock could not be valued on the basis of the underlying assets, even though these shares were listed on the New York Stock Exchange, because the buyer of the stock would be unable to obtain these underlying assets. Instead, the value of the corporation was valued at a discount of 33.33 percent.

In the case of a manufacturing company, as opposed to an investment company, liquidating value has little relevancy, for the company is not likely to be liquidated, being in most instances worth more alive than dead.

4. *Comparison with other corporations.* Where the value of stock and securities of a corporation cannot be determined with reference to actual sales, or to meaningful bid and asked prices, the Internal Revenue Service has said that consideration should be given to the value of stock or securities of corporations engaged in the same or a similar line of business that are listed on an exchange, or that sell in a free or open market. This approach, of course, assumes that information is available on similar or comparable businesses at the critical valuation date.

The Internal Revenue Service, with its vast computerized files on "other companies," is in far better position than is the executor to draw comparisons. If the I.R.S. seeks to establish the value of a stock by comparing it to the shares of another corporation with active trading or other indications of value, the executor has the opportunity to show factors that would diminish the purchase price that the shares of *his* company would command. In one case, for example, the supposedly comparable company had its own export staff to effect foreign sales, whereas the company to be valued had no such export department of its own. And when the I.R.S. sought to value the stock of a family-owned meat packing company by comparing it to the market values of the four giant corporations in the meat industry, the court rejected these figures as unrealistic for the purpose.

In another case, it was held that the stock of a corporation should be valued at a discount from the value of the shares of a supposedly comparable corporation because the former company was characterized by these factors: Its products were few in number; it was engaged in a luxury type of business that was subject to fluctuation; it was engaged in lively competition with larger companies; throughout the years, it had been unable to develop new products; and the services of key personnel in the sales area recently had been lost.

An unlisted, closely-held stock is less attractive to an investor than a similar stock listed on an exchange, where there is ready access to the investing public. So the marketability factor of the stock of the closely-held corporation must be taken into account. A discount may be in order when comparing unlisted shares with those of a listed corporation, so that the cost of publicly underwriting the shares is represented. In one case, a 12.17 percent discount factor was applied.

It is not possible to compare all unlisted corporations with listed ones; some stock must be characterized as unique. Sometimes a court ascertains that there are no publicly traded companies that are comparable to the corporation, the shares of which must be valued.

On occasion, the management team of a closely-held corporation, anticipating the death in the not-too-distant future of an important shareholder, will try to solve the forthcoming valuation problem by merging into another corporation with less controversial valuation problems.

The comparison method also is used in the case of properties other than stock and securities. In one case, the court was unwilling to accept sales of supposedly comparable industrial properties as really being comparable, because there were significant differences in access to railroads, sewer facilities, rights to waterways, and size.

The property to be valued was substantially smaller than other properties where actual sales had taken place, and the court noted that the range of possible uses of the property under scrutiny was more limited.

5. *Depth of a corporation's management team.* Where a corporation is in effect a one-man corporation, the death of that person can reduce the value of the stock. The ages of the whole executive cadre also may be considered.

The valuation of shares of a decedent need *not* be written down to reflect the corporation's loss of its guiding spirit and chief executive. In one case, the evidence revealed that an extremely able and experienced management team was capable of assuming the decedent's duties. His death would not have led a willing buyer to believe that the general outlook of the corporation was unfavorable. (Certainly the prospects of some corporations might be improved greatly if their chief executives should die.)

6. *Narrowness of a corporation's product line or sphere of activity.* In setting the valuation of stock in a closely-held corporation, one court considered the fact that the company's activities were not diversified. This served to lessen the valuation.

7. *Existence of substantial financial commitments.* The value of stock is lessened for valuation purposes by the existence of a heavy bond-retirement commitment or early maturities. Stock of a closely-held corporation was affected adversely by the fact that it was known widely that the company was to be subjected to Federal income taxes. Stock also would tend to have a lower value if the corporate assets were primarily securities and there was a "built-in" capital gains tax.

8. *Dispute among shareholders.* A purchaser of an interest in a corporation where there is dissension, in the words of one decision, "would know that, at best, he was 'buying a fight.' " What he would be willing to pay for the stock had to reflect this fact. In fact, *any* property is subject to valuation at a discount if its ownership or usage is subject to litigation.

9. *The dividend record.* A policy of liberal dividend payments is likely to make the shares of a corporation more attractive to persons of moderate or modest means. An individual in a high tax bracket might prefer to invest in a corporation that ploughs its earnings back into the business, for he is not desirous of getting dividends that are taxed in his stiff bracket. Dividend payments by a corporation do not set a value for the stock when distributions in recent years exceed corporate earnings.

10. *Breadth of customers.* If a corporation's earnings are imperilled by the possible loss of an important customer, the stock must be valued at a figure that reflects this hazard. A corporation with diverse customers would look more attractive to an investor in most situations.

Where a corporation relies primarily on government contracts, a potential buyer of the stock would be disturbed by cutbacks if the economy changed or by shifting currents in the political or international scene.

11. *The nature of the business and the history of the business from its inception.*

12. *The economic outlook in general, and the condition of the specific industry in particular.*

13. *The existence of good will and other intangibles.*

14. *Ability of management.*

15. *Condition of the corporation's physical plant and of its distribution methods.*

16. *Nature of the competition.*

17. *Valuation of the same corporation's stock that the decedent had placed on gift tax returns filed in the recent past.*

18. *Any other adverse factors that could disturb a potential buyer.*

Examples include poor public relations or a history of labor unrest.

Even after there has been agreement as to the valuation determined under these or other yardsticks, the question remains as to the weight to be given to each method.

## MINORITY INTERESTS IN CLOSELY-HELD CORPORATIONS

After a per-share valuation of stock in a closely-held corporation is arrived at, there is a question of how realistic this valuation is when the shares do not represent control. A person might be inclined to buy stock in a closely-held corporation if he felt that his policies could make the company more successful, or if he thought that his investment would enable him to become a senior officer, or to determine dividend policies, or to set his own compensation package, or to get jobs for his relatives. But if his interest does not represent control, he may realize that the other shareholders could "gang up" against him. In consequence, he would be inclined not to purchase shares unless he could get them at a bargain price. Accordingly, minority stock interests in a closely-held corporation usually are worth much less than the per-share value of the stock.

In the case of a 17 percent interest in a closely-held corporation, one court allowed a 50 percent discount from the estimated fair market value of the shares. Another decision permitted a 33.33 percent discount to an estate that owned 50 percent of the stock of a family corporation. Discounts ranging from 30 to 50 percent for minority interests are not unusual, 30 or 33.33 percent seeming to be the most common.

A minority interest in a closely-held corporation was not entitled to a discount, however, where the actual purchaser was not an outsider but the owner of the largest block of shares.

Discounts have been allowed in many instances to holders of a minority interest in an undivided real estate tract, because of the disadvantages of joint ownership with other parties who exercise complete dominion in all decisions. One decedent's undivided interest in real estate was given a 10 percent discount where this interest was a minority portion. Other decisions have allowed discounts of 12.5 percent and 15 percent in the case of urban real estate.

## MUTUAL FUNDS

For many years, the Internal Revenue Service insisted that the shares of open-end mutual funds must be valued at the "ask" price, which includes the enterprise's costs or profits. But the United States Supreme Court has held that such shares are to be valued at their redemption value, that is, at "bid."

## DETERMINING HIGHEST AND BEST USE

In order to determine the market value of a property according to its highest and best use, the required standard in virtually all situations, three techniques generally are accepted by the courts: income capitalization, reproduction cost minus depreciation, and comparative sales.

The technique used by courts in any particular case depends on the nature of the property to be valued. If more than one technique can appropriately be applied to a property, a court often will utilize all suitable techniques and base its valuation on the average of these results.

The *income capitalization* technique usually is applied to income-producing properties, such as apartments, hotels, and office buildings. An appraiser takes the estimated annual rent that can be obtained from the property (calculated from prior rentals of the same property or rentals of comparable properties) and multiplies it by a capitalization rate (determined by the rates of income and valuation of comparable properties) in order to obtain the market value of the property.

The *reproduction-cost-minus-depreciation* technique can be applied only to buildings or other improvements. The appraiser estimates the current replacement cost of the buildings and subtracts from that the estimated depreciation on the original cost of the property. This method is not useful if land is the chief value of the property.

The *comparative sales* technique uses the price of recent sales of comparable properties and general real estate price trends in order to estimate value. This method, of course, is most reliable when comparable properties have been sold in recent years.

## SPECIAL-USE VALUATION OF FARM AND OTHER REAL PROPERTY

As was mentioned earlier in this chapter, fair market value of property is based upon the highest and best use to which the property can be put, even if it is being used less productively.

But under carefully described conditions, certain real property used for farm or closely-held business purposes can be valued for tax purposes according to the use to which it has been put. This is the subject of Chapter 5.

## SPECIAL FACTORS IN VALUING REAL ESTATE

In the case of real property, one court stated that it had considered the topography of the land and the difficulties and costs of preparation attendant upon its zoned use, the availability at that time of a buyer with a unique interest in the land, the indication that a willing buyer would pay a lesser price for its use as zoned as compared to the price for park use, and access characteristics of the land.

The value of a building is lessened by an unfavorable lease, if this limitation upon earnings potential or saleability can be established.

Obsolescence and the need for physical improvements are limiting factors on a plant's value.

No consideration is given, however, to any temporary decline in the market value of land damaged by the impact of a storm.

The Internal Revenue Service may not increase the value of property by reason of a rezoning possibility if no application for rezoning was pending at the time of the decedent's death.

The worth of property as determined by valuation procedures can be reduced by a showing of such factors as:

☐ A possible cloud upon title.

☐ The likelihood that the ownership, use, or accessibility will be involved in litigation.

☐ The quality of police and fire protection.

☐ The availability of mortgage money.

Rather similar to the blockage theory in the valuation of securities, which was discussed earlier in this chapter, is the *absorption* theory in real estate. This is a price depressant caused by the disposition of the parcels of land in a short period of time, creating competition among the parcels that otherwise might not exist.

Neither insurance coverage nor assessed value must be considered as a basis for property valuation. There is no assurance that the property owner will insure his property in an amount equal to the fair market value; he may not even know what that is. And because of varying professional backgrounds of and pressures on local property tax assessors, their assessed values are not determinative of fair market value for tax purposes.

An individual may list his home with a broker at an inflated value, with the purpose of establishing that this is property held for the production of income so that he can deduct insurance and maintenance charges even though he is not in the real estate business. This can be dangerous. The exorbitant price was selected so that no one actually would rent or buy the property. But for tax purposes, the Internal Revenue Service may value it at the figure that the owner himself had placed upon his property, regardless of the reason for it.

## NOTES

Where a note is secured by collateral, or where the signer has some assets, it will not be regarded as having no fair market value, even though it may not be worth its face amount. In the absence of evidence to the contrary, notes are deemed to have value equal to their face amounts.

## CLAIMS

Claims are presumed to be worth the full amount stated, unless there is evidence to the contrary. Obviously, a disputed claim is of less value than one that is uncontested.

## WORKS OF ART

A ten-person advisory panel of art experts advises the Internal Revenue Service on the valuation of works of art. A court, however, can if it chooses overrule the aesthetic and market judgments of the art experts.

The valuation of a gift ordinarily is determined from the known facts when it was presented. But if the donee of a work of art sells it shortly after receipt, the proceeds customarily determine what the art was worth for tax purposes.

The taxable value of property is what can be obtained from a sale, not the net which can be retained when the property is sold. Thus, *taxable value is not reduced by the commission* (such as 33.33 percent) that an art gallery would charge for selling property.

## VALUATION BY ACTUARIAL TABLES

In some instances, property owned by a decedent can only be valued for estate tax purposes by taking into account the length of time over which payments will be received or the length of time until some specific event happens. Here are some examples.

## ANNUITIES

If an annuity is for the life of the decedent only, payments stop when his life does, and no valuation remains. But if the valuation of the interest involved is dependent upon the continuation or the termination of more than one life, or upon a term dependent upon one or more lives, a special factor must be used. The factor is computed on the basis of interest at a specified rate, such as 6 percent a year, compounded annually. Life contingencies are determined, as to each male and female life involved, according to actuarial tables.

## LIFE ESTATES

The decedent may have been entitled to certain property, such as in a trust fund, after the death of a designated person who will receive income each year for as long as he lives. Valuation of the decedent's interest is based upon the total value of the property less the value of the interest of the so-called *life tenant*. The latter interest is based upon his actuarial life expectancy. But if the income beneficiary's life span, according to competent medical testimony, cannot possibly be as long as the tables indicate, the value of the interest will be computed according to the length of expected life indicated by medical testimony. A life beneficiary suffering from cancer in inoperable form and a person who is helpless, without memory and almost completely paralyzed as the result of a cerebral attack, are the types of exceptional case that can justify by-passing. The second situation brought about the so-called ''Jennings Rule,'' which provides that when a valuation depends on the length of somebody's life, actuarial computations must be used unless it is shown medically that the result is so unrealistic and unreasonable that value must be determined in another manner.

## REVERSIONARY INTERESTS

The decedent may have transferred property for another person's benefit in trust for as long as the other person lives. If a man under a divorce decree sets up a trust account for the benefit of his ex-wife for as long as she lives, the principal to return to him should she die first, he has a reversionary interest. Here, again, actuarial tables determine the value of his interest in the trust fund, unless medical testimony indicates that the length of his ex-wife's life will be shorter than her supposed life expectancy.

The fact that someone, such as a life tenant, actually dies shortly after the decedent does not justify valuing the decedent's interest other than by actuarial tables based on the tenant's life, if death actually results from a cause not covered by a sound medical prophecy.

## AFTEREVENTS

The valuation of property held by a decedent when he died must be made on the date of his death or six months later, according to the executor's election, without regard to events occurring subsequent to the crucial dates. Thus, evidence of a sale of property taking place after the crucial date has no bearing on the originally indicated valuation where there was some material change of conditions or circumstances after that date. Such was the situation when, less than a year after a decedent's death, a large national corporation decided to acquire a huge tract in which the decedent's property was located, and the community agreed to install sewer and water systems to accommodate the corporation. Even the most optimistic of real estate speculators could not reasonably have foreseen these circumstances.

## VALUE SET BY EXPERTS

Where only one party to a tax dispute, either the taxpayer or the Internal Revenue Service, introduces testimony of a professional appraiser, the court usually will accept this as the true value. But a court may disregard professional testimony that seems to be lacking in true disinterested opinions. Sometimes a judge himself will examine the property in question or will in some other manner decide what the true value really is.

It is important for an executor to select an appraiser with sufficiently imposing qualifications. In one case, both the taxpayer and the I.R.S. used real estate experts. How could the court decide which of the professional consultants knew better what he was talking about? The court decided to rely on the government's expert witness because the records of the two specialists showed that he had passed the examination of the American Institute of Real Estate Appraisers, while the taxpayer's expert had failed to pass it. In another case, the valuation of the I.R.S. expert was rejected. Said the judge: "He stumbled over the definition of fair market value. His reasoning and conclusions are not convincing."[1]

Clearly, a court is put in a difficult spot when each party has a thoroughly trained expert and the experts cannot agree as to the proper valuation to use. Sometimes a judge recommends that the parties get together and come to an understanding, so that he is not placed in a Solomon-like role. Such a procedure, observed one judge, is "a process clearly more conclusive to the proper disposition of disputes such as this."[2] Another judge, in a dispute involving the valuation of a minority interest in a closely-held corporation, commented that, "Cases of this kind would be better disposed of by honest bargaining of the experts rather than by lengthy trials and conflicting testimony of those experts."[3]

If a valuation dispute is submitted to a court for judgment because the taxpayer and the Internal Revenue Service cannot agree, it is indeed possible that neither of the parties will be satisfied by the result.

## ALTERNATE VALUATION

The executor may elect to value the estate's assets at the date of death or six months later. This is a valuable privilege if prices have gone down in this six-month interval. Where estate assets have been sold in arm's length transactions during the six-month interval, the actual selling price of the property sold will be the value.

This election must be made on an estate tax return that was filed on time. The election does not count, and valuation as of the date of death must be used, when the estate tax return on which the election was manifested is filed tardily, even though the executor relies on the advice of an accountant who is unclear about dates. The election cannot be made when the value of the estate does not exceed the applicable credits and, therefore, a return is not required.

## NEW PENALTY FOR VALUATION OVERSTATEMENTS

In the case of tax returns filed after December 31, 1981, there is a new penalty applicable to certain income tax "valuation overstatements." This applies only to the extent of an income tax underpayment that is attribut-

[1] Nellie I. Brown, T.C. Memo 1966-92, filed April 28, 1966.
[2] Morris M. Messing, 48 T.C. 502 (1967).
[3] Airdrie K. Pinkerton Estate, T.C. Memo 1974-71, filed March 26, 1974.

able to an overstatement where the taxpayer is an individual, a closely-held corporation, or a personal service corporation. There is a valuation overstatement if the value or the adjusted basis of any property claimed on any return exceeds the amount that should have been used.

| *If the valuation claimed is the following percent of the correct valuation:* | *The applicable percentage is:* |
|---|---|
| Under 150 | 0 |
| More than 150 but not more than 200 | 10 |
| More than 200 but not more than 250 | 20 |
| More than 250 | 30 |

In consequence, when a person sells property that he has received by gift or by inheritance, and he uses a valuation figure that is too high so that reported gain on the transaction is less than it should have been, the new penalties may apply.

# 5

## SPECIAL-USE VALUATION OF CERTAIN FARMS AND OTHER REAL PROPERTY

If certain conditions are met, an executor may elect to value real property in a decedent's estate that is devoted to farming or to other closely-held businesses at its fair market value determined in the customary way rather than on the basis of the highest and best use to which it can be put.

Although this opportunity has been available in appropriate situations since the Tax Reform Act of 1976, many changes made by the Economic Recovery Act of 1981 have enlarged the scope of the provision to such an extent that a fresh look should be taken at the possibilities.

Valuation of land on the basis of its highest and best use rather than actual use could result in the imposition of substantially higher estate taxes. In some cases, the greater estate tax burden would make continuation of the farming or other activities carried on quite infeasible because the income potential from these activities is insufficient to service extended tax payments or loans obtained to pay the taxes. Thus, the heirs might be forced to sell the land for development or other purposes that are more productive than the present use.

## QUALIFYING FOR CURRENT-USE VALUATION

If all of the requirements can be met, a decedent's gross estate may be reduced by employment of a lower valuation. The reduction, however, cannot exceed $600,000 for persons dying in 1981, $700,000 for those dying in 1982, and $750,000 for those dying in 1983 and later years.

An estate may qualify for current-use valuation if:

1. The decedent was a citizen or resident of the United States.

2. The adjusted value of the farm or closely-held business assets in his estate, including both real and personal property, is at least 50 percent of

the adjusted value of the decedent's gross estate. The value of property here and in item 3, below, is determined without regard to its special-use value.

3. At least 25 percent of the adjusted value of the gross estate is qualified farm or closely-held business real estate.

4. The real property qualifying for current-use valuation passes to a *qualified heir*. That means a member of the decedent's family, including his spouse, parents, brothers, sisters, children, stepchildren, and spouses and lineal descendants of those individuals.

5. The real property has been owned by the decedent or a member of his family and used or held for use as a farm or closely-held business (a "qualified use") for five of the last eight years prior to the decedent's death. This qualified-use requirement may be satisfied if either the decedent or a member of his family uses real property otherwise eligible for current-use valuation in the qualified use. There must be an active trade or business use, as opposed to a passive or an investment use.

6. There must have been a material participation in the operation of the farm or closely-held business by the decedent or a member of his family for periods aggregating at least five of the last eight years in the period ending before the earliest of (a) the date of the decedent's death, (b) the date on which he became permanently disabled, or (c) the date on which he began receiving Social Security retirement benefits. There is an alternative to the material participation requirement for qualification of real property for current-use valuation in the estate of surviving spouses (here called "wives" for simplicity's sake) who die within eight years of the decedent if they receive the property from a decedent spouse in whose estate it was eligible to be valued on the basis of current use. The wife is treated as having materially participated during periods when she was engaged in the active management of the farm or other business operation. Active management for this purpose means the making of business decisions other than the daily operating decisions.

7. The executor makes an election on the estate tax return when it is filed. All parties with any interest in the property must enter into an agreement consenting to the election. The required agreement must be binding under the laws of the state in which each party resides. This could require that a guardian be appointed for minor heirs solely for the purpose of signing the agreement.

In order to determine whether property had been held long enough to meet the time requirements for ownership, qualified use, and material participation, the holding periods are combined where there has been a like-kind exchange or the replacement of what had been lost through an involuntary conversion, as where land had been seized by a municipality for public use and had been replaced.

Property is considered to be acquired from a decedent only if (1) the qualified heir receives this property by inheritance, (2) it is received in satisfaction of a right to a monetary bequest, or (3) it is purchased by a qualified heir from the decedent's estate.

## PROPERTY THAT QUALIFIES

In the case of qualifying real property where the ownership, use, and material participation requirements are satisfied, the real property that qualifies for current-use valuation includes the farmhouse, other residential buildings, and related improvements located on qualifying real property if the buildings are occupied on a regular basis by the owner or lessee of the real property (or by employees of the owner or lessee) for the purpose of operating or maintaining the real property or the business conducted on the property. Qualified real property also includes roads, buildings, and other structures and improvements functionally related to the qualified use.

Property owned indirectly through ownership of an interest in a partnership, a corporation, or a trust qualifies for current-use valuation to the extent that it would qualify if directly owned.

Property meeting the other requirements for current-use valuation can be specially valued if it passes to a discretionary trust in which no beneficiary has a present interest because of the discretion in the trustee to determine the amount to be received by any individual beneficiary, so long as all potential beneficiaries of the trust are qualified heirs.

In general, a "farm" includes stock, dairy, poultry, fruit, fur-bearing animals, and truck farms; plantations, ranches, nurseries, ranges, and greenhouses or similar structures used primarily for the raising of agricultural or horticultural commodities. Farms also include orchards and woodlands, which are subject to certain special rules. In deciding whether real property is used as a farm for farming purposes, the activities engaged in on the real property determine the question. In addition to cultivation of the soil, raising or harvesting of agricultural commodities, and preparing such commodities for market, farming purposes also include the planting, cultivation, caring for, or cutting of trees, and the preparation (other than milling) of trees for market.

## DETERMINING CURRENT-USE VALUE

The current-use value can be determined under either of two methods:

1. The *multiple factor method* takes into account those factors normally used in the valuation of real estate (for example, comparable sales)

and any other factors that fairly value the property without regard to any use other than its current use.

2. The *formula method* is used where there is comparable land from which the average gross cash rental may be determined. Farm property (but not property used in other trades or businesses) may be valued under the formula method, which involves complex comparisons relating to property taxes, interest rates, capitalization of income yields and of rentals, and other factors. Net crop rentals may be substituted for cash rentals if the executor cannot identify actual tracts of comparable farm property in the same locality as the decedent's that are rented solely for cash.

The determination of whether property is comparable is factual and is made on a case-by-case basis, with no single factor being conclusive. Different parcels of real property need not be exactly alike to be compared, however. Comparability requires only that the value of the different parcels be equivalent or similar in their farming use.

## RECAPTURE OF FARM OR CLOSELY-HELD VALUATION ADJUSTMENT

It would be a windfall to the beneficiaries of an estate to allow farm or other closely-held business property to be valued for estate tax purposes at a value other than its highest and best use, *unless* the beneficiaries continue to use the property for a reasonable period as the decedent did before he died. To forestall that possibility, there is a recapture provision. If, within ten years after the death of the decedent (but before the death of the qualified heir), the property is disposed of to nonfamily members or it ceases to be used for farming or other closely-held business purposes, any tax benefits obtained by virtue of the reduced valuation are to be recaptured by means of an "additional estate tax" imposed upon the qualified heir. The qualified heir owning the real estate after the decedent's death must use the property in the qualified use throughout its recapture period in order to avoid the tax. But there is a two-year grace period during which his failure to commence use of the property in the same manner will not result in imposition of the recapture tax. If the qualified heir dies without having disposed of the property or converting it to a nonqualified use, or if a period of ten years from the decedent's death elapses, the potential liability for recapture ceases.

But if an involuntary conversion of qualified real property takes place (such as a state's exercise of its right of eminent domain), no recapture of the estate tax benefit occurs where the property is replaced by other real property of at least equal value that is to be given the same use. To the extent that involuntary conversion property is not replaced, the recapture tax is taken into account in determining gain or loss for income tax purposes in a manner similar to the adjustment made on account of estate taxes.

## SPECIAL LIEN

If an election is made to value property according to its current use, the qualified heir's income tax basis in the property is the current-use value. No adjustment is made to this basis if the additional estate tax is imposed. Where the recapture tax is paid, a qualified heir is permitted to make an irrevocable election to have the income tax basis of qualified real property increased to fair market value as of the date of the decedent's death or the alternate valuation date if that had been chosen by the executor. If the heir elects this basic adjustment, he must pay interest on the amount of the recapture tax from the date nine months after the decedent's death until the due date of the recapture tax.

Where the election is made to value qualified property according to the actual use rather than its highest and best use, a special lien arises on the property that continues until the earlier of the recapture of the tax benefit or the termination of the potential liability for recapture, such as the death of a qualified heir or the expiration of a ten-year period from the decedent's death. A qualified heir may be discharged from personal liability and is entitled to a receipt or writing that shows this discharge if he furnishes a bond that meets certain requirements. In order to comply with this bond procedure, he must make written application to the Secretary of the Treasury for a determination of the maximum amount of additional tax that may be imposed by the special-use-valuation provision with respect to his interest. The Secretary must notify the heir of the maximum amount of the recapture tax as soon as possible and, in any event, within one year after the making of the application. If the qualified heir furnishes a bond in this amount and for such period as may be required (which, in general, should be no longer than the period to which the recapture tax applies), he will be discharged from personal liability. The maximum amount of the bond does not include interest on the amount of his personal liability, even though interest may accrue on the amount of the recapture tax imposed from the date of the imposition until the date the tax is paid.

# 6

## THE TOOLS OF ESTATE PLANNING

Estate planning is the game plan by which one arranges to transmit his wealth at appropriate times to parties of his choice in order to meet his own objectives in the most effective manner. To help him in this endeavor, various tools are available, some of which have become more effective because of new provisions in the Economic Recovery Tax Act of 1981. The order in which these tools are used will vary from person to person, and the following sequence is more or less arbitrary.

## THE WILL

A will leaves directions for an individual's deathtime transfer of his interests in property. It also expresses other wishes he has concerning, for example, funeral and bill-paying arrangements. There need not be immediate dispositions to beneficiaries; money or other property can be transferred for their benefits to testamentary trusts. The names of the beneficiaries, what each will receive, and when may not even be spelled out if trustees are provided with discretionary powers.

Even if a person has a valid will, he does not have full discretion as to how his wealth is to be apportioned. Under law, which varies from state to state, a surviving spouse is entitled to a specific portion of the decedent's property (called "dower" in the case of a widow and "curtesy" in the case of a widower). If that proportion, expressed in terms of dollars, is not left to the survivor, he or she can "take against the will" at the expense of the named beneficiaries. In a few states, minor children automatically are entitled to a specific portion of a parent's deathtime wealth, regardless of whether the will has made provision for this.

Actually, a considerable portion of the wealth of all decedents does not pass under the provisions of wills. Life insurance proceeds customarily are distributed according to policy provisions. Trusts set up during a person's lifetime make their distributions according to the trust agreement. Jointly-held property may go to co-owners or survivors under arrangements made many years ago. What happens to an individual's interest in a business could be controlled by buy-sell agreements or other arrangements. But an individual should have a will, because he cannot be certain that all of his property will be covered by some other distribution procedure.

A will has been defined as "a dead giveaway." But it can be more than that. For example, if a parent makes no provision for the naming of a guardian for minor children should they be orphaned, a court will take over that responsibility, with results the parent may not have intended.

The validity of a will depends upon the laws of the state where the decedent was domiciled. Probably the most common reason for a will's being invalid is failure to comply with state law on the number of witnesses to the document. Should a person die without a will, or without a valid will, here are some consequences:

☐ His property will be divided according to his state's intestacy laws. This means that his property will not go to the persons of his choice, or in the amounts he desired, distribution being in accordance to a sequential scheme based, in general, upon defined next-of-kin relationships. Thus a decedent's wealth can go to persons to whom he would not have left a kopeck. Example: Howard Hughes.

☐ Property may go to his next-of-kin, as he could have wanted, but not in the manner he would have chosen. For example, cash or complex business interests might pass directly to relatives who lack the experience or capacity to handle what is dumped into their laps in a lump sum.

☐ There will be no equalization of inequitable lifetime gifts, an imbalance that the decedent might have pledged to rectify.

☐ Property may go to a person who does not need or even want it because of burdensome administrative headaches.

☐ Wealth may pass to someone who is very old or who is critically ill, with the result that this property soon will be subjected to transfer taxes again.

☐ A state court will name an administrator to handle the estate instead of the carefully selected executor that the decedent could have named or perhaps even did name. This administrator all too frequently is completely ignorant of the decedent's affairs and aspirations, and his qualifications, experience, and even honesty may have had nothing to do with his appointment.

A will should make provisions for contingencies. It should specify what happens if a beneficiary dies before the testator, or if he refuses the inheritance, or if he cannot be found. It should make reference to a successor or contingent executor if the person named cannot or will not serve; otherwise, that administrator fellow will be named by a court.

Wills should be reviewed frequently. Have your priorities changed?

Are needs of your relatives the same or, for that matter, have the persons who are your relatives changed? New legislation, such as the Economic Recovery Tax Act of 1981, demands a review of all existing wills. A review may be required if you move to another state where property rights or other matters are treated differently.

Married persons frequently have the following problem when wills are being prepared: The husband would like to leave all or a substantial part of his property to his wife. But he fears that should she survive him, none of what had been his property will go to his friends when she dies. The wife is likely to have comparable feelings when her will is prepared. A joint will may be used to cope with the problem(s): After discussion or negotiation, the will, to be signed by each spouse, provides how property will be distributed to the nominees of each upon the death of the second spouse. Mutual wills are two separate instruments, separately signed, with the same ultimate allocations.

Prior to 1982, joint and mutual wills were regarded with some distaste by many persons because the marital deduction was lost to the estate of the first spouse to die, being a terminable interest, that is, the second spouse did not receive the property to dispose of as she saw fit. But with the greatly increased unified transfer tax credits of the Economic Recovery Tax Act of 1981 and the enlarged marital deduction possibility, this objection now seems far less serious.

## SIMULTANEOUS-DEATH PROVISIONS

A will customarily makes provision for what happens upon the death of the testator. But because of such factors as longer vacations and the taking along of one's spouse when going on a business trip, there is increasing likelihood that both parties will die in a common disaster. If it is not possible to determine the exact sequence of dying there are problems as to what happens in the case of property passing to the spouse if she survives the testator, insurance proceeds on the husband that are payable to the wife if she still is living, the passage of property that is owned jointly with right of survivorship, and the like.

To solve the usually unanswerable question of rights when the order of death is unknown, the various states have adopted variations on the Uniform Simultaneous Death Act. Wills, life insurance policies, joint ownership agreements, and other documents should make provisions for what happens when there are simultaneous deaths. State laws make certain assumptions in the absence of other guidelines. But if you do not like the way the standard arrangement would work out in your case, it is possible to utilize a reverse simultaneous-death clause.

This subject will be discussed in Chapter 15.

## THE TRUST

Of all estate planning tools, the trust is most versatile. A person can part with property without turning it over to young, inexperienced, untrustworthy, or unwilling recipients. The actual, ultimate recipients may not even be known when a trust is created. Meanwhile, the grantor of the trust can postpone questions of ultimate enjoyment of the property or its income until a later date. He can avoid Federal income taxes on income-producing property even, if desired, until his retirement years, when he again will need more income and would like to get back the property. He can insulate property from the claims of his creditors in most instances. He can obtain the advantage of professional, permanent administrators for the property or its income.

This important subject will be discussed in Chapter 7.

## THE MARITAL DEDUCTION

In the case of married persons, the biggest reduction of gross estate usually is the marital deduction. Its use is possible, but it is not always desirable.

The marital deduction, in the case of gifts made and decedents dying after December 31, 1981, can provide for unlimited spousal transfers if the ground rules are met. But the usually oversimplified explanations of this apparently straightforward subject do not hint at the traps and pitfalls that must be avoided.

This is the subject of Chapter 8.

## A CONTINUOUS, ANNUAL-GIFT PROGRAM

Because of the $10,000-per-donee annual gift tax exclusion (that can be doubled in the case of married persons who consent to this treatment), a considerable amount of wealth can be transferred to persons other than one's spouse without any gift or estate tax liability. Under appropriate circumstances, this now includes more than direct gifts.

But there is no carryover of unused annual gift tax exclusions. That means that, in order to qualify, gifts must be made each year, starting as soon in one's life as possible. Gifts can be made with borrowed money, in noncash form, or as the result of a corporate reorganization.

Further consideration of the subject will appear in the chapter on gift taxes (Chapter 9) and elsewhere in this book.

## UNIFORM GIFTS TO MINORS ACT

If a gift is made to a minor, there are two principal problems: (1) It will be difficult if not impossible to sell the property should funds be required or should the market appear to be deteriorating, because a minor can repudiate any business transactions he makes once he becomes of age; in consequence, purchases from him present grave difficulties; and (2) The value of the property is likely to be includible in the gross estate of the parent or other person who controls the property while the recipient still is a minor.

But a procedure exists for making gifts, annual or otherwise, to the minor, while avoiding the two problems identified here. It will be discussed in Chapter 9.

## POWERS OF APPOINTMENT

Under a well-thought-out arrangement, a person is able to have distributions of his property made after his death in the light of circumstances as they exist at that time. He also is enabled to avoid having to make difficult intra-family or other decisions.

The methodology will be considered in Chapter 12.

## POWERS OF ATTORNEY

A person may be incapacitated by an illness or accident, as a result of which he is unable to institute business, investment, or other actions that can affect the amount of his wealth or the conduct of his affairs. But with some advance planning, it can be arranged that decisions are made, perhaps within guidelines which he had set, while he is unable to participate in the action.

This will be reviewed in Chapter 12, along with powers of appointment.

## LIFE INSURANCE

There are may ways in which life insurance can be used as a tool in estate planning: increasing what will be one's ultimate estate, giving liquidity to the estate, funding business continuation agreements, leaving one's family without mortgage indebtedness, providing flexibility in family financial areas. But a person's life insurance can create a widely overlooked estate tax liability when he dies if proper steps are not taken.

Chapter 13 is devoted to this question.

## OTHER INSURANCE AND INDEMNIFICATION ARRANGEMENTS

An estate planning tool need not be one that is used affirmatively. Negative or defensive tools are equally useful. A person can protect the size of the estate he would leave to his beneficiaries by taking steps to see that it is not eroded or eliminated by what happens to him or to his property. Where appropriate, he should take out malpractice and other liability insurance. If he is a businessperson, he should endeavor to have his employer adopt a reimbursement program to cover the financial consequences of decisions or acts he undertakes in the company's behalf. Directors' and officers' liability policies are available both to a corporation and to an executive. He should take out hospitalization and major medical coverage.

Chapter 22 covers these issues.

## ENSURE THAT YOUR INSURANCE IS IN EFFECT

A lapsed insurance policy can be very expensive to your estate. Keep follow-up files so that there is a reminder to pay premiums even if notices are not received or if they are misfiled. Frequently, arrangements can be made so that unpaid premiums automatically are paid from cash surrender value or other cash values. A funded life insurance trust can see that premiums are paid, while at the same time insulating the insurance from creditors' claims.

## ANNUITIES

There are many uses of annuities, commercial or family, in estate planning. Chapter 14 discusses this subject.

## CORPORATE REORGANIZATIONS

The tax-free reorganization is an estate planning tool with many uses: making contributions for income tax purposes or charitable bequests without loss of corporate control, redemption by a corporation of a decedent's stock without dividend implications, assuring continuity of management, establishing a fair market value for stock in a closely-held corporation.

See Chapter 17, "The Uses of Tax-Free Reorganizations."

## FORM IN WHICH PROPERTY IS HELD

Selection of the form in which property is held has both tax and other consequences: joint ownership, co-ownership with right of survivorship, and others. The Economic Recovery Tax Act of 1981 has had significant impact upon husband-wife co-ownership.

This subject will be treated subsequently in Chapter 10.

## BUSINESS CONTINUATION ARRANGEMENTS

To a businessperson, there may be no more serious problem than what happens to his interest in a closely-held corporation upon the death of himself or of another important shareholder.

Several solutions are examined in Chapter 16, "Problems When a Major Stockholder Dies."

## RETIREMENT PLANS

A person can obtain various advantages through a tax-favored retirement plan. What otherwise would be taxable income in high bracket years of maximum productivity may be deferred until retirement, when the wage earner predictably will be in a lower tax bracket. Arrangements can be made to have the deferred income paid out in the form of a survivorship annuity that includes his spouse.

Through the medium of an executive search agency, it may be possible to find employment with a corporation that, as part of its compensation package, will offer a worthwhile retirement program. The form in which employer-provided annual benefits are made may be selected afresh each year if there is a cafeteria plan.

## GOOD RECORDS

A fine tool of estate planning is the defensive one of good records. Proper documentation and back-up records can explain transactions and avoid unnecessary Federal income tax disallowances. Ideally, these records should be in such a form that your executor or someone engaged by him can satisfy the Internal Revenue Service examiners when you no longer are available to explain your tax return entries. (See Chapters 21 and 22, which discuss how to make it easier for your executor and for your beneficiaries.) Beneficiaries' Federal income tax treatment upon sale of gifted property and inheritances can depend upon the records you make available on cost basis and other matters. Beneficiaries can avoid unnecessary transferee liability if the documentation of your own tax returns is good.

## SELECTION OF PROPER EXECUTOR(S)

The choice of the proper person can do much to ensure that the decedent's properties are located and gathered in for the beneficiaries, are properly managed, and are effectively distributed. Once an executor has been chosen, the matter should not be forgotten. The decedent-to-be should reconsider his selection regularly, in order to see that the person is still willing to serve, and is interested, competent, and abreast of present-day conditions.

## PURCHASE OF "FLOWER BONDS"

Where it is apparent that Federal estate tax will have to be paid, the decedent-to-be should consider the purchase of "flower bonds." These are certain issues of United States Treasuries that can be presented for payment of estate taxes at par. Because of their very low interest rates, these bonds are selling well below par. So there is an assured savings if these securities are part of one's estate when he dies.

This subject will be considered in Chapter 20, which covers procedural requirements.

# 7

## THE TRUST: THE MOST VERSATILE TOOL OF ALL

In the past, one of the principal uses of trusts was to keep as much of a person's property as possible out of his estate when he died, the property at that time belonging not to him but to a separate legal entity, the trust. With the virtual phasing out of an individual's estate tax liability by 1987 under the provisions of the Economic Recovery Tax Act of 1981, this one aspect of the use of trusts in estate planning has lost its primary importance, except in the case of very large estates. But the trust form has many estate planning uses other than the saving of estate taxes.

## NATURE OF A TRUST

Most of the uses of a trust center on the fact that its principal or the income that it generates is insulated from the person who has created the trust. His wealth is being used to effectuate his desires, but he is protected from important tax and other consequences of property ownership.

The starting point is definitional. The person who sets up the trust is known by several names, most frequently as the *grantor* or *settlor*. A trust is set up for the benefit of one or more *beneficiaries*. A *testamentary trust* is created under the terms of a decedent's will, while an *inter vivos* trust is set up by a person who still is alive, such as through the instrumentality of a deed or declaration of trust. The principal of a trust is known as the *corpus*. The *trustee*, sometimes referred to as the *fiduciary*, may be one or more persons; a corporate trustee most commonly is a bank or trust company. One or more beneficiaries may get some or all of the trust's income under the terms of a trust agreement; they are the *income beneficiaries*. When a trust terminates, what remains after specific bequests goes to a *remainderman* or, as a trust agreement frequently provides, back to the grantor or his estate. A trust that must distribute all of its income currently, without any discretion on the part of the fiduciary, is a *simple trust*. Any other trust, such as one where the trustee is empowered to accumulate income or to exercise certain discretion, is a *complex trust*. If the grantor may terminate a trust, it is *revocable*. If he lacks this power, it is an *irrevocable trust*. Where a trust agreement provides that under specified conditions or after a given period of time, the corpus goes back to the grantor, this is a *reversionary trust*.

A function of the trust form is to separate the legal title, such as held by the fiduciary and the equitable title, such as held by the beneficiary or beneficiaries. Inasmuch as the grantor has parted with his interests in the property he has transferred to the trust, he no longer has any interest in the trust property or income. But he may have a reversionary interest.

## THE FEDERAL TAX ASPECTS OF A TRUST

Although a trust is created under the laws of a particular state, Federal tax treatment of the trust is governed by Federal law. A trust will not be recognized for Federal tax purposes unless steps have been taken to avoid the dangers of the three R's:

- ☐ Revocability
- ☐ Reversionary interests
- ☐ Retained powers

If a trust can be revoked by its grantor at will, it could be said that he really has not let go of the property. Otherwise, he would not have any power over it. Hence, the income from the trust property is taxable to him, and the value of the property is includible in his gross estate when he dies.

A trust may be characterized as revocable by the Internal Revenue Service simply because there is nothing that declares it is irrevocable. In some states, such as California, it is provided that unless a trust specifically is made irrevocable, it is a revocable trust.

There may be good reasons why a grantor would like to have the opportunity of revoking a trust that he had created. But he should consider whether these reasons are more meaningful to him than the additional taxes that could be involved.

Although the law of the state where it was created may not impose such a requirement, a trust will not be recognized for Federal tax purposes if it lacks economic reality. The familiar rule of form versus substance is particularly applicable to trusts because they easily are susceptible to manipulation.

A grantor may learn of the danger of the three R's or of lack of economic reality after he has created a trust. But a trust instrument can be modified only if a power of modification is included in the trust agreement, and the grantor may not modify the trust unless he has reserved that power to himself in the instrument. This reservation is likely to be characterized as a retained power, because if he has the ability to make changes affecting the property that allegedly no longer is his, he has not really let go of it.

Usually, a Federal court will tax a trust in accordance with the way it was constituted in the taxable year, without reference to the fact that a state court subsequently permitted a retroactive modification of the trust agreement.

Despite the importance of intent in deciding many tax questions, intent to create a trust is not enough to afford recognition of the trust for Federal tax purposes.

## WHY A TRUST?

Here are a number of ways in which a trust may be used advantageously:

1. If a person's property, during his lifetime or at his death, goes to one or more beneficiaries, they may quickly lose the wealth that he wanted them to have because of their inexperience or ineptitude. A properly thought-out and executed trust agreement will enable a person to part with his property or income without giving a beneficiary unqualified control over what is transmitted. A professional trustee or a competent friend or relative may serve as a trustee or co-trustee. Trusts for the benefit of children customarily terminate when a child becomes twenty-one, but there is no requirement for that. A trust may be for the benefit of a grantor's children until they attain what he considers to be a state of maturity, for example, age fifty.

2. A trust may be used in order to reduce Federal income taxes by the transfer of income-producing property to a fiduciary for some other party's benefit. A trust that is valid for tax purposes is a separate taxable entity. Thus, income of the trust may be taxed at lower rates than if it were taxed to the grantor. If several trusts are used properly, income is spread and the higher tax brackets never need be reached. Special scrutiny of any arrangement is necessary lest what is in reality but one economic unit be multiplied into two or more by devices that though valid under state law, are not conclusively genuine as far as the Federal law is concerned. A person may use a short-term trust (to be discussed later in this chapter) in order to reduce his income taxes during his years of greatest productivity (and highest income-tax brackets) without depriving himself of the use of this property after retirement or in other later years when his income will probably be less.

3. The employment of a trust can save the grantor from paying

property taxes on many forms of tangible or intangible property that had been transferred to a fiduciary.

4. A grantor may be saved custodial, insurance, management, and conservation expenses of property transferred to the trust.

5. A trust may be utilized to set up funds for the support of a dependent for life. Property can be placed in an irrevocable trust, for the benefit of aged dependents, handicapped children or other persons, and thus escape being thrown into the grantor's gross estate when he dies. One mother transferred stock to a trust for the benefit of her invalid and mentally retarded daughter, the shares to go at the daughter's death to the grantor's nieces. This irrevocable trust gave the grantor peace of mind and assured her that her daughter would be taken care of.

6. Property may be placed in trust so that this property or its income are subject to the discretion of a trustee, to be used in accordance with guidelines set up by the grantor or, if so provided, the judgment of the trustee or trustees (the so-called "sprinkling" or "spray" trust). These picturesque terms come from the language of a court decision that referred to a trustee's right "to sprinkle the income among the beneficiaries he may select (as if he were playing a hose). . . ." In a sprinkling trust, the trustee is given the discretion to ascertain which member or members of a family or a *defined class of beneficiaries* is to receive principal or income of a trust, and to what extent. Income may be accumulated instead of being distributed, if so provided.

A definite standard may or may not be provided in the trust agreement. Flexibility is not only one of the most attractive attributes of a gift to a class of beneficiaries. It is also universally accepted as a prerequisite to the creation of a *class gift;* that is, the size of the group usually must be able either to expand or to contract, with a resultant increase or decrease in the size of the share of an individual member.

The grantor of a sprinkling trust should not name himself as the trustee. He may be taxed on trust income if he has the right to sprinkle income to any member of a family and that includes himself. The annual gift tax exclusion is not available to the donor, inasmuch as no beneficiary's right to income can be evaluated.

7. A trust may be used to reapportion income among various other trusts (the so-called "pour-over" trust). For example, a grantor set up four trusts by will. Three of the trusts had named beneficiaries and successor beneficiaries, and provision was made that after the death of the last surviving beneficiary, the remaining trust funds would be transferred to the fourth trust, which was to have entirely different objectives. The first three trusts were of the "pour-over" character. Or an individual could set up several trusts, with different objectives and needs for funds. At the same time he sets up a "pour-over" trust, the sole function of which is to be a source of funds for any of the other trusts that had exhausted its own resources.

8. A trust may be employed in order to keep property under the ultimate control of the grantor or his beneficiaries. For example, when money is set aside as security for alimony payments, the principal may return to the grantor or to his estate when the spouse dies or remarries, if the trust instrument so provides. An individual may wish to leave property or its income to his widowed daughter-in-law, but only as long as she does not remarry. That, in the grantor's mind, might relieve him of any further moral responsibility for providing what his deceased son had failed to provide.

9. One use of a trust is to hold insurance policies on the grantor's life, to pay the premiums, and to make decisions, if desired, as to settlement options on these policies. If a grantor has transferred all of his interest in the policies irrevocably to the trustee, the cash surrender value of the insurance cannot be reached by his creditors, including the Internal Revenue Service. Payment of premiums could be from funds or income-producing securities transferred to the trust for this purpose.

10. Although a grantor customarily regards a trust he creates as being for the protection of someone else, he may also provide for his own protection by transferring assets irrevocably to a trust for his own benefit, thereby safeguarding the assets from the consequences of faulty judgment, carelessness, poor perception of character, or undue influence of other parties as he gets older.

11. A trust may be used by an individual so that an income tax deduction is available before a decision is made concerning who will get the contributions and what the amounts will be.

12. Through the mechanism of a trust, it can be provided that a charitable organization will get periodic income after the grantor's death, in line with what had been his lifetime custom (the so-called "charitable" trust). The fact that a state court recognizes an entity as a charitable trust is not controlling for Federal tax purposes. A charitable trust properly may discriminate in favor of relatives, friends, or ex-employees of the grantor, as long as the class of beneficiaries is a legitimate classification. For example, a trust may be set up for the benefit of families whose incomes are below the poverty level set by a stipulated governmental agency, preferences to be given to relatives of the grantor. Similarly, an educational fund could be set up to send to college qualified youths who cannot afford to pay tuition, preference to be given to members of the grantor's family.

13. A trust may be used in order to make deductible contributions to a foreign charity, such as the birthplace of the donor. An individual is not entitled to a deduction for a charitable bequest to a foreign political subdivision. But such a bequest can be made to a trust set up for purely charitable purposes.

14. One use of a trust is to make money available for the use of dependents without having the principal subject to claims of a dependent's credi-

tors (the so-called "spendthrift" trust). State laws vary as to whether spendthrift trusts will be recognized. In some jurisdictions, such trusts are considered to be a fraud against creditors. Various state courts, such as in Maryland, have upheld spendthrift trusts against the claims of creditors, but *not* against Federal tax claims. The right of the United States to collect unpaid taxes prevails over spendthrift trusts notwithstanding state statutes that exempt a portion of the beneficiary's support payments from creditors' claims. If a spendthrift trust instrument provides that the trustee is to have discretion to decide whether trust income should be distributed to a beneficiary, this is not a present interest that would qualify for the annual gift tax exclusion of $10,000 per donee per year.

A spendthrift trust may be supplemented by an incentive trust, income from which would be payable in amounts equivalent to what the "spendthrift" earns each year.

To guard against the extravagant spouse of a son or daughter, a parent could provide that when the son or daughter dies, the spouse would receive only a life interest, the remainder then going to the parent's grandchildren.

15. A trust may be used in appropriate circumstances to skip a generation of estate taxes. When an individual dies, there is an estate tax to be paid in many instances. If much of his property goes to this spouse, very likely there will be a second estate tax to be paid upon her death. By using a trust, the property can be held for the ultimate benefit of the children, his wife meanwhile receiving a life interest in the trust's income. When she dies, there is no estate tax upon the value of what he had provided for her, because all she had owned was the life estate, which, of course, ceases with her death. An interest may be maintained in trust for as long as permitted by the state's rule against perpetuities. (See a more extended discussion of skip-a-generation trusts later in this chapter.)

16. A trust may be an effective mechanism to continue to operate the grantor's business after his death, something his executor might be unwilling or unqualified to do. The trustees could include key employees, the firm's accountant, and other persons knowledgeable in this area. Instructions might be left that the business is to be operated for a minimum number of years, possibly with an escape clause, which would take effect, for example, should there be operating losses in two or three successive years. Often an executor is disinclined to operate a business and may be tempted to sell or to liquidate at the wrong time or for an inadequate price just to be rid of the time-consuming responsibility. To prevent a crippling liquidity problem that can arise upon the death of a major stockholder of a closely-held corporation, the controlling shareholder's estate sometimes includes an irrevocable trust.

17. In order to keep the voting power intact in the case of corporate shares given or bequeathed to plural beneficiaries, a trust may be used. The trustee or trustees hold the stock and exercise voting power in a block,

giving voting trust certificates (without voting power) of comparable amount to the beneficiaries. The voting trust should be established with an eye on a state's law against perpetuities.

18. A trust can be utilized in order to set aside funds for purposes that might not be taken care of unless specific arrangements had been provided. The will of the eminent author Lucius Beebe set aside in trust $15,000 for the support of his dog, which was said to have acquired very expensive eating habits from its gourmet owner. Another individual set up a $10,000 trust fund in her will to provide $100 a month for the upkeep of her cat.

19. Funds may be set aside for minor children, as will be discussed in Chapter 9. In order to get the funds out of a parent's ultimate estate and to insulate them from claims by the parent's creditors, a custodianship is a simple vehicle to use. But a trust may seem to be more foolproof, with professional management and supervision if desired.

20. A trust sometimes is used in order to keep certain properties intact, so that the greatest value can be preserved for the intended future owners. Property may be transferred to a trust for the benefit of the beneficiaries, thus avoiding fragmentation of, say, real estate, an interest in an oil well, or an art collection among various parties, whose views on management or disposition could well be disharmonious. Most frequently, the whole is worth more than the sum of the parts. The trustee predictably would receive a greater price upon sale, for the benefit of the beneficiaries, than they could have gotten individually.

21. Where trusts are used, specific properties may be administered by specialists in various fields, instead of having one's entire estate subject to the management of one or more executors whose areas of expertise necessarily are limited. Properties of different character can be transferred by gift or will to separate trusts, the trustees of which are, respectively, experts in such fields as urban real estate, suburban realty, securities, tax-exempt bonds, mortgages, foreign shipping, and the like.

22. In order to eliminate the delays, costs, and publicity of probating a will when decisions already have been made as to who is to get certain properties, a trust may be useful. An individual can transfer property from what would be his ultimate estate to a trust. If the trust is irrevocable and there are no retained interests, the property will be distributed automatically in accordance with his desires, but it will not be a part of his gross estate even if his wealth is very large. Where the trust terminates with his death, the pre-programmed dispositions will be without exposure to outside parties. Where property is not part of the decedent's estate, there will be no executor's and estate lawyers' fees, which are based upon the size of the estate to be administered.

23. A trust can enable a person to avoid a conflict of interest situation. For example, a prominent industrialist might be offered a cabinet position in Washington, where business transactions with his corporation

could be involved. He may avoid having to sell his stock with a large capital gains tax by having the shares transferred to a trust "for the duration," with independent trustees making all business decisions without his participation (the co-called "blind" trust).

24.  In order to keep his beneficiaries from knowing how much other beneficiaries are receiving, an individual may set up a separate trust for the benefit of each beneficiary. That could eliminate any beneficiary's seeking to obtain, by court order if necessary, relevant information to establish that he was getting his full entitlement.

25.  A trust may be used to represent one's minor children in a business transaction. For example, a physician may give the professional building he uses in his practice to a trust for the benefit of his minor children in order to free it from possible malpractice claims against him by disenchanted patients. As the children lack the legal capacity to negotiate terms and to carry out the business aspects of the transaction, an independent trustee could represent them and thus provide the arrangement with tax respectability.

26.  By setting up a trust at this time, a person can test how parties he intends to have serve as trustees of substantial portions of his wealth will function and how beneficiaries will respond to the situation. He can commit to this experiment only a modest fraction of the money and other property ultimately to be transferred by gift or by will. If this "trial balloon" does not work to his complete satisfaction, he has time (one hopes) to make other arrangements with the bulk of his property.

## "SKIP-A-GENERATION" TRUSTS

The Tax Reform Act of 1976 financially discouraged skip-a-generation trusts *except for the most popular form* of this technique, namely, where one spouse sets up a trust with the other spouse as life tenant and their children as remaindermen. Under the law, both spouses are deemed to be of the same generation, and hence there is no generation-skipping under this procedure.

A tax is imposed on generation-skipping transfers. This occurs where, under a trust, life estate, or similar arrangement trust *assets* are distributed to someone of a younger generation than the creator of the trust. This could be, for example, a transaction where a trust was set up with the grantor's niece to get the income for life, after which the trust principal would go to the niece's son. The generation-skipping tax is triggered when the niece dies, because the property (the trust principal) has gone to a younger generation.

An exception to this rule permits a generation-skipping transfer to a grandchild of the grantor. The tax is *not* imposed on the termination of the life estate of the child of the grantor where the trust provided a life estate for the child and the remainder to the grandchildren of the grantor. The maximum amount that can be transferred under this exception without the imposition of a generation-skipping tax, however, is $250,000 for each child of the original creator of the trust.

The generation-skipping tax is substantially equivalent to the estate tax that would have been imposed if the property actually had been transferred outright to each successive generation. For example, a trust can be created for the benefit of the grantor's grandchild, with the remainder to the great-grandchildren. Upon the death of the grandchild, his portion of the trust assets is added to his estate, and tax is computed at the grandchild's marginal estate tax rate. In other words, the grandchild is treated as the transferor of the trust property. But the grandchild's estate is not liable for the payment of the tax. Instead, the tax generally is payable out of the proceeds of the trust property.

The marginal estate tax rate is used as a measuring rod for purposes of determining the tax imposed on the generation-skipping transfer. The trust is entitled to any unused portion of the grandchild's unified transfer tax credit, the charitable deduction (if any part of the trust property was left to charity), the credit for state inheritance taxes, and a deduction for certain administrative expenses.

The generation-skipping tax rate is not imposed in the case of outright transfers. As a rule of administrative convenience, the tax is not imposed in the case of distributions of current income from a generation-skipping trust.

*The tax under these rules is imposed only once each generation.* Generally, a generation is determined along family lines, where possible; the grantor, his wife, and his brothers and sisters are one generation; their children are a second generation; the grandchildren are a third generation.

Where generation-skipping transfers are made outside the family, generations are measured from the grantor. Individuals *not more than 12.5 years younger than the grantor* are treated as members of his generation; individuals more than 12.5 years younger than the grantor, but not more than 37.5 years younger, are considered members of his children's generation; and the like. In cases where generation-skipping transfers are made outside the family, the deemed transferor (that is, the base for purposes of determining the tax) is the estate of the person having the closest relationship to the grantor or the person having the intervening life interest or power (generally, the person named in the grantor's will or in the trust instrument).

There are special rules relating to *disclaimers* for purposes of generation-skipping trusts, as well as for other Federal gift and estate tax purposes. This subject will be discussed in Chapter 11, "Retained Interests: A Danger and an Opportunity."

The generation-skipping tax is not imposed in the case of outright transfers. In addition, the tax is not imposed by reason of the death of a member of an older generation if the decedent is not treated as a beneficiary because he had nothing more than a right of management over the trust assets, or a limited power to appoint the trust assets along the lineal descendants of the grantor. An individual trustee is not treated as having a power in a trust if (1) he has no interest in the trust, and (2) he does not have a present or future power in the trust other than a power to allocate the principal of the trust or to distribute or to accumulate the income to or for a beneficiary or class of beneficiaries designated in the trust agreement, and (3) he is independent of the grantor of the trust.

An independent trustee for this purpose is an individual trustee who is not related or subordinate. A trustee is treated as being related or subordinate if he or she is (1) a spouse of the grantor or of any beneficiary, or (2) the father, mother, lineal descendant, brother, or sister of the grantor or of any beneficiary, or (3) an employee of a corporation in which the stock holdings of the grantor, the trust, and all beneficiaries are significant from the point of view of voting control, or (4) an employee of a corporation in which the grantor or any beneficiary is an executive.

An alternate valuation date may be used to value the assets of a generation-skipping trust where the death of an older-generation beneficiary causes a taxable termination. In such a situation, the assets may be valued either as of the date of the death of the the older-generation beneficiary or on the appropriate alternate valuation date.

The tax imposed on a beneficiary with respect to an accumulation distribution is adjusted to take into account the estate tax or generation--skipping tax attributable to the accumulated income.

## GRANTOR TRUSTS

A grantor trust is one that is set up for the benefit of the person who creates the trust. A grantor will be taxed on the income from property that he transfers to a trust unless he *avoids* all three of the following:

1. Return of the trust principal to himself. This can be done by making the trust irrevocable and by reserving no reversionary rights of any kind. If he already has such rights, he should renounce them soon enough so that the renunciation will not be too late to avoid an estate tax. In this type of situation, he must have parted with the rights within three years before his death.

2. Power to say who is going to enjoy the trust's principal or income. If the grantor's power to control the person or persons who will enjoy

these forms of wealth is limited by reasonably definite standards set forth in the trust instrument, the grantor is not treated as the owner of the trust property, because he cannot redirect the flow of money through mere whim. For example, provision may be made that trust principal can be used for the education, support, maintenance, or health of a beneficiary; or to enable him to maintain his accustomed standard of living; or to meet an emergency.

3. Administrative powers exercised for his (the grantor's) benefit. The grantor is treated as the owner of any portion of a trust if he can divert trust income without the approval or consent of any party with conflicting economic interests (such as beneficiary or the person who will get whatever is in the trust fund when the trust ends) and (a) distribute it to himself; (b) hold or accumulate the income for future distribution to himself; or (c) use the income applied to pay premiums on insurance policies on his own life, except policies irrevocably payable to a tax-exempt organization.

The grantor also is treated as the owner of any portion of a trust in which the income may be held or accumulated for further distribution without the approval or consent of a person with conflicting interests. For example, if an individual's sister is to get the income for the remainder of her life from a trust fund he had set up, his decision to have some of the income accumulate instead of being paid to her would be in conflict with her interest.

Any amount that, under the terms of a trust instrument, may be used in full or partial discharge of a legal obligation of the grantor is included in his gross income. For example, if an individual sets up a trust and transfers income-producing properties to it, he has received an economic benefit to the extent that trust income is used to discharge his legal obligation of supporting his minor children. So he is subject to income tax on the money so used.

A grantor should not be a trustee for a grantor trust, as this strongly suggests that he never really parted with the trust property or its income.

## SUPPORT TRUSTS

A support trust is nominally for the benefit of the named beneficiary. Actually, it benefits the grantor, such as by providing for the support of someone who the grantor has the legal obligation to support. Income of a support trust is taxed to the person whose legal obligation of supporting a dependent is met by the trust's income. Where one spouse sets up a trust for the benefit of the other, the grantor is taxed on all trust income that may be used for the benefit of the beneficiary spouse. But this does not apply when, under some other provision of the tax law, the trust income must be reported by the beneficiary spouse, such as in the case of periodic payments of alimony.

When it is clear that the grantor's interest in a support trust is of a limited nature, as when the trust has more income than is required for support, only that portion necessary to satisfy the support requirement is taxed to the grantor.

In setting up a trust for the benefit of his children, one grantor wrote into the trust agreement that creation of the trust would not discharge him of his duty of support. But the trust could have been used precisely for that purpose. Inasmuch as he, as trustee, had the authority to pay out principal and income for education, maintenance, and health of the beneficiaries, he was discharging his obligations with trust principal, or at least he had the authority to do so. As such, he really had not let go of the trust principal. Upon his death, the principal would be includible in his gross estate.

## GRANDFATHER TRUSTS

Grandfather trust is a term used to describe a trust set up by an individual for the benefit of someone he is not legally obligated to support, even though the income is in fact used for support purposes. Thus, when a trust's income is used to provide support for a grantor's grandchild, whom he is not legally obliged to support, trust income is not taxed to the grantor. The trust principal would not be included in the grandfather's estate when he dies, so his tax situation benefits from such an arrangement in another respect. The grandchild also benefits, receiving support he otherwise might not receive. And so does the grantor's son, who has been relieved of the obligation of providing support for his child.

If an individual sets up a trust with a third party, such as a bank, serving as trustee, and the trustee has the authority in its sole discretion to use trust income for the support of a person that the grantor must support, such as his wife or minor child, the grantor is not regarded as the owner of the trust fund.

## SHORT-TERM TRUSTS

A grantor is considered to be the owner of any portion of a trust in which he has a reversionary right to get back either the trust principal or its income, if this right may be expected to take effect within ten years. Whether or not the grantor contemplates reversion within ten years is irrelevant. He will not be considered to be the owner of a trust because of a reversionary interest that is to take effect only on the death of the person or persons to whom the incomes is *payable*. This rule applies even though the beneficiary has a short life expectancy and the reversionary interest reasonably may be expected to take effect within ten years. This kind of trust can be set up, for instance, for the benefit of a mother, with the trust principal to return to the grantor when she dies.

When the grantor of a trust has a life expectancy of more than ten years according to mortality tables and a reversionary interest in the principal, which will come back into his estate at his death, the trust *income* is not taxable to him.

An attractive advantage of a ten-year trust is that a person can transfer income-producing securities or other property to such a trust for the benefit of someone else, including a charity. During the minimum permissible period of ten years and a day, the beneficiary alone is entitled to the income and any income tax liability from it. Thus, an active person can provide that a portion of the income he receives during his high-earnings years will go directly to another party, perhaps one that the grantor is interested in helping although under no legal obligation to do so. Later in the grantor's life, when he may be retired, he again will get this income.

The tax advantages of a ten-year trust primarily are in the savings of income taxes. An estate could hav enough assets to make it taxable (or more highly taxable) even after the Economic Recovery Tax Act of 1981 to the extent of the value of a reversionary interest. This means value that would be part of gross estate because, at the end of this ten-year or longer period, the trust principal would revert to the grantor's estate after his death. The value of the property held by the trust would be reduced in accordance with actuarial tables, for what the grantor owned at the time of his death was not the trust principal but the right to get it after a certain number of years. Even ignoring the realities of inflation, the right to get back a dollar after a specified number of years is worth less than owning that dollar today.

A valid trust is supposed to insulate the grantor from tax consequences during the period it exists. But the creator of a ten-year trust for the benefit of his children had a reversionary interest in the trust principal. Therefore, the Internal Revenue Service could enforce a tax lien by reason of his delinquency in tax payments against the trust fund to the extent of the value of his reversionary interest at the time.

## MULTIPLE TRUSTS

Multiple trusts may be used in order to fragment income so that it will not get into maximum tax brackets. Where a trust is taxable on its income, the same system of rising tax brackets exists as in the case of individuals. But if the income is spread among a number of trusts, income that would be taxed at a high rate in the case of a single taxpayer is subject to much lower rates. In addition, a trust's exemption can be multiplied if each of several trusts is entitled to a separate exemption.

The courts have held that there is nothing to prevent the use of several trusts despite the obvious tax motivation. All that is necessary is to show that the trusts were indeed set up and operated as separate entities.

Nontax reasons can be cited for the use of multiple trusts and can lessen the chance of difficulties with the Internal Revenue Service. For example, trusts can be used:

☐ To allow the creation of trusts for the same beneficiaries at different times and in different manners.

☐ To implement various objectives of estate planning, such as conferring different degrees of discretion on several trustees or setting up different remaindermen after the death of a person entitled to receive the income for life.

☐ To separate trust principal into "packages," with specialized experts to administer each one.

## THE TRUSTEE'S INDEPENDENCE

A person certainly can insulate himself from taxes and other consequences of owning property by transferring it to a trust, which is a separate entity. But an important question is whether the trust *really* is not the same creature as its creator. Income and property that are subject to an individual's complete command and that he is free to enjoy at his own option may be taxed as though it were his, whether he used them or not. A donor who keeps a strong hold over what presumably he has put beyond his power to take back actually has not divested himself of the benefits of ownership.

Any competent person (including a bank) can serve as the trustee of a trust. Nothing in the tax law prohibits the grantor from making himself trustee or co-trustee of his trust. But in many decisions the courts have indicated that the separate tax existence of a trust can be disregarded by the

Internal Revenue Service if the grantor is also the trustee. In some cases, this finding also has been made where the trustee was the grantor's spouse. The reason is that in such situations, despite compliance with state formalities in the formation of a trust, the grantor actually has not lessened his control over the trust's principal or income. In refusing to recognize the separate existence of one trust where the grantor's wife was the trustee, the court declared that "There is no evidence that she did anything more than passively acquiesce in [the grantor's] wishes."

In one case, an individual had named his wife and a bank as co-trustees. On the surface, it would appear that the necessary independence of the trustees had been safeguarded. But the trust agreement stated that if at any time during the wife's lifetime there should be a difference of opinion between her and the bank, *her* wishes would prevail. So the lack of independence of the bank trustee meant that the trust could not be recognized as a separate entity.

Some courts have held that it cannot be assumed that a trustee who also is a grantor would exercise his powers for personal advantage in violation of his fiduciary obligations. Most courts have held, however, that if the grantor has the power to use trust property in accordance with his own whim, he really has not let go of anything.

There is no reason why the grantor cannot be trustee of his own creation, if under the trust agreement his powers clearly are set forth and he has no discretionary power. For example, a grantor may serve as trustee without hazard to the trust's independence if he has no power to say who is to enjoy property or its income, or when distributions will be made.

In one case, the United States Supreme Court found that the grantor really was an independent trustee even though he had reserved the right to vote the stock he had transferred to the trust. True, he could have used his majority stock voting power to influence the corporate directors in their payment of dividends, most of which would go to the beneficiaries of the trust. But if he caused the corporation to retain earnings beyond the reasonable needs of the business, and thus regulated what beneficiaries would receive, the corporation would be subjected to an accumulated earnings tax by reason of undistributed earnings, and he personally could have been compelled by a minority shareholder to reimburse the corporation for this unnecessary corporate tax out of his own pocketbook.

A grantor who makes himself trustee of a trust that he creates is not considered to be the owner of trust principal or income merely because he has retained managerial and investment powers over the trust principal.

## TRANSFER OF STOCK WITH RETAINED VOTING RIGHTS

Where an individual transfers stock to a trust but retains the voting power of that stock, the shares' value is includible in his gross estate if the corporation is controlled by the decedent and his relatives. A controlled corporation for this purpose means a corporation where the decedent and his relatives owned or had the power to vote stock possessing at least 20 percent of the total combined voting power of all classes of stock. Shares that are deemed to be "constructively owned" because they are owned by certain parties are taken into account. A corporation is said to be controlled where the 20 percent of the total combined voting power of all stock exists at any time after the transfer of the property and during the three-year period ending on the date of the decedent's death.

The rule requiring inclusion in the gross estate of stock of a controlled corporation applies where the decedent retained the voting rights of the stock that was directly or indirectly transferred by him. Thus, where the decedent transferred cash or other property prior to his death to a trust of which he was trustee within three years of his death, and then the trust used that cash or other property to purchase stock in a controlled corporation from him, the value of his stock is included in his gross estate.

In addition, the indirect retention of voting rights in the case of reciprocal transfers of stock in trust results in the inclusion of stock with respect to which the decedent had voting rights as trustee. Voting rights in stock transferred in trust by the decedent, however, will not be considered to have been retained by the decedent merely because a relative was the trustee who voted the stock.

In these cases, the voting rights are considered to have been indirectly retained by the decedent if, in substance, he had retained such voting rights. For example, there may have been an arrangement or agreement for the trustee to vote the stock in accordance with instructions from the decedent.

## TAX MOTIVATION AND THE INTERNAL REVENUE SERVICE

A taxpayer may act in a manner that will minimize his taxes if he acts in a manner that the law permits. A grantor's purpose in establishing a trust is irrelevant to the question of whether he will be taxed on the trust's principal or income.

## THE FEDERAL GIFT TAX

Property transferred by an individual to a trust for the benefit of another individual or individuals is subject to the Federal gift tax, just as property directly transferred to the beneficiary would be.

When a grantor releases any reversionary interest in trust principal to an individual, that also constitutes a taxable gift. If he releases his reversionary interest in favor of a charitable organization on the approved Treasury Department list, he is entitled to a charitable deduction on his income tax return.

## THE FEDERAL INCOME TAX

The income taxability of trust income will be discussed in Chapter 19, "The Income Aspects of Estate Planning."

# 8

## THE "UNLIMITED" MARITAL DEDUCTION AND ITS PRACTICAL LIMITATIONS

The marital deduction should be regarded as an estate planning tool available for use when careful thought indicates it is desirable. It is a tool because its effectiveness depends upon how it is used. There is nothing automatic about the marital deduction; it does not just happen except to the extent that it operates for that portion of a decedent's wealth that may be claimed by a surviving spouse under a state's dower or curtesy laws. These laws, it will be remembered, specify that a surviving spouse is entitled to a stipulated percentage of the estate, whether the will so provides or not. But for this exception, there is no certainty that anything that goes to one's spouse will be eligible for the marital deduction. A person must take steps to see that it will apply, or, stated differently, he has to make plans to ensure that the deduction will not fail to qualify as a reduction of gross estate.

In its report on the bill that was to become the Economic Recovery Tax Act of 1981, the Ways and Means Committee of the House of Representatives stated that it "believes that an individual should be free to pass his entire estate to a surviving spouse without the imposition of any transfer tax." But the usual oversimplified explanation of that legislation can be dangerous. Among the biggest traps is the frequent statement that in the case of gifts made or decedents dying after December 31, 1981, there is an unlimited marital deduction. Actually, that is only partially true, for there are some very important exceptions.

## LIMITATIONS ON THE "UNLIMITED" MARITAL DEDUCTION

Here are the limitations on the marital deduction:

1. The interest is a terminable one. There is a terminable interest where, upon the occurrence of an event or contingency, the interest of the

transferee will terminate and an interest in such property passes from the transferor to some other person who might possess or enjoy some part of the property after the termination of the tranferee's interest. Property is not eligible for the marital deduction where all that is given to the recipient (here, solely for simplicity's sake, called the wife) is an income interest for a specified number of years or until the occurrence of some specific happening, such as remarriage. But see the new exception to this rule, discussed later in this chapter under the heading "Qualified Terminable Interest."

2.  The property interest transferred is not a completed transfer.

3.  The recipient is not, under state law, the transferor's spouse.

4.  The recipient files a valid disclaimer.

5.  In the case of a bequest, the named transferee does not survive the transferor.

6.  There is a Federal tax lien (a right against the property until a debt has been paid), so that transferee receives the property subject to encumbrance of part or all of its value.

## TERMINABLE INTERESTS

In order to qualify for the marital deduction, the general rule is that property passing to the other spouse (called the wife here) must have the potential of being included in her gross estate when she dies, unless she has disposed of it *according to her own wishes.* So property interests passing from a person to his spouse ordinarily do not qualify if they are *terminable interests,* that is, interests that terminate at the moment of her death.

A terminable interest for this purpose covers most situations in which the wife gets less than outright possession of property because someone else has rights in its ultimate ownership, or the possibility exists that some other person will have possession or enjoyment of the property in the future without the wife being able to do anything about it.

An individual may be concerned that his wife will be too generous to her relatives or others, so he tries to curb the possibility in his will. Typically, such a will may provide that his property will pass to his wife at his death, to be used or disposed of by her without restrictions; but if any of this property remains in her possession or ownership when she dies, it is to go to their children or to named contingent beneficiaries who will get the property should the children die before receiving it. This represents a terminable interest, ineligible for the marital deduction, because the wife did not get the property as her very own. When she dies, any of the property that the husband had made available to her that remains will be disposed of according to his will and not hers. Her interest in the property ceases at her death, for she cannot dispose of it by will. Without the power to dispose of the property, her inheritance does not meet the requirements for a marital deduction.

The marital deduction can be lost where a will is drawn up by an attorney who is thoroughly familiar with testamentary draftsmanship but not with the marital deduction. Typically, a husband's will may leave his property, or a specified portion of it, to his wife "in fee simple, to be disposed of by her as she may provide in her will." So far, so good. But elsewhere in his will he provides that if she should remarry, certain property rights are to pass to the children. This does not qualify for the marital deduction, because she did not receive the property with the full right to do with it as she pleased. He could have written with impunity that he was leaving her his property, adding "It is my wish and desire" that any of what had been his property that was left after her death should go to his brother and sister. Here she had received the property as absolutely her own, with only a non-enforceable suggestion concerning the ultimate disposition of the assets.

There is a terminable interest if property goes to his wife without strings except that she will forfeit further rights to it if she remarries. Such also is the situation where she receives property outright for life but upon her death the property is to go to *her* next of kin, which presumably would not include a new husband.

Allowance of the marital deduction can depend upon the wife's ability to follow simple instructions. One person left property to his wife, subject to her executing a valid will. If she did not, the property would go to the children when she dies. After her death, her executor claimed the marital deduction, alleging that she indeed had made a legally aceptable will; but it could not be found. There was no marital deduction, for she had only a contingent interest when she died.

One of the most successful of mystery writers was Erle Stanley Gardner, whose fictional character, Perry Mason, was a lawyer who repeatedly demonstrated his mastery over the law. Unfortunately, Mr. Gardner, who himself was an attorney, failed to consult Perry Mason, Esq. The eminent author's will left his property to his wife, with the provision that if she failed to designate who was to receive her wealth when she died, people named by Mr. Gardner would receive it. Inasmuch as the husband's designees received the property after her death, there was no marital deduction.

In ascertaining whether there is a terminable interest, it does not matter what the property passing to the surviving spouse is called. For example, an insurance agent bequeathed to his wife any renewal commissions he might earn in the next nine years. Commissions that remained unpaid at her death were to go to their son. This was a terminable interest, in spite of the fact that she had the right to dispose of her interest in the commissions at any time by sale or by gift.

A bequest to one's spouse conditioned on her surviving until the distribution of his estate is common. Under the laws of many states, a beneficiary is not entitled to property until a decedent's will is probated. If she dies before his will is probated, a process that in some states might take several years, the wife will not get the property.

An interest in property terminable upon the happening of contingency, as here (the probating of the will) does not qualify for the marital deduction, whether or not the contingency does in fact occur. The property passing to her would not be subject to estate tax when she died if she dies before it was hers, so allowance of the marital deduction could mean that neither his estate nor hers would pay estate tax on the property willed to her. Thus, his estate is not entitled to the marital deduction.

An interest passing to the surviving spouse is not considered an interest that will terminate or fail on the death of the surviving spouse if (1) the death will cause a termination or failure of an interest to pass only if it occurs within a period of not more than six months after the first decedent's death, or only if it occurs as a result of a common disaster resulting in the death of both spouses, or only if it occurs in the case of either such event; and (2) such termination or failure does not in fact occur. For example, a husband's will could provide that property will go to his widow unless she fails to survive him by more than six months. This is not regarded as a terminable interest if she *does* survive him by that time.

## EXCEPTIONS TO THE TERMINABLE INTEREST RULE

An important exception to the rule that a terminable interest will not qualify for the marital deduction is where there is a power of appointment in the surviving spouse. That is, she has been given the right to say who will get her property upon her death even though she cannot use it during her lifetime; the income it produces is all that she gets. For example, a husband may have set up a trust providing that his wife is to get the income for as long as she lives. Up to his point, she is entitled only to a life income, a terminable interest. But the husband's property going to the trust will qualify for the marital deduction if these five conditions are met:

1. The wife must be entitled for life to all of the income from the entire estate, or all the income from a specific portion of it. (If the entire property transferred to the trust is not to be used to provide the wife with a life income, the "specific portion" may be a dollar amount or even an amount determined by actuarial computation of a life expectancy. For example, a wife gets income from certain property after the death of the husband's mother, who meanwhile is to get the income. Feasible computation of a "specific portion" is the key to marital deduction status in this situation.)

2.  The income must be payable annually or at more frequent intervals.

3.  The wife must have a power of appointment over the trust principal of the entire interest or the specific portion. This means the power to dispose of property by gift, deed, or will. A surviving spouse must be given the unrestricted power to name the principal to herself as unqualified owner or to designate the principal as part of her estate. This means, in effect, that she must be able to dispose of it to whomever she pleases. She must have unlimited power to make use of the principal, to the extent of being able to cut off remainder interests in a trust fund by withdrawing the principal at any time. A wife was deemed not to have power over the entire principal where her husband's will specified that she was to make use of trust principal for the education of the children. If the right to make use of the principal is limited, there is no general power of appointment. If only limited powers are provided, no matter what name the state law ascribes to these powers, the transfer to the trust by the husband does not qualify for the marital deduction.

4.  There must be no power in any other person to name any part of the interest to go to any other person other than the surviving spouse.

5.  The power must be exercisable by the wife alone and in all events. The power of appointment must be absolute and unconditional, exercisable by the wife by deed or by will at any time after the death of her husband. The power must be exercisable *in all events*. The "all events" test was not met when a wife was entitled to trust income for her support, maintenance, welfare, and comfort, but had no right to further income once these requirements had been met. Another wife was deemed to be able to exercise power over trust principal "alone and in all events" where principal could be used for purposes other than her own if the trustees so desired, but only with her consent.

Another exception to the terminable interest rule exists in the case of an interest passing from the decedent that consists of the proceeds under a life insurance, endowment, or annuity contract.

All five of the following conditions must be met:

1.  The proceeds, or a specific portion, must be held by the insurance company to an agreement either to pay the entire proceeds or a specific portion of them in installments. Or the insurance company must be required to pay interest on these amounts. All or a specific portion of the installments or interest payable during the life of the surviving spouse must be payable only to her.

2.  The installments or interest payable to the surviving spouse must be payable annually, or more frequently, commencing not later than thirteen months after the decedent's death.

3.  The surviving spouse must have the power to designate all or a

specific portion of the amounts so held by the insurance company for herself or for the estate.

4. The power in the surviving spouse must be exercisable by her alone. It must be exercisable in all events, by will or during life.

5. The amounts or the specific portion payable under the policy must not be subject to a power in any other person to designate any part to any person other than the surviving spouse.

## QUALIFIED TERMINABLE INTEREST

Under the Economic Recovery Tax Act of 1981, if certain conditions are met, a life interest granted to a surviving spouse is not treated as a terminable interest. The entire property subject to this interest is treated as passing to the surviving spouse, and no interest in this property is treated as passing to any person other than the spouse (consistently referred to here, for convenience, as the wife). Accordingly, the entire interest qualifies for the marital deduction.

In the case of gifts made, or decedent dying, after December 31, 1981, transfers of terminable interests are considered to be *qualified terminable interests,* eligible for the marital deduction. There are three conditions for allowance of the deduction here:

1. The wife must be entitled for a period measured only by her life to all the income from the entire interest, or to all of the income from a specific portion of it, payable annually or at more frequent intervals.

2. No person, including the wife, can give away any part of the property during her lifetime. If the husband had left property in trust, with the wife to get the income for life, this rule permits the existence of powers in the trustee to use principal for her benefit but ensures that the value of the property not required for her use is subject to tax upon her death or the earliest disposition of the property. By will or otherwise, she only can say what happens to the remaining principal at or after her death.

3. An irrevocable election for this treatment must be made by the donor in case of a gift or by the executor in case of a bequest. *There is no automatic marital deduction in the case of a qualified terminable interest.*

Property subject to an election to be treatd as a qualified terminable interest will be subject to transfer taxes at the earlier of (1) the date on which the wife disposes (by gift, sale, or otherwise) of all or part of the qualifying income interest, or (2) upon her death.

If the property is subject to gift tax as a result of the wife's lifetime transfer of the qualifying income interest, the entire value of the property, less amounts received by her upon disposition, is treated as a taxable gift.

In general, no annual gift tax exclusion is permitted with respect to the imputed transfer of the remainder interest (to a person other than the income beneficiary) because the remainder is a future interest. (The terms "annual exclusion" and "future interest" will be discussed in Chapter 9.) But if the wife makes a gift of the qualifying income interest, this is considered a gift to the donee, eligible for the annual exclusion and marital deduction, if applicable.

If the property subject to the qualifying income interest is not disposed of prior to the death of the surviving spouse, the fair market value of the property subject to the qualifying income interest determined as of the date of her death (or the alternate valuation date, if so elected by her executor) is includible in her gross estate.

Apportionment provisions describe how the additional estate taxes attributable to the taxation of the qualified terminable interest property, other than the wife's life estate, are borne by that property. Unless she directs otherwise, she or her estate has a right to recover the gift tax paid on the remainder interest as a result of a lifetime transfer of the qualifying income interest, or the estate tax paid as a result of including any penalties or interest paid that are attributable to the additional gift or estate tax. But if, as a result of the lifetime disposition of the qualifying income interest, the inclusion of the entire property as a taxable transfer uses up some or all of her unified credit, she is not permitted to recover the credit amount from the remaindermen.

Similar rules apply with respect to lifetime transfers to a spouse that are qualifying terminable interests if the donor makes an irrevocable election at the time of gift.

## INCOMPLETE TRANSFER TO SPOUSE

A transfer of property to one's spouse qualifies for the marital deduction only if this transfer is a completed one. Where there are conditions or contingencies, the transfer may not qualify. In the case of the estate tax, the will may be in question because of allegations concerning the decedent's mental competence at the time he made his will. The decedent may have had less than a complete interest in the property bequeathed.

In the case of the gift tax, there are many factors that could make the gift incomplete. There may have been requirements under state law that had not been met, such as a rule that a conveyance of real property must be in writing or that the deed has to be recorded in a county office before the transfer is effective. Transfer of stock may not have met state requirements on endorsements. Various United States Treasury Bonds, for another example, cannot be given away by delivery of certificates or a letter of gift; the certificates must be sent to the appropriate agency for reissuance in the name of the new owner.

## IMPACT OF STATE LAW UPON SPOUSAL RELATIONSHIPS

There cannot be a transfer of property to one's spouse that will qualify for the marital deduction for Federal gift or estate tax purposes unless, under state law, the transferor and the transferee are married.

In the words of one court, "It is a curious anomaly of life that the status of holy matrimony should be decided by the taxing agencies of the United States; but anomalies are not new to the federal courts."[1]

If the husband's earlier divorce was not recognized under the state law, he still is considered to be married to his prior wife. So transfers he makes to his present "wife" do not qualify for the marital deduction inasmuch as the present spouse is not recognized as such. Similarly, if the recipient wife had been married previously but the divorce that allegedly had terminated that relationship is not recognized under state law, she did not receive property from her husband #2 as his spouse, and the marital deduction is not available.

Property passing to a surviving spouse under a state's dower provisions qualify for the marital deduction. But if what her husband had provided for her in his last testament was less than the amount of her dower rights, she may "take against the will," the amounts going to her being eligible for the deduction. Her election to do this will not permit the payment to qualify for the marital deduction, however, if made after the last date set by state law for claiming dower rights.

The giving of property to one's spouse will not qualify for the marital deduction if the transfer is void under state law as a fraud against creditors.

## EFFECT OF DISCLAIMERS ON THE MARITAL DEDUCTION

A disclaimer is the repudiation or renunciation of a right. If an interest passes to the surviving spouse because a disclaimer to the property is filed by a third party who otherwise would have gotten the assets, then, for pur-

---

[1] Amy Ann McGinnis Spalding Estate v. Commissioner, 537 F. 2d 666 (2d Cir. 1976).

poses of the marital deduction, the interest is considered as passing from the decedent to his surviving spouse, provided that the disclaimer had been made before the filing date of the Federal estate tax return and provided also that the person making the disclaimer had not accepted an interest in the property before making his disclaimer. For example, a father's will may have bequeathed his residence to his son. If the son disclaims his interest in the property before the due date of the father's estate tax return, under state law the property has passed to the surviving spouse for marital deduction purposes.

If the property is willed to the decedent's spouse, and she promptly disclaims her interest, the property passes to the person or persons (most commonly, the couple's children) who receive it from the decedent. Consequently, the marital deduction is not available. Had the widow accepted the property and then given it to her children, the marital deduction would have been allowed. But her transfer of the property would have been subject to the Federal gift tax.

The marital deduction is not available if property passes to the surviving spouse because of a disclaimer filed by a minor child who had the right to repudiate any of his acts upon reaching age twenty-one.

## THE TRANSFEREE MUST SURVIVE THE TRANSFEROR

The estate tax marital deduction applies in the case of property that passes to the surviving spouse. If the latter dies before the husband, she is not the surviving spouse. So there can be no marital deduction.

For a discusssion of what happens when both spouses die in a common disaster, see Chapter 15, which deals with the Uniform Simultaneous Death Act.

## EXISTENCE OF FEDERAL TAX LIEN CAN INTERFERE WITH MARITAL DEDUCTION

If the Internal Revenue Service has imposed a lien against a husband's property for unpaid taxes, this property will still be encumbered by the lien when it passes to another party. Property received by his wife therefore will have its value reduced or even eliminated by the amount of the lien. Inasmuch as the marital deduction is passed upon the value of property passing to the spouse, that deduction may be wiped out.

## EXAMPLES OF PROPERTY THAT "PASSES" TO THE SURVIVING SPOUSE

The estate tax marital deduction applies to property that passes from decedent to his surviving spouse. Property is considered to pass from the decedent to any person only if:

☐ The interest is bequeathed or devised. The latter word is the legal term for a "bequest" of land.

☐ The interest is inherited by a person from the decedent.

☐ The interest is the dower or curtesy interest, or the equivalent, under the language of a particular state's law, of a person as surviving spouse of the decedent.

☐ The interest has been transferred to the person by the decedent at any time.

☐ The interest was, at the time of the decedent's death, held by the person and the decedent in joint ownership, with the property to belong to the survivor.

☐ The decedent had a power to designate the owner of an interest and he actually designated the person as the owner of the property.

☐ The interest consists of the proceeds of insurance on the life of the decedent receivable by the person.

☐ The will provided that upon the decedent's death, a reorganization would take place in a corporation of which he owned stock, so that instead of the previous one-class stock there would be issued preferred stock and voting common stock. Where his widow receives preferred stock, this is considered property that is passing to her by reason of the decedent's death, even though the preferred stock did not exist at the time he died.

Where a decedent's will had made property dispositions to specified persons, but the beneficiaries had agreed to accept other amounts, here is the pattern of treatment:

☐ The husband of a decedent threatened to challenge his wife's will. The amount paid to him by her estate in settlement of his claim was held to have passed to him from his deceased wife, thus qualifying for the marital deduction.

☐ On the other hand, when a surviving spouse relinquished his claim to property he otherwise would have received from his spouse's estate, the property was not considered to have passed to him from the decedent for the purpose of the marital deduction.

☐ If a surviving spouse assigns or surrenders a property interest in settlement of a controversy involving the decedent's will or any bequest under it, the interest so assigned or surrendered is not considered to have passed from the decedent to his surviving spouse for purposes of the marital deduction.

## PECUNIARY BEQUESTS

To implement a bequest of a specific dollar amount to the surviving spouse, an executor might distribute assets having a fair market value of no less than the amount of the bequest. The marital deduction will be allowed to the full amount of the *dollar* bequest, even though the executor did not make the payment in the form specified in the will. For example, if there was a bequest of $50,000 and the estate is short of cash, the executor may offer the spouse certain noncash assets worth at least that much. The marital deduction is for $50,000.

## IT MAY BE ADVISABLE TO LIMIT THE UNLIMITED MARITAL DEDUCTION

The so-called marital deduction really is not unlimited if the parties decide to limit gifts or bequests. Reasons for self-imposed limits include these:

1. For personal reasons, a husband does not want to give too much property to his wife. The future of the marriage may appear to be dubious. Or he thinks that she wouuld be recklessly generous in the making of gifts or in the sharing of her new wealth. Or he does not want to make things too easy for his own successor.

2. The husband may not want to leave all or a very substantial part of his property to his wife because he wishes to make dispositions to other parties, such as his children (especially children by an earlier marriage, who might be ignored by his wife), his sisters, or any other people or institutions.

3. The wife's wealth may be far greater than the husband's. Any saving on estate tax if he dies first would be far less than the additional estate tax when she dies subsequently, at which time she is the owner of her own wealth plus what she gets from him.

4. The wife may be quite elderly or sickly. Predictably, property that he leaves to her may soon be subjected to a second estate tax.

5. The husband may feel that if his wife inherits too much wealth, she will be an easy target for fortune hunters. It should be remembered that wills are available for inspection by the public at large.

# 9

# USING LIFETIME GIFTS TO MINIMIZE OR WIPE OUT TRANSFER TAXES

Lifetime and deathtime transfers are subject to a coordinated Federal gift and estate tax system. There is a unified credit for the purpose of both taxes. This credit is utilized first against gift tax liability. But there is no gift tax liability to the extent that a person can use the annual exclusion, the making of split-gifts with a spouse, the gift tax marital deduction. Liberalization of the annual exclusion and the so-called unlimited marital deduction provided by the Economic Recovery Tax Act of 1981 have increased greatly the utility of gifts in the formation of an estate plan.

## BENEFITS FROM THE MAKING OF GIFTS

The tax advantages of making gifts are:

☐ The reduction of gross estate by removing property from it. Even under the unified structure that aggregates lifetime and deathtime transfers, tax-free gifts will permit reduction of ultimate gross estate.

☐ Avoidance of income tax on the appreciation of property. By giving appreciated-value property to relatives or friends in lower tax brackets, the gain on eventual disposition will be taxed at a lesser rate.

☐ Avoidance of income tax on income-producing properties that are given away.

☐ Avoidance of property taxes (including taxes on intangible property) in the case of assets that are given away.

☐ Avoidance of loss of the estate tax marital deduction if the spouse dies first.

☐ Freezing of transfer taxes at present values if it is anticipated that values will rise because of inflation or other factors.

☐ There is no depreciation recapture in the case of gifts, as there is for other dispositions of depreciable property.

☐ Recovery of the cost of a property. If an individual sells property at cost to someone else, this is a combination sale and gift. The sale is tax-free, inasmuch as realization equalled cost. The recipient benefits to the extent that he receives a gift of the difference in value.

☐ The $10,000 per donee per year gift tax exclusion, joint gifts by married persons where there is a proper consent, and the marital deduction can remove property from both gift and estate tax liability.

☐ In order to obtain the tax benefits, a person who had been negligent about making estate plans now can make most forms of gift when he literally is on his deathbed. The former rule that an individual's gifts within three years of his death are includible in his gross estate does not apply in the case of decedents dying after December 31, 1981, except in a few specialized situations.

☐ If a person plans to make a gift of a cash-value insurance policy on his life to anyone, the longer he waits to make the gift, the higher the gift tax is likely to be. Tax is based upon the interpolated terminal reserve at the time of the gift. (Interpolated terminal reserve can be likened to "cash surrender value.") If no cash is withdrawn by the policyholder, this figure will rise each year.

There also are nontax reasons for making a gift, such as the pleasure of seeing beneficiaries enjoy what you have given them, the desire to help someone who is in need or who could use some assistance, the saving of insurance and custodial costs, freedom from the responsibility of caring for possessions, the confidentiality that is preserved if dispositions are not made by will, the effectuation of present disposition plans before senility sets in.

By making gifts of property to the intended beneficiaries at this time, the assets can be protected against creditors or damage suits.

Where a person already has used up his unified credit (cumulative transfers exempt from both gift and estate taxes), gifts in excess of annual exclusions may seem less attractive. The accompanying gift tax then amounts to a prepayment of estate tax.

## REQUIREMENTS FOR A GIFT

In order to be recognized for tax purposes, these ingredients must be present:

1. A donor competent to make a gift.

2. A donee capable of accepting a gift.

3. The clear and unmistakable intention on the part of the donor to divest himself completely and irrevocably of the title, ownership, and control of the subject matter of the gift at the present time.

4. Delivery to the donee of the subject of the gift. Jewelry can be transmitted physically. Realty can be conveyed by means of a deed. Stock certificates can be handed over by an endorsement of the certificate or instructions to the transfer agent of the security.

5. Acceptance of the gift by the donee. If the donee does not know that a gift has been made, he cannot accept it.

## FACTORS THAT SHOULD BE CONSIDERED

A transfer is regarded as a gift if it is not intended as an exchange of value for something else. The transfer cannot represent an intent to repay another person what is his due or what he had a moral right to receive. A gift is bestowed because of personal affection, or regard, or pity, or from general motives of philanthropy. Desire on the part of the donor to save taxes does not prevent an otherwise qualifying transfer from being characterized as a gift.

There is a presumption that a transfer between closely related parties is a gift. A husband may make a gift to his wife without the presumption that such a gift is in discharge of marital duty.

A gift was not recognized where a husband set up a trust for the benefit of his wife, and the trust agreement provided that the income was for her support and maintenance.

The Internal Revenue Service views with suspicion any "settlements" between relatives that involve transfer of property that otherwise would be subject to gift or estate taxes.

An individual transferred property in order to prevent a lawsuit in a will contest. There was arm's length bargaining to arrive at the settlement, and it was ruled that there had been no intent to make a gift.

In many cases, questions have arisen as to whether a sum of money given by a man to a woman was a gift or was payment for services. In the first situation, gift tax could be involved; in the second, income tax. Decisions seem to hinge on whether the payor had wanted to make a gift to a nonrelative or whether the payments were of a compensatory character.

Even in a transaction between related parties, there could be the question of gift or compensation.

A father gave stock in the family business to his son, who had expressed the desire to work elsewhere. The Internal Revenue Service labeled the transfer of stock as taxable compensation. But the court agreed with the son that the transfer was a gift. The evidence indicated that for some years the father had intended making a gift and hesitated only because he felt the son would ignore him thereafter. The transfer took place only when the son actually had been offered a position elsewhere.

## INCOMPLETE GIFTS

For Federal tax purposes, a gift can be like a boomerang. One cannot get rid of property unless he knows how.

A gift does not take place, for tax purposes, when the necessary elements of a gift are lacking. For example, United States Treasury Series EE Bonds cannot be transferred; if the owner wishes to make a gift, the only way in which he can part with the property is to send the certificates back to the Treasury for reissuance in another name or names.

A gift of stock is not recognized for tax purposes where the donor merely makes a verbal assignment or states in a letter to the donee that a gift is being made. Transfer of stock by a form of assignment or on the transfer agent's books is required.

An individual who gives bank passbooks and time certificates of deposit to another person, but who retains his name on the accounts and certificates, has not made a gift. He has retained the power to withdraw funds and to use them for his own purposes.

Gifts of insurance on the donor's life are not effective until the proper endorsement is made by the insurance company, or an assignment is furnished to the insurance company on its own form. Where the original owner of property continues to pay the insurance premiums, there is a strong inference that the property merely had been loaned to someone else.

Customarily, land can be given away only by means of a written conveyance. In some states, a transfer is not effective until recorded in a designated office.

If a person deeds the family residence to his wife but continues to live there, courts generally interpret this to mean that he intended his gift to become effective at a later date, such as his death should he still be residing there at that time.

A gift will not be recognized for tax purposes when the donor retains the power to alter, to amend, to modify, or to revoke the property transfer.

An earnest desire to confer the benefits of ownership on someone else is not enough to accomplish a gift. One must pay a price for making a gift—namely, divestiture of ownership and control. The mere statement of a wish to make a gift has little bearing on whether a gift really has been made. The parties' expectations or hopes as to the tax treatment have nothing to do with the matter.

## TRUST

Even though an individual places property beyond his power to reacquire it when he creates an irrevocable trust, he may have retained significant interest by way of powers to alter arrangements or to change the flow of income between named beneficiaries. He would not have these powers if he had made a complete gift.

A transfer of property in trust is a completed gift if the grantor retains no power to change its disposition, whether for his own benefit or for the benefit of someone else. Retained power to change contingent remainder interests (such as who is to get a trust's property when the named beneficiaries and the remaindermen have died) will prevent a gift from being complete.

If a gift is not complete, even though both donor and donee believe that it is, the supposed donee can lose the property because of seizure by the Internal Revenue Service by reason of unpaid taxes of the donor.

# KINDS OF GIFTS

It is necessary to know what the tax law includes in the term "gift" so that transactions will not result in penalties and interest for unpaid taxes because a person did not realize that he had made a gift. The word covers far more than the mere bestowal of property. Here are other common forms of gift:

☐ Transfer of property to a trust for the benefit of someone else.

☐ Permitting a beneficiary, other than the grantor himself, to receive the income from a trust created by the grantor, where he retains the power to get back the property or to change the beneficiaries or their respective proportions. Here the grantor is deemed to have retained ownership of the trust property, and permitting someone else to get income is deemed a gift.

☐ Purchase of a life insurance policy, or payment of a premium on a previously issued policy, if the proceeds are payable to a beneficiary other than the estate of the insured person, and if the insured person retains no rights in the policy.

&#9633; Permitting another person to withdraw from a joint bank account funds that were deposited by the donor. No gift is made if one person simply puts money that another party may withdraw into a joint bank account. The gift is made when the person who did not deposit money withdraws funds without having to account to the donor. (An individual who opened a joint account with a brokerage office, and provided all of the funds and securities, was held not to have made a gift by permitting the other joint owner to withdraw funds at pleasure. Gifts were made only when this other person actually did withdraw funds.)

&#9633; Conveyance of title to property to oneself and another as joint owners. No gift is made when bonds simply are registered in joint names, although one party supplied all of the funds. A gift is made when the party who did not furnish any of the money sells the bonds or has them reregistered in his own name.

&#9633; Transfer to another person by a remainderman of a trust of his remainder interest, without consideration.

&#9633; Transfer without consideration of a reversionary right, that is, the power to get back property under certain circumstances. For example, an individual may transfer property to a trust for the benefit of his former wife, but he retains the right to get back the assets should she remarry. He has retained a reversionary right in the property.

&#9633; Acceptance by an annuitant (the person entitled to receive an annuity) of a lesser amount so that another person will be entitled to receive an annuity should the original annuitant die. The value of the gift is the value of the survivorship annuity received by the second person. But there is no gift element where a similar arrangement is made by a person covered by a Treasury-approved employee benefit plan.

&#9633; Forgiving a debt.

&#9633; Assignment without consideration of a judgment, a Federal income tax refund claim, or anything else to another person.

&#9633; A transaction, in the language of instructions on the Federal gift tax return, "by another method, direct or indirect." This refers to all transactions where property or property rights or interests are passed without recompense or are conferred on another person, regardless of the means or devices used.

## INDIRECT GIFTS

Sometimes the transfer of property is not obvious. But the Internal Revenue Service successfully has held that many such indirect gifts are taxable.

When a divorced person voluntarily increased the amounts of

court-ordered alimony that he paid to his former wife, the amounts of his generosity were gifts.

A father reimbursed his son for the cost of gifts that the son had purchased for the father. This was an indirect gift.

In a family corporation, the father owned 1,509 shares of stock. Each of his three sons owned *one* of the remaining shares. The father transferred, without consideration, 1,508 of his shares to the corporation, which then held them as treasury stock. This was held to be a gift by him to each son of one-fourth of his stock, as the one share which he kept now represented a one-fourth interest in the corporation.

A mother lent money to her son. She was deemed to have made a taxable gift when she permitted the statute of limitations on the collection of debts to expire without taking steps to enforce repayment.

## PROPERTY SETTLEMENTS

Certain property settlements are not regarded as gifts if divorce follows within two years. This applies also in the case of a child-support agreement.

Transfers of interests in property made under the terms of a written agreement between spouses in settlement of their marital or property rights are deemed to be for full and adequate value. They do not represent taxable gifts, whether or not the agreement is approved by a divorce decree, if the spouses obtain a final decree of divorce from each other within two years after entering into the agreement. Transfers to provide a reasonable allowance for the support of the children, including those legally adopted, are not subject to gift tax if made pursuant to an agreement meeting the requirements above.

## RENUNCIATIONS

A donee of a gift cannot be compelled to accept property he does not want. So he can disclaim it without incurring Federal gift tax liability even though the effect of this disclaimer is to pass the property to another person, such as his daughter. This disclaimer must be made within nine months after the gift was made and before the intended donee accepts the gift or any of its benefits. In the case of gifts made after December 31, 1981, requirements of a state disclaimer law do not have to be met.

A right created by law cannot be renounced. Disclaiming the right amounts to the making a gift of any property covered by it.

> A wife held property jointly with her husband, the property to go to the survivor on the death of either spouse. She filed a petition with a county probate court renouncing all her interest as surviving joint tenant, so that the property would go to their children as next of kin if her husband died first. But she could not refuse to accept property rights that already were hers, for she had accepted the property at the time of the contractual creation of the joint interests. Thus, she was subject to gift tax on a transfer of property to her children without consideration.

> A husband and wife owned certain securities jointly. When the wife died, the husband executed a disclaimer, renouncing any interest that he had in the securities, and stating that he was renouncing ownership in favor of his children. It was held that he had made taxable gifts to the children of his interest in the securities. He had become the complete and unqualified owner by reason of his wife's death. The execution of the disclaimer amounted to nothing more than a transfer of property that he owned absolutely, and, hence, it was a taxable gift.

## TRANSFERS FOR INSUFFICIENT CONSIDERATION

A transfer of property is taxed as a gift to the extent that the payment or other consideration for the transfer is less than an adequate payment.

Transfers for insufficient consideration include transfers for consideration that is not reducible to a figure that can be expressed in terms of money. Examples of this are transfers of property for love and affection, or in return for a promise of marriage. The "consideration" for such a transfer is wholly disregarded, and the entire value of the property transferred is regarded as a gift.

Transfer of property of substantial value is not kept from being a gift when an inadequate or merely nominal price is paid for it. Bargain sales may be treated as gifts to the extent of the bargain, if there had been an intent to make a gift. When a father sells a home worth $65,000 to his son for $1,000 because he wants the son's family to enjoy the house even though the son cannot afford to pay for it, a $64,000 gift has been made. But if a person receives less for property than it is worth because he is overly anxious to sell or because he has made a bad bargain through ignorance of the fact that there was a uranium deposit beneath his pasture land, this does not result in the making of a taxable gift.

A woman transferred stock in a family corporation to her children in order to settle a lawsuit. The value of the shares was not regarded as a transfer for insufficient consideration. The full and adequate consideration was the ending of litigation. There had been no intent to make a gift. The transaction represented the exchange of something of value in return for something deemed to be of equivalent value.

## TRANSFERS TO EMPLOYEES

Transfers from employers to employees may be made without incurring gift tax liability. For example, a majority stockholder of a corporation transferred some of his stock in the company to employees. The number of shares given to each person depended on his length of service. These shares were not treated as gifts in a tax sense. The majority stockholder stood to benefit economically from the transfer of stock through the increased initiative of the employees resulting from their ownership of stock. And the fact that the number of shares given was based on years of employment showed that his intent was recognition of past services rather than the detached and disinterested generosity that is expected in a gift.

## RESIDENT OR NONRESIDENT ALIEN?

If the donor is a citizen or resident of the United States, the gift tax applies to all gifts, regardless of where the property is located.

If the donor is a nonresident who is not a citizen of the United States, the tax is imposed only if the gift consists of real estate or tangible personal property situated within the United States at the time of the transfer. Kinds of property considered to be situated in the U.S.: shares of stock issued by a domestic corporation (one whose charter was issued by a state or territory of the U.S.); debt obligations of a United States person; debt obligations of the United States, a state, or a political subdivision thereof.

Gifts made by citizens of the United States who were residents of a U.S. possession at the time the gifts were made are subject to the gift tax, unless the donor acquired United States citizenship solely by being a citizen of the possession or because of his birth or residence in the possession. (A donor who is a citizen of the United States and a resident of one of its possessions is regarded as a nonresident and not a citizen of the United States, if he acquired his U.S. citizenship solely by reason of one of the circumstances mentioned in the preceding sentence.)

## ANNUAL EXCLUSION

The first $10,000 of gifts made to any one donee during a calendar year are excluded in determining the total amount of gifts for that year. For purposes of allowance of the $10,000 per donee exclusion, the donee is deemed to be the beneficiary when transfers are made in trust.

If husband and wife consent, all gifts made by them to third persons may, for the purpose of the gift tax, be considered as having been made one-half by each. This in effect raises the $10,000 per donee exclusion to $20,000, that being the amount of gifts that can be given away each year without tax. In addition, in the case of gifts made after December 31, 1981, any amounts paid on behalf of any individual (1) as tuition to certain educational organizations for his education or training or (2) as payments for medical care to any person who provides medical care with respect to such individual will not be considered as transfers by gift. This exclusion for tuition and medical expenses is in addition to the $10,000 annual gift tax exclusion and is permitted without regard to the relationship between the donor and the donee.

The exclusion for medical expenses (including medical insurance) applies only with respect to direct payments made by the donor to the individual or organization providing medical services (i.e., no reimbursement made to the donee, as intermediary, is excludible). Qualifying medical expenses are limited to those used for the medical expense deduction on the income tax return, that is, those incurred essentially for the diagnosis, cure, mitigation, or prevention of disease, or for the purpose of affecting any structure or function of the body. Medical expenses, however, are excludible from gift tax without regard to the percentage limitation of the income tax law.

The unlimited exclusion is not permitted for amounts that are reimbursed by insurance. Thus, if a donor pays a qualifying medical expense and the donee also receives reimbursement, the donor's payment, to the extent of the reimbursement, is not eligible for the unlimited exclusion whether or not this reimbursement is paid in the same or a subsequent taxable year.

With respect to educational expenses, an unlimited exclusion is permitted for any tuition paid on behalf of an individual directly to the qualifying educational institution providing these services. A qualifying organization is an institution that normally maintains a regular faculty and curriculum and normally has a regularly enrolled body of students in attendance at the place of its educational activities. The exclusion is permitted with respect to both full-time and part-time students, but is limited to direct tuition costs, that is, no exclusion is available for books, supplies, dormitory fees, and the like.

No gift is recognized if the person providing the medical expenses or the tuition is under an obligation under local law to provide such items to the recipient. No reference is made in this provision as to the income tax consequences otherwise applicable to these payments.

# PRESENT INTEREST

In order for a gift to qualify for the annual $10,000 per donee exclusion, two requirements must be satisfied:

1. The gift must not be of a future interest, that is, the donee's benefit is immediate.

2. The gift must have an ascertainable value at the time it is given.

A *present interest* is one where the donee is entitled unconditionally to the immediate use, possession, or enjoyment of the property transferred. If a gift is made in trust, the income from the trust must be distributable absolutely to the beneficiary in all circumstances.

To achieve spendthrift protection, a trust provided that the trustee would have discretion to decide whether the income would be distributed to the beneficiary when a creditor was lurking in the wings. Under these conditions the trust income was not a present interest.

The critical test is whether there has been a postponement of the rights of the donee to use, to possess, and to enjoy the property.

A gift of a present interest does not qualify for the $10,000 exclusion where the value of the interest is not reasonably certain.

Stock in a closely-held corporation was given in trust for the benefit of the donor's minor grandchildren. No dividends had been paid on the stock for a dozen years; hence, the income interest had no ascertainable value.

A gift of life insurance where the beneficiary has no rights until the death of the insured is a future interest. But if current dividends may be used for the benefit of a beneficiary, the value of the dividends is a gift of a present interest.

## FUTURE INTEREST

A future interest is one where the donee's enjoyment of rights, powers, and privileges is postponed, despite the definiteness of the amounts of the gift or of the immediate acquisition by the donee of his rights. This includes any interest that the donee cannot enjoy until some future time. The *certainty of postponement* of the donee's rights to property or interests, *not the length of its duration,* determines whether the gift is of a future interest.

> Gifts to a trust were of future interests because the trust income was to accumulate until the beneficiaries reached age twenty-one. At that time, their interests could be paid to them. That the beneficiaries' interests could not be taken away from them was immaterial.

A donor who conveys ownership of real estate, but reserves the right to live there until he dies, makes a gift of a future interest. The donee's possession and enjoyment of the property is postponed until a later date, namely, the death of the donor.

The gift of a remainder interest in a trust is a future interest, because the recipient will have to wait until the trust is terminated to get his property. No exclusion is allowed for gifts to a sprinkling or spray trust because a beneficiary's right to income is not immediate, being dependent on the trustee's discretion.

A donor should keep an eye on the calendar in making gifts in order to make sure that they meet the criteria for present interests.

> A woman made a gift of real estate to her eight children and two grandchildren. But the properties were subject to leases by unrelated parties and the gifts were made *three months before the leases expired.* Poor timing of the gifts cost the donor ten times the per donee gift tax exclusion, which would be $100,000 under present law. That was equivalent to $33,333 per month for giv-

ing away interests that in three months' time automatically would have become excludible present interests. But the donees could not *immediately* enjoy the use or possession of the property. Even though the postponement of the gifts was of short duration, and the fact that the recipients could have sold them at once to outsiders, did not change the fact.

## MAKING GIFTS TO MINORS A PRESENT INTEREST

A gift to a minor is not regarded as a future interest in property if the property and the income from it may be expended by, or for the benefit of, the minor before he reaches age twenty-one. The nonexpended portion of the gift also must pass to the donee when he reaches twenty-one (or to his estate should he die before that time). Congress, in effect, has removed gifts in trust for a minor's benefit from the classification of future interest, if the transfer meets these prescribed guidelines.

This special provision declares that the trustee or other person authorized to administer the gift may have discretion from the time the gift is made until the donee reaches twenty-one years of age to expend the property for the benefit of the minor to the extent that it is needed.

The transfer will not be disqualified as a present interest merely if the trustee has discretion to distribute the amounts to be expended for the benefit of the minor, and there are no substantial restrictions under the trust agreement on the exercise of this discretion.

A limitation on the use of trust income to provide "for accident, illness, or other emergency affecting the beneficiary" was held to be a substantial restriction on the exercise of the trustee's discretion. Thus gift status as a present interest in the property was destroyed.

It is not necessary that the property or income from it actually be expended by or for the benefit of a minor during his minority, as long as all such amounts not so expended will pass to him when he attains majority or are payable to his estate.

## UNIFORM GIFTS TO MINORS ACT

It is easy to make gifts to minors. It is not so easy for the minor to dispose of the property. If it is stock, real estate, jewelry, etc., no one is going to be willing to buy from a child, who can repudiate the transaction when he becomes of age if, in the meantime, prices have gone up. A trust or guardianship could be set up, but that involves expense and red tape. If the gifted property remains under the donor's control, it will be included in his gross estate for Federal estate tax purposes when he dies.

In order to simplify these problems, most states have adopted some variation of the Uniform Gifts to Minors Act. Any adult, *except the donor or his spouse,* can be named custodian for the minor under the terms of this act. When a gift is made to the custodian, the property rights belong completely to the minor. The custodian is authorized to apply as much of the income of principal held by him for the benefit of the minor as he (the custodian) may deem advisable in his sole discretion. Income and principal not so applied are to be delivered to the minor when he reaches age twenty-one or, in the event of his prior death, to his estate.

Allowance of the annual exclusion is not affected by the changing of a state's version of the Uniform Gifts to Minors Act that lowers the age of majority to eighteen and therefore mandates that property be distributed to him at that age.

Gifts to a minor under the act qualify for the annual gift tax exclusion.

Income that is derived from property transferred under the act that is used in the discharge or satisfaction, in whole or in part, of a legal obligation of any person (such as a father) to support or to maintain a minor is taxable to this person to the extent so used. Otherwise it is taxable to the minor donee.

The value of property so transferred to a minor donee is includible in the donor's gross estate if he names himself custodian and dies while serving in that capacity and before the donee reaches age twenty-one. Gross estate includes assets transferred by another person to a custodianship for the transferor's minor children with himself as custodian, if he has retained such rights as revocation of the arrangement, especially where state law permits custodial assets to be used to satisfy the custodian's legal obligation of support.

> An individual owned all of the stock of a corporation. He gave 50 percent of the stock to his children in the sense that he had certificates made out in the name of each child, followed by the words: "Under the New York Uniform Gifts to Minors Act." The tax ruling was that the shares remained his property for Federal income tax purposes. He still had the full voting control of the corporation, and dividends that allegedly had been paid to the stockholders did not appear anywhere as the property of his children; no bank accounts or book entries had been established for them.

## MARITAL DEDUCTION

See the discussion on this subject in Chapter 8, "The 'Unlimited' Marital Deduction and Its Practical Limitations."

## GIFTS BY SPOUSES TO THIRD PARTIES

Gifts made by a husband and wife to a third party can be considered, for purposes of the gift tax, as having been made by one-half each, if both spouses consent.

If the consent is effective, all gifts by husband or wife to third parties that year must be treated in the same way. For this purpose, an individual is considered to be the spouse of another individual only if he is married to that individual at the time of the gift, and he does not remarry during the remainder of the calendar year. The rule does not apply if either spouse was a nonresident and not a citizen of the United States on the date of the gift.

The value of the gift must be ascertainable at the time of the gift.

A husband transferred to a trust for the benefit of his grandchildren certain property that the trustee could make use of for the benefit of his wife for her proper support, care, and health, or for any emergency affecting her or her family. As there was no ascertainable standard for the trustee's use of principal for the benefit of the wife, the value of the gift could not be measured. Gift-splitting was not allowed.

Consent to gift-splitting is made by the spouse filing the gift tax return by answering "Yes" to Question B on the face of the return and, by the other spouse, by executing the "Consent of Spouse" appearing on the face of the same return form. But it is sufficient if:

1. The consent of the husband is signified on the wife's return, and the consent of the wife is signified on the husband's return.

2. Or the consent of both spouses is signified on one of the returns.

Consent cannot be signified after the fifteenth day of the second month following the close of the calendar year, unless no return has been filed before that day for the calendar year by either spouse. Consent may not be signified after a return for that calendar year if filed by either spouse.

## CHARITABLE AND SIMILAR GIFTS

A donor who is a citizen or resident of the United States at the time a gift is made may deduct any of the following kinds of gift in determining the taxable gifts for a calendar year.

Gifts to:

☐ The United States or any state or political subdivision thereof exclusively for public purposes;

☐ Any corporation, trust, community chest, fund, or foundation organized and operated exclusively for religious, charitable, scientific, literary, or educational purposes, including the encouragement of art and the prevention of cruelty to children and animals, if no part of the net earnings of the organization are for the benefit of any private shareholder or individual, and no substantial part of its activities is carrying on propaganda or otherwise attempting to influence legislation;

☐ A fraternal society or order, operating as a lodge, if gifts are to be used exclusively as stated above; or

☐ Any post or organization of war veterans or auxiliary unit if organized in the United States or any of its possessions, and if no part of its net earnings is for the benefit of any private shareholder or individual.

The deduction is not limited to gifts for use within the United States, nor to these kinds of organization. But no deduction is allowed if the donor is not a citizen or resident of the United States, unless the charitable purposes of the benefitted organization will be accomplished in the United States.

## REQUIREMENTS

In the case of gifts made after December 31, 1981, a gift tax return is filed annually; previously, returns had been filed on a quarterly basis. But for a calendar year in which a donor dies, the gift tax return must be filed no later than the due date (including extensions) for the donor's Federal estate tax return.

## PENALTIES

There is a penalty of one-half of 1 percent per month, up to a maximum of 25 percent, for failure to pay gift tax when due or to pay a deficiency within ten days of the day of notice and demand.

Where a wife participates in gifts made by her husband, she is fully liable for gift taxes if he fails to pay.

Penalty can be imposed where no gift tax return was filed because the donor did not realize that the value of the gifted property was high enough to require the filing of a return.

One person purchased a house. There were several cases of wine in the cellar. He gave away the wine and failed to file a gift tax return although the items had considerable value. He was subected to a negligence penalty. In effect, this was not for his failure to file a gift tax return but for his negligence in not consulting a knowledgeable expert about the value of the wine.

## LIABILITY OF PERSON RECEIVING A GIFT

The Federal gift tax is a lien on all gifts in the calendar year for a ten-year period if the donor fails to pay the tax. If the donee gives away the property in the meantime, the lien is lifted as to this particular property. But a lien in the same amount applies to his other property, including assets acquired after the lien was imposed. The transferee is liable for the transferor's unpaid taxes to the extent of the property he receives, even if the transferor was not insolvent at the time of the transaction nor was rendered insolvent by the transfer.

## NET GIFTS

Sometimes an individual makes a gift subject to an understanding that the donee will pay the Federal gift tax. This is regarded as a net gift on which the donor owes no gift tax, if it can be established that payment of the tax by the donee was a condition of the transfer, or that the tax was to be paid from the value of the property transferred.

Ordinarily, a person derives taxable income to the extent that he has been relieved of an obligation. On June 15, 1982, the Supreme Court stated that this applies to a donor where the donee agrees to pay the gift tax.

As far as the donee is concerned, the gift tax is imposed on the net amount he receives. So the tax he pays is based on the property value less this gift tax. His basis in the gifted property, for the purpose of determining gain or loss when subsequently he sells it, is increased by the amount of gift tax he pays.

The gift tax is imposed on the donor for the privilege of giving away property. The donee's liability arises only if the donor does not pay the tax when it is due. If neither pays the tax, the "gift" may be deemed as never having actually been made, and the I.R.S. can seize the property should the donor have any unpaid taxes.

A gift tax return was not filed by an alleged donor, and the so-called donee also failed to file a return. The Internal Revenue Service was permitted to take this property away from the re-puted donee to satisfy unpaid taxes of the donor, on the theory that there was no proof that the asset ever had passed from donor to donee and hence it remained the former's property, subject to seizure to satisfy his tax arrearages.

## VALUATION

The valuation used for gift tax purposes is fair market value at the time of the gift. That also is the donee's basis. Valuation rules are the same as used for Federal estate tax purposes.

If a person makes a gift of stock that represents such a large propor-tion of a corporation's total outstanding shares that the market could not absorb this quantity without a drop in the quoted price, the blockage rule is applied, just as in the case of the estate tax. Valuation will be reduced by the cost of having a broker make a secondary distribution, so as not to break the regular market. (See Chapter 4 for a discussion of the blockage rule for estate tax purposes.)

But if a person gives away a very large number of shares in a corpora-tion to each of several donees, the blockage rule will not be applied. Valua-tion then is made on the value of the property covered by each gift, not on the value of all gifts made at about the same time.

The gift tax valuation may be increased to reflect a control premium when appropriate.

When a life insurance policy is given away, its value for gift tax purposes is the *interpolated terminal reserve,* which is rather akin to the better known term "cash surrender value." The insurance company can provide this figure and, in fact, is called upon to supply it to the Internal Revenue Service for use in checking on the gift tax return.

## GIFTS WITHIN THREE YEARS OF DEATH

In the case of decedents dying after December 31, 1981, the former rule that all gifts within three years of the donor's death automatically are included in his gross estate does not apply. Now, the only gifts within three years of death that are includible in the donor's gross estate are (1) gifts of life insurance and (2) interests in property that are regarded as incomplete, such as transfers with a retained life interest or those subject to the donor's power to alter, to amend, or to terminate.

All transfers within three years of death (other than gifts eligible for the annual gift tax exclusion) are included in the decedent's gross estate for purposes of determining the estate's qualification for redemption of stock to pay death taxes, eligibility to utilize the special-use valuation, and ascertainment of property subject to estate tax liens.

## SURVIVING SPOUSE'S GIFTS

This subject has been discussed in the section on qualified terminable interests in Chapter 8.

## RECORDS' RETENTION

A donor is required to keep permanent records to show the gifts he has made and the determination of the value of these gifts.

# 10

## THE WAY YOU OWN PROPERTY IS A FORM OF ESTATE PLANNING

The owning of property jointly with one or more other persons serves several estate planning purposes. If A and B hold assets in joint ownership with right of survival, there is no question of who gets the property when one co-owner dies. This can assure a beneficiary that she will receive specific property. For example, joint ownership of the family residence by two spouses with right of survivorship enables a wife to know that her children cannot deprive her of the home. *Joint ownership also can avoid the delay, publicity, and expenses of the customary probate of a decedent's estate.* It can provide incentive to another person, for example, where a father puts some or all of his business in joint ownership with his son, so that the latter, without having made an investment, has "a piece of the action" to stimulate his participation in the enterprise. It can provide an instant source of funds as required, as where a father opens a joint bank or brokerage account with his daughter.

But although joint ownership with right of survivorship can establish how property will be distributed upon a person's death, such an arrangement should not be regarded as a substitute for a will. All of an individual's assets may not be held in this form of ownership at the time of his death because he may have been unaware of everything he owned, or he may have been careless, or there may have been practical considerations such as a bank's requirements that property not be conveyed in any way while indebtedness remains unpaid. Joint ownership lacks the flexibility of a will. And it does not cover all points that a will could encompass, such as naming a guardian for his minor children should they be orphaned by his death.

## ESTATE TAX CONSEQUENCES OF JOINT OWNERSHIP

The Internal Revenue Service uses a rule of expediency: In the case of jointly-owned property, the value is attributable entirely to the first party to die. The estate has the burden of rebutting this presumption. The executor must be prepared to prove that the decedent was not entirely responsible for the accumulation of the property or that he has made valid dispositions of some of it.

In the case of decedents dying after December 31, 1981, where a husband and wife owned property in joint tenancy, with right of survivorship, the estate of the first spouse to die includes one-half of the value of the property, regardless of which spouse had furnished the consideration for its acquisition. At first flush, this appears to be good news for married couples, as it eliminates the sometimes impossible job of endeavoring to trace the financial history of the property and to prove the relative contribution of each spouse. On the other hand, the first spouse to die may have paid little if any of the cost, so that his gross estate may include half the value of property that had been obtained through the work or purchase of the survivor. Where property has increased in value since acquisition, the tax cost or basis for determining gain or loss on subsequent sale by the surviving spouse will be value at the time of death or six months later, as elected by the executor, in the case of inherited property. Where the husband dies first, his assumed one-half of the property will have a stepped-up basis in the hands of his surviving spouse, while the half she is assumed to own will have its cost as its basis. If more than one-half of the property is presumed to be the husband's here, a greater part (perhaps all) of the property will receive a stepped-up basis. Where the fifty-fifty split provided by the Economic Recovery Tax Act of 1981 is not what the parties want, consideration should be given to changing these proportions by such means as interspousal gifts, which now can be regarded as tax-free under most circumstances.

## FORMS OF CO-OWNERSHIP

The principal forms of joint ownership are (1) joint tenancy, (2) tenancy in common, (3) tenancy by the entirety, and (4) community property.

### JOINT TENANCY

Each of the parties to a joint tenancy has an undivided interest in the entire property. If one party dies, the survivor or survivors own the property. Some state laws limit survivorship rights. A joint tenant who survives does not take the interest of the other tenant from him as his successor, but takes it by right under the instrument by which the tenancy was created. Thus, joint tenancy passes outside of a will, even though the interest that the survivor gets is limited by the terms of the instrument.

As was mentioned earlier, joint ownership with right of survivorship is a convenient method of transferring property that takes these assets out of *probate* (the proving of a will before the appropriate state court). Property that goes from the estate to a beneficiary by means of a will is subject to delay in transmission, for the probate court will have to get and review a full accounting from the executor. Where there will be Federal estate tax liability, or there seems to be a likelihood of this, a timid executor may delay making any distributions of assets to beneficiaries until the tax liability is finalized, lest he (the executor) incur personal liability by distributing the assets without having made sufficient provision for payment of estate taxes. There may be additional expenses, inasmuch as executors and estate lawyers customarily charge according to the total dollar value of the property that passes through their hands. Publicity is avoided in the case of assets that do not go through probate. Wills that are probated become a matter of record; what passes outside of probate enjoys the advantage of confidentiality.

Where a joint tenant (such as a daughter or brother) is the survivor, a new basis is given to that portion of the joint property that is included in the decedent's gross estate: fair market value at the date of death or at the alternate valuation date, if that legitimately had been elected by the executor.

Where two joint tenants die under circumstances where it is not possible to determine whether they died other than simultaneously, the property so held is distributed one-half as if one co-tenant had survived and one-half as if the other had survived.

## TENANCY IN COMMON

Each of the tenants in common owns a stipulated share of the property. If one co-owner dies, his share goes to his *estate,* rather than to the surviving co-owners.

Some states recognize a form of tenancy in common for joint lives with a remainder to the survivor. This survivorship right usually cannot be changed by one owner acting alone.

Property in the estate of a tenant in common does not increase through a co-tenant's death, unless a specific bequest is made. The survivor's basis, consequently, is the cost to him of his original proportion, plus (if applicable) the value on the estate tax return of any property that he inherits from a deceased tenant in common.

## TENANCY BY THE ENTIRETY

This type of ownership is restricted to legally married spouses, and in some states it is further restricted only to realty. Husband and wife share the property in a single ownership and title. Each has an undivided interest in the entire property. Upon the death of one spouse, the survivor does not succeed to the right and title of the deceased spouse, inasmuch as she already has title to the entire estate.

In the case of simultaneous deaths of both spouses, where the deaths presumably took place at the same instant, the property is divided one-half as if one had survived and one-half as if the other had survived, as in the case of joint tenants.

When property was held in tenancy by the entirety at the time of the husband's death and there is no evidence to indicate that the wife had furnished any consideration for the property, the full value is includible in the husband's gross estate.

## COMMUNITY PROPERTY

In a community property state, each spouse legally owns one-half of the property acquired by either spouse after the marriage. It does not necessarily follow that 50 percent of the property owned by a married couple in a community state belongs to each spouse. For example, property acquired before the marriage does not qualify.

The share of the first spouse to die takes as its basis its fair market value at the date of death or the alternate valuation date, if applicable. If at least one-half of the community property was includible in the estate, the survivor is considered to have acquired his one-half under the state community property tax law. The basis of that property is one-half of the fair market value as shown on the Federal estate tax return filed on behalf of the decedent.

The Economic Recovery Tax Act of 1981 has removed the former disallowance of the marital deduction for transfers between spouses of community property.

The community property states are Arizona, California, Idaho, Louisiana, Nevada, New Mexico, Texas, and Washington.

# CREATING OR ENDING A JOINT OWNERSHIP MAY TRIGGER GIFT TAX

Reference has been made previously to the fact that under most circumstances, there is a virtually unlimited marital deduction. But there can be Federal gift tax liability in transactions that are not between spouses.

If one party contributes more than the value of his joint interest when title to property is transferred to two persons (other than joint tenancies with right of survivorship), there may be gift tax liability. Similarly, a gift results where a joint tenancy is terminated and the property is not divided among the parties in accordance with their rights as joint owners.

# DISADVANTAGES OF CO-OWNERSHIP OF PROPERTY

Before entering upon co-ownership of property, consider these potential shortcomings in such an arrangement:

1. There may be deteriorating relations with a co-owner. Examples include marital discord or an increasingly disenchanted business partner.

2. Where property has more than one owner, problems of sale may be insuperable.

3. An inexperienced co-owner may have to take over the administration and other ownership problems if the co-owner who is knowledgeable in this area dies suddenly.

4. Where a husband and wife file a joint Federal income tax return, each spouse can be held personally liable for the entire tax. Ordinarily, one party (here called the wife for sake of simplicity) is free of personal liability for tax on income that had been unreported if she can show (a) that omitted income of her husband had been in excess of 25 percent of gross income shown on the return, (b) she had not known and had no reason to know of the omission, and (c) she did not profit materially from the omission. But she forfeits this status of *innocent spouse* where the omitted income was deposited in a joint bank account to which she had access.

5. Jointly-owned property may be subjected to serious problems in the case of action by the creditors of one co-owner.

A father and son jointly owned a garage and service station. In an attempt to collect unpaid taxes owed by the son, Internal Revenue Service agents seized the premises, padlocked the place, and posted a sign announcing the proceedings had been brought on by the son's tax liabilities. The father brought suit against the Revenue Agents, claiming that they wrongfully had excluded him from his own property (including tools in which the son had no interest), deprived him of the right to conduct his business, and defamed him by posting the seizure notice for customers to see—when *he* owed nothing. It was held that jointly-owned property of a delinquent taxpayer may be seized when any co-owner owes taxes, and the fact that the father's personal property happened to be inside the building did not prevent its being padlocked to ensure that the son's interest in jointly-owned property stayed firmly in government hands. The father's name was not deemed to have been defamed in the seizure notice, for customers and the public at large could have noted that only the son's name was mentioned . . . provided that anyone actually read the small print.

## REQUIREMENTS

Where the I.R.S. seizes jointly-owned property and sells it to recoup unpaid taxes of one co-owner, the Service can retain only that portion of the proceeds allocated to that one co-owner's interest. But the other co-owners are hurt if property in which they have an interest is sold at a time and under circumstances not of their own choosing.

# 11

# RETAINED INTERESTS: A DANGER AND AN OPPORTUNITY

A person's gross estate includes the value of property owned at the time of his death, to the extent of his interest in that property. With a moderate amount of advance planning with regard to keeping records of acquisitions, co-ownership arrangements, and current inventories and locations, establishing the value of owned property is usually not a difficult matter. But gross estate also includes the value of property that an individual has disposed of during his lifetime if, at the time of his death, he still holds significant strings that could control the use, apportionment, or distribution of assets that no longer are his. He may not realize the implication of retained powers and hence may have never told his professional advisor about their existence. The result of such an oversight is that even after the Economic Recovery Tax Act of 1981 is phased in fully by 1987, his estate may be subject to tax—despite the virtual elimination of the estate tax by that time. Such taxation could be completely unnecessary in those cases where he no longer has reason to retain these powers but has forgotten that they exist (assuming he had realized the implications) or their costly consequences.

Before the Tax Act of 1981, conflicting pressures affected the use of retained powers in estate planning. A person may wish to keep open for as long as possible his options concerning how his property and its income will be used. For example, he may feel unqualified to decide which of his children should get property or income, or the form in which each should receive it, until each child has demonstrated his earning power and capabilities, financial and other aspirations, health, and "attitudes." So property may be transferred, in trust or otherwise, with the transferor retaining the right to channel funds or to select beneficiaries as he deems appropriate in the light of changing circumstances and personalities. A tax-conscious estate planner would advise, "Sever those strings and you will cut down on estate tax." That is true but it may not supply the complete story. The saving of estate tax very likely is not so important to a person as is the power to reserve decisions about his property until he feels that he is in better position to make those decisions. He may want to postpone his decisions for as long as he lives.

The Economic Recovery Tax Act of 1981 invites the rethinking of present intentions. Because of a higher unified credit, lowered tax rates, and other liberalizing changes, the decision on whether to retain one's choice as to property dispositions now can be made with less attention to the estate tax consequences and more attention to a person's real concerns, such as the desire to keep open his alternatives in the disposition of his wealth. Because of the diminishing estate tax consequences, he may decide not to let go of significant strings to property. But if the property remains subject to his control, the assets may be lost to his beneficiaries because of claims against him by the Internal Revenue Service or other creditors, such as in the case of a malpractice suit. And as he gets older, he may become increasingly less competent to make the best decisions. He may become more susceptible to undue influence of other parties.

## TRANSFERRED PROPERTY THAT REMAINS IN ONE'S ESTATE

As a general rule, property that is not owned by a decedent when he dies—because he has divested himself of it during his lifetime—is not considered part of his estate when he dies. But a donor who keeps a hold over the actual and immediate enjoyment of what he puts beyond his own control has not rid himself of the degree of control required to avoid the tax. Transfer of property subject to a retained interest usually is an *incomplete transfer* that fails to take the property out of the transferor's estate when eventually he dies.

The estate tax cannot be avoided where there is a transfer in excess of the credits and exceptions, except when an owner transfers absolutely, completely, and without possible reservations, and parts with all of his ownership, possession, and enjoyment of the property. After such a transfer has been made, he must be left with no legal title in the property, no possibility other than a minimal one that the property will come back to him, and no right to possess or to enjoy the property then or thereafter. In other words, the transfer must be immediate, out-and-out, and unaffected by whether the transferor lives or dies.

For this purpose, the tax statute is not concerned with property laws relating to ownership; it is interested only in who had the actual economic benefit of property. And psychological benefits may be involved, such as the pleasure of controlling the dispositions of property or income.

The three principal types of transfer that wind up being included in an individual's gross estate are:

1. *Transfers with retained life estate or the right to designate the enjoyment of property or the income from it.* A retained life estate refers to a transfer, such as in trust, where the transferor still holds on to significant rights in the transferred property until the moment of his death. The most common form of this is where a person reserves the right to use or to enjoy property, for example, by getting the income it produces, for the remainder of his life. The property really has not been transferred until he dies, so its value is included in his gross estate at that time.

2. *Transfers taking effect at death.* This includes all property transfers that a person makes during his lifetime (as a substitute for a will) that become operative only at his death. This sweeps into a person's gross estate all property the final possession or enjoyment of which is held in suspense until the moment of his death. For example, an individual transfers property for the benefit of someone else, the latter to get the income for as long as she lives, the property itself to belong to her only if she outlives the transferor.

3. *Transfers that can be revoked, altered, or amended until the moment of death.* The transferor still has the right to enjoy the property or to say who will enjoy it. Thus, the property is still his in a very meaningful sense up to the instant he dies. When a person holds property on a string, the statute does not require that he pull the string or even intend to pull it; all that is necessary is that the string exists. As long as it does, he has a very significant incident of ownership of this property. At the moment of his death, the property passes out of his control to someone else "without strings." This is the event that triggers the estate tax.

A person can have excellent reasons for retaining interests in property he has transferred. A father might choose to give stock in the family business to his son, provided the son remains with the business. If the son becomes disinterested, the father legitimately would like to have the opportunity of saying who *will* run the business if he wants the income for his family. Or an individual may transfer income-producing property to persons he would like to own it, but reserves to himself the income for the remainder of his life because he may need it. There is nothing morally wrong and nothing that smacks of tax evasion about such motivations.

Funds transferred to an irrevocable trust for the benefit of an individual's existing children are includible in his gross estate when he dies if he has reserved the right to add the names of children who may be born after the transfer to the trust. Here the transferor has reserved the right to amend the original transfer, as the addition of new beneficiaries will reduce the proportions originally made available to the beneficiaries named in the first instance.

A vital area of estate planning is recognition of retained interests that will trigger the estate tax, periodic review of whether it still is necessary to retain strings that once were considered necessary, and timely severance of those strings when circumstances change. *But one must consider carefully whether it is best to accept vulnerability to estate taxes so that a person may continue to retain strings that are important to him, such as the keeping open of his options or the making of decisions that he believes are to the best interest of his beneficiaries.*

## TRANSFERS WITH RETAINED LIFE ESTATE

Here is the general rule: The value of one's gross estate when he dies includes the value of all property that the decedent had *at any time* transferred, by trust or otherwise, where he retained for his life or for any period that does not in fact end before his death (1) the possession or enjoyment of it, or (2) the right, either alone or in conjunction with any person, to designate those who will possess or enjoy the property or the income from it.

The transfer may have been made many years before death; there is no statute of limitations that protects transactions after a specific period of time. The rule applies in the case of any transfer except a sale for adequate and full consideration in money or the equivalent.

> An individual's will provided that she would retain the power to allocate rights to named beneficiaries for as long as she lived. The property subject to this power was included in her gross estate when she died, sixty-seven years later.

"Enjoyment" refers not only to the transferor's actual possession of property or his right to the income it produces. It includes also the use of the property or its income to pay his obligations. A person is said to enjoy property, even if under no circumstances it can come back to him, when he retains the ability to say who will possess the property, or its income, or any part of its income.

The purpose of this part of the tax law is to impose an estate tax on property in which the decedent retained the right to economic benefit during his lifetime. Economic benefit might relate to an understanding or agreement reached at the time of the transfer:

> A person transfers stock certificates to his daughter, saying, "I'll continue to cash the dividend checks myself."

> An individual gives savings bank books to his nieces, arranging for signature cards for withdrawal purposes to be furnished to them. But because of forgetfulness or otherwise, he keeps his own signature card on file.

The existence of such an understanding can be inferred from the facts and circumstances surrounding the transfer and subsequent use of the property; the agreement need not be legally enforceable, nor evidenced by the deed or other instrument of transfer. For example, if by prearrangement a transferor receives the income from transferred property until his death, the value of the property will be includible in his gross estate, even though he had no enforceable right to that income.

An individual consulted her attorney about the amount of property she could convey to her daughter without gift tax liability. He told her about the annual exclusion and the unified credit for gift and estate tax purposes, warning that gifts must have "no strings attached." The mother then conveyed to her daughter an undivided fractional interest in some income-producing lands. A Federal gift tax return for the value of the property less the exclusion was filed. The mother continued to pay all the property taxes on this land and to receive (and report) all its income. The daughter later explained to the Internal Revenue Service that she understood that she was entitled to a proportionate part of the total income from the property, but she never asked for it because she did not need it. The property allegedly the subject of the gift was included in the mother's gross estate when she died on the ground that she had retained for life the possession or enjoyment of, or the right to, the income from the property conveyed to her daughter. All the daughter had was bare legal title, which was not enough to overcome the requirement that the property be includible in her mother's gross estate.

A father deeded substantial timberland acreage to his children. But he continued to live in his old home there and to run the business as before. He also continued to pocket all of the revenues and to pay income taxes on them. The value of the property was included in his gross estate when he died, as a transfer with a retained life estate. There was no record that the transferor caused any material change in his relationship to the land. The children merely accepted the fact that he would get the income as long as he lived. Whether a transferor has the legal right to income he continued to receive is irrelevant for this purpose. A beneficiary's acquiescence in the transferor's retention of income from transferred property implies that some pretransfer agreement or prearrangement for such retention existed.

If a decedent reserves the right to receive income from transferred property after the death of another person who was, in fact, enjoying the income at the time of the decedent's death, the amount to be included in the decedent's gross estate does not include the value of the outstanding income interest of another person. But if the other person had died before the decedent, the reservation by the decedent may be considered to be either for his life or for a period that does not in fact end before his death.

An individual's gross estate does not include the value of a house that he had given to his daughter, merely because he continues to live there, if he pays a reasonable rent or it can be shown that he lives there merely by an invitation that, realistically, can be withdrawn at any time.

> When a mother transferred the house in which she lived to her children but continued to live there, the value of the property was included in her gross estate when she died. True, she had not specifically retained the right to live there. But, as a daughter subsequently admitted during the trial, "We weren't about to kick her out." One procedure that would have indicated that the mother indeed had given up all rights to the house would have been for her to have worked out any rental obligation by performing baby sitting, custodial, and other chores.

The tax law applies also when the transfer is neither direct nor obvious.

> An individual was entitled to receive the income from a trust for the balance of her life. She renounced her right to stock dividends received by the trust and deliberately passed control over these dividends for the benefit of the remainderman, retaining only a life interest in the income. This was a transfer subject to tax.

> A person entitled to receive an annuity from a governmental agency, such as a father, elects to receive a reduced amount in order to benefit a second annuitant, his son. This is deemed to be a transfer.

The value of a retained right is included in a transferor's gross estate when he dies, not only where he is the one who can designate the person who can possess or enjoy property, but also when he has a right to do so in conjunction with any other person. But this is true only if he retained the right himself, not if it was conferred by a third party.

> An individual set up a trust and served as co-trustee. In that capacity, he had the authority to direct that payments of trust principal be made to the person who was entitled to receive trust income for life. Possession of this power made it possible for the

creator of the trust to diminish or to wipe out the principal so that the remaindermen would get nothing, thus changing the enjoyment of the trust property. This reserved power was exercisable by the creator of the trust in his capacity as co-trustee, rather than as the original transferor, but that was immaterial. The principal was includible in his gross estate.

If a person transfers property but retains rights and powers that are so circumscribed by a *determinable external standard* that actually he has no discretion concerning the exercise of these powers, the property subject to the powers is not includible in his gross estate when he dies. The underlying concept in the definition of an ascertainable standard is that a person who holds the power to make decisions, such as the discretion given to a trustee to make distributions out of trust income or to accumulate this income for the benefit of the remainderman, really does not have a power; he has a *duty*. There is an ascertainable standard and the trustee can be *compelled* to follow it.

An individual transferred property to a trust, of which he was a co-trustee. Under the trust instrument, the co-trustees could use principal funds in the event of sickness or similar emergency, or when the person entitled to trust income for life had insufficient income from all sources during a period of illness or other incapacity. Here the creator of the trust had retained no powers of his own, for application of the trust funds to the needs of the person entitled to the trust's income was set by a determinable external standard, enforceable in a court if he sought to exceed his authority.

Words such as "support," "education," "maintenance," "care," "necessity," "illness," and "accident" generally are regarded as providing ascertainable standards. Words such as "happiness," "pleasure," "desire," "benefit," "best interest," and "well being" customarily are not regarded as being sufficiently definite to provide ascertainable standards.

An individual set up a trust with himself as co-trustee, for the benefit of his wife, who was to receive trust income for the remainder of her life. The trustees had the right to make use of principal funds if, in their discretion, this was necessary to ensure the wife's "happiness." The value of the principal was includible in his estate as the reservation of an interest without an ascertainable standard. No external standard, said the court, could possibly set a dollar value on a woman's happiness.

There are certain clearly defined powers that an individual may retain over property he has transferred without having this property included in his gross estate.

> An individual transferred property irrevocably to a trust, with a bank as trustee. Trust principal could be used by the bank for a beneficiary's needs on the basis of defined ascertainable standards, but there could be no such use of principal during this individual's lifetime without his prior written consent. No request for use of trust principal ever had been submitted to the creator of the trust during his lifetime. The principal was not includible in his gross estate when he died by reason of his having retained veto power. He had no power to say who would get income or principal under any circumstances nor could he modify any arrangements of the trust instrument.

The grantor of a trust may reserve purely administrative powers where he has no discretion as to what he will or will not do. The creator of a trust may retain the right of portfolio management of the trust principal. The transferor may have the right to be "consulted" by the trustee. Transferors sometimes become aware of the tax consequences of their retained interests and then endeavor to correct the situation. But in these circumstances a transferor may not go far enough.

> One individual set up a trust, with a bank as trustee. He reserved the right to revoke the trust as well as the right to get back the trust principal under certain conditions. Later, he amended the trust instrument to make the trust irrevocable. Possibly because of oversight or carelessness, he did not revoke or renounce his power to get back the trust principal under any circumstances. But that caused the trust principal to be included in his gross estate.

## TRANSFERS THAT TAKE EFFECT ONLY AT DEATH

When the ultimate possession or enjoyment of a property interest is held in suspense until an individual dies, that property will be included in his gross estate. If he has the *power* to change the enjoyment of property up to the date of his death, the value of the property goes into the gross estate.

Thus, gross estate includes the value of all property to the extent of any interest in it when the decedent had, at any time after September 7, 1916, made a transfer (except in the case of a genuine sale for full consideration), by trust or otherwise, if (1) possession or enjoyment of the property can, through ownership of the interest, be obtained by the transferee only by surviving the decedent and (2) the decedent has retained a reversionary interest in the property, that is, the right to get it back under certain circumstances. A transfer made before October 8, 1949, is included in the gross estate only if the reversionary interest arose by the specific terms of the instrument of transfer, that is, the deed, letter of transmittal, or the like.

Retention of a reversionary interest throws the property into the decedent's gross estate only if the value of the interest immediately before his death exceeds 5 percent of the value of the property. This is an area where a person generally requires professional guidance.

The term "reversionary interest" includes a possibility that the property transferred by the transferor (1) may return to him or to his estate, or (2) may be subject to a power of disposition by him. But the term does not include a possibility that the income alone from the property may return to him or become subject to a disposition by him. Nor does the term include the possibility that the transferor may receive back an interest in transferred property by inheritance during his lifetime through the estate of another person.

A person has a reversionary interest at the time of his death if he creates an irrevocable trust that fails to provide for the disposition of the trust assets after the death of the last survivor getting lifetime income from the trust.

The amount to be included in the estate of a decedent who had retained a reversionary interest in property he transferred is not the value merely of the reversionary interest itself, but rather the total value of the property subject to this interest. The value of his reversionary interest is computed as of the moment immediately before his death, without regard to whether the executor elects to value the assets at the date of death or six months later.

A decedent's reversionary interest is valued by recognized valuation procedures and without regard to the fact of the decedent's death. Where it is apparent from the facts that property could have come back to the decedent under contingencies that were not remote, the reversionary interest is not necessarily to be regarded as having no value merely because a value cannot be measured precisely. Upon the presentation of adequate medical testimony, the possibility of a reversion need not be computed strictly upon actuarial tables of normal life expectancy. Physical and mental conditions may be taken into account.

When a transferor procures the transfer of property to his beneficiary by another party for a valuable consideration, the value of that property goes into his gross estate.

Payments to a decedent's widow are deemed to be transfers by him at the time of his death if they were made in return for some consideration by the decedent. An employment contract provided that the employer would make such payments if the employee died while on the job or after retirement. By supplying consideration (he agreed to work for the company), he had caused the corporation to make a transfer or property, namely, post-death payments to his widow.

An agreement between a corporation and two officer-stockholders provided, among other things, that upon the respective deaths of each officer, the company would pay $5,000 benefits to his widow or legal representative. The agreement was part of a package deal by which the officers transferred assets to the corporation for its stock, an employment contract, and the death benefit plan. Inasmuch as the contract provided that if there was no widow, the right to the payments would go to the decedent's legal representative, the decedent was deemed at the time of his death to have had a reversionary interest in the death payment, to be included in his estate if the mathematical possibility that the money would come back to him was greater than 5 percent. Because the wife was three years older than the decedent, actuarial tables valued this possibility as amounting to more than 5 percent.

## TRANSFERS THAT CAN BE REVOKED, ALTERED, OR AMENDED

A transfer of property that an individual makes subject to the power of revoking the transfer at any time until he dies is not a complete disposition of that property. Until he dies, he is holding the assets on a string that he can pull back.

Accordingly, the value of a decedent's gross estate includes the value of any interest in property that he had transferred at any time after June 22, 1936, except in the case of a genuine sale for full consideration, where at the time of death he had the power to alter, to amend, to revoke, or to terminate this arrangement. It is immaterial whether he could exercise this power alone or in conjunction with any other person. Nor does it matter when or from what source the decedent had acquired this power, or in what capacity he is acting; for example, he might have this power as an individual or as a trustee. This also covers a situation where the decedent-to-be had relinquished a power within three years of his death.

The essential elements of this provision are:
1. A transfer by the decedent without full consideration.

2. A power enabling him to change the enjoyment of the transferred property.

3. The existence of the power at the date of his death.

A donor who keeps this strong a hold over the actual and immediate enjoyment of what he has transferred has not divested himself of the degree of control that would take the property out of his gross estate.

The existence of this power and not its use is what throws the property covered by the power into a decedent's gross estate. The holder of a power who expressly declines to exercise it holds it nevertheless. The provision is not applicable, however, to a power subject to a contingency beyond the decedent's control.

> An individual set up spendthrift trusts for the benefit of his sons so that they would not be able to waste the money. He reserved the right to revoke the trusts, in which event the principal was not to come back to him, but would go to other named parties. When he died, the trust property was included in his gross estate, even though he could not have exercised the power in his own favor. Power to change the names of beneficiaries is enough to bring trust principal into the creator's gross estate. So is a change in the amounts the beneficiaries are to receive.

Where a person transfers property to a trust for the benefit of named persons for as long as they live, but he reserves the right to say who is to get the property when all these persons die, only the value of the remainder interests is includible in his gross estate.

If a person's power to alter, to amend, or to revoke transfers of property is limited by an ascertainable standard, the property subject to this power is not includible in his gross estate.

> An individual transferred property to a trust for the benefit of a named party, but he retained the right to order that trust principal be used if the beneficiary or his children "suffered prolonged illness, or be overtaken by financial misfortune, which the trustees seem extraordinary." The trust property was not includible in his gross estate because the limitation on his power was specific.

The degree of control must be decided on the *possibilities* within the language of a document creating the arrangement, not on the probabilities. The question is: Was the power, however improbable its use, limited by a determinable standard, one that was enforceable in the courts?

The creator of a trust was permitted by the trust agreement to direct the trustee to use principal for amounts the creator might "require," up to 50 percent of the amount of the trust's principal. The trust principal was not includible in her gross estate when she died, for there was little likelihood that she ever would "require" any of these funds. When the trust was created, she was sixty years of age and owned about $5,000,000 in property, in addition to which she was entitled for life to the income of a trust with assets of about the same amount.

An individual transferred property to a trust but retained the power to direct the trustee to sell, to exchange, to invest, or to reinvest any of the trust property. The power retained did not constitute a power to alter, to amend, or to revoke the transfer. A trustee must act in good faith in accordance with his fiduciary responsibility and, accordingly, must act to safeguard the trust property in accordance with his authority.

In another case, retention of the power to name a substitute *corporate* trustee, such as a bank or trust company, was not regarded as power to alter or to amend. It is so regarded when an individual trustee may be replaced by the grantor at will, such as where the present trustee is not sufficiently complacent about accepting "suggestions."

Even though the creator of a trust may reserve the right to order the trustee to make changes in the trust's investment portfolio without being deemed to have retained powers to alter, etc., he should review the situation periodically. As he gets older, is he likely to be as competent as once he had been to select the property securities? Perhaps the bank or another trustee now might be able to do a better job in this respect.

An individual, in setting up a trust, may choose to retain the authority to alter, to amend, or to revoke the trust, for the purpose of keeping his options open for a while despite the estate tax consequences. He may wish to see how the objectives and needs of his beneficiaries take shape, after which he might change beneficiaries or amounts and simultaneously renounce his powers to alter, etc. In such a case, that property will not be includible in his gross estate if he dies three years or longer after this new arrangement. But circumstances may interfere with these plans.

An individual set up a trust for certain beneficiaries with the reserved power to revoke it. Nine years later he became insane. Forty years after the trust was created, he died. The trust property was included in his gross estate because he still had the power to revoke the trust. Of course, he could not have revoked it in the last thirty-one years because he no longer had legal competence to do so. In addition, he could not repudiate his right of revocation.

A trust creator reserved the right to modify, to alter, or to amend the trust. Subsequently, she was declared incompetent by the state where she resided, and a committee was appointed to handle her property and affairs. The trust principal was included in her gross estate when she died. Even though the power to modify, etc., was held by the committee at the time of her death, the committee was acting in her behalf.

## RETAINED VOTING RIGHTS

A transfer of stock where the transferor retains voting rights may be treated as a retention of the enjoyment of stock. The value of this stock is includible in a decedent's gross estate if, at the time of his death, he or immediate members of his family owned shares in the corporation amounting to at least 20 percent of the voting power.

But retention of the stock may be more important to a person than potential estate tax liability. For example, voting power may affect his position with the corporation, his compensation, his ability to make corporate decisions, his say in the naming of his own successor.

## TRANSFERS WITHIN THREE YEARS OF DEATH

In the case of decedent's dying after December 31, 1981, the value of property transferred within three years of death no longer is automatically treated as part of the gross estate. But this exclusion does not apply to retained interests, such as discussed in this chapter, that would be part of the decedent's gross estate had he not made the transfer within three years of his death.

## OTHER FORMS OF RETAINED INTERESTS

In addition to those forms of retained interest specifically identified in the tax law as includible in gross estate, comparable treatment is given to other forms of retained interest. Consideration of this will be given in the chapters in this book where the subjects are discussed, such as powers of appointment (Chapter 12) and the retention of significant incidents of ownership of life insurance (Chapter 13).

# 12

# POWERS OF APPOINTMENT AND POWERS OF ATTORNEY

## POWERS OF APPOINTMENT

Many tools can be very dangerous in the hands of a person who has not read the instruction manual. The power of appointment is an estate planning tool that can be most helpful to the individual who creates this power (the "creator"). But it can be very expensive—in taxes, inconvenience, and unpleasantness—to the person who accepts the power (the "holder"). Before accepting a power from someone, be certain that you understand the implications.

The Economic Recovery Act of 1981 calls for rethinking the employment of powers of appointment. Because of the phased-in, virtual elimination of the Federal estate tax, a person may with equanimity ask a close relative or friend to accept such a power, possession of which will have far less estate tax danger than in the past. On the other side of the coin, an individual, even if he understands the dangers, may be more willing to accept the responsibility, believing that the estate tax hazard has been lessened substantially if not eliminated entirely. Where large amounts of wealth are involved, estate tax liability remains a factor to be reckoned with.

## OVERVIEW OF THE POWER OF APPOINTMENT

One of the objectives of estate planning is *flexibility*. A person often would like to provide for his beneficiaries in the light of circumstances that develop when he no longer is here to make decisions, choices and allocations of his wealth. One method of doing this is utilization of a *power of appointment*. Power of appointment is a procedure by which a person can delegate

123

to somebody familiar with and sympathetic to his goals and desires the authority to bestow his assets or the income from them in the light of circumstances existing at that time.

There are no tax consequences to the person who gives or leaves property in such a manner; there are simply the regular gift or estate taxes that are imposed when someone gives or bequeaths property in amounts larger than the authorized exemptions, exclusions, deductions, and credits. For example, there may be gift tax when property is transferred to a trust for the benefit of other persons. So the individual who transfers property under a power of appointment has no tax penalty for the privilege of controlling his wealth from the grave, assuming that the person to whom he has given the power (the holder) is understanding and faithful in carrying out the allocations that the decedent himself would have made had he lived. (The words donee" or "possessor" sometimes are used instead of "holder.")

## TAXABILITY OF HOLDER'S ESTATE

*The estate of the holder of a power of appointment can be taxed heavily.* This fact must be kept in mind before an individual asks a relative or a close friend (and who else would be intimate enough with a person's wishes, dreams, prejudices, and beneficiaries to undertake this chore?) to accept a power of appointment. And anyone who agrees to make property or income dispositions for someone else should understand what this favor is apt to cost his own estate. The reason is that *a decedent's estate is taxed on the value of all property that he was in a position at the time of his death to divert to his own use.*

The exercise of a general power of appointment created after October 21, 1942, and, under certain circumstances, the exercise of a special power created after that date, is regarded as a taxable gift. Under some circumstances, the failure to exercise a power created after that date within a specified time, so that the power lapses, constitutes a gift. (The terms general power and special power are distinguished below, under the heading "Kinds of Powers of Appointment.")

## ADVANTAGES OF POWER OF APPOINTMENT TO ITS CREATOR

The chief use of a power of appointment is to entrust another person, the holder of the power, with decisions that the decedent was not yet in position to make at the time of his death. An individual might not know what his spouse's needs for funds will be. He might have several children or other young persons for whom he feels varying degrees of responsibility; but he cannot predict how their financial needs will be affected by business or professional ambitions, marriage, health, or contingencies. Personal friends or business associates may be in desperate but hopefully temporary need of assistance. There may be dependents or other relatives who are not known to the individual at the time he is making property divisions. The amount to be distributed, and the division of this amount, will depend to a large degree on the performance of his business or investments, the courses of which are uncertain.

Sometimes a person gives a power of appointment to an understanding party so that the latter will make difficult decisions that the creator cannot face up to making himself. An individual may feel, for example, that he simply cannot disinherit his own child. But the holder of a power of appointment could be the one to decide not to give a cent to a derelict son or to a daughter whose way of life distressed her late father.

A power of appointment also is useful where a person feels that someone else, the holder, can be more objective than he is in making distributions. The creator's own favoritism or prejudices thus may be avoided.

The creator of the power may gain peace of mind because present dispositions of his property, for the purpose of reducing his ultimate estate tax or to protect the property against claims of future creditors, can be made without solidifying the actual dispositions at this time.

## KINDS OF POWERS OF APPOINTMENT

A power of appointment authorizes the holder to control, within whatever guidelines are set in the power, the ultimate disposition of designated properties.

For Federal estate tax purposes, powers of appointment fall into two categories: *general* and *special*.

A *general* power of appointment is a power that the holder can exercise in favor of himself, his estate, his creditors, or the creditors of his estate. That is, the possessor of such a power has the authority to designate himself or any of these other parties to receive property covered by this power. The value of any property covered by a general power of appointment at the time of the holder's death is included in the gross estate of a decedent if the power was created after October 21, 1942, regardless of whether this power had been exercised or not. (If the power was created on or before that date, the value of the property covered by it is includible in his gross estate *only* if the power is exercised.) The complete release of such a power (where, for example, it had been transferred to somebody else to exercise, or where it had been renounced under conditions to be described later in this chapter) is not considered to be the exercise of a general power of appointment, and no estate tax liability is involved.

A *special* power of appointment is a power that does not have the characterization of a general power of appointment because the holder cannot designate ("appoint") himself, his estate, his creditors, or the creditors of his estate to get any of the property subject to the power. *There is no danger of estate tax liability from holding a special power.*

## RECOGNIZING A GENERAL POWER OF APPOINTMENT

One should not blissfully assume that a power of appointment that he holds is not a general one, because his estate could have tax liability when he dies. He might have been given the authority to bestow or to allocate property to the decedent's spouse, his children, his grandchildren, or any other relative—a classification into which the holder himself could fall. The authorization might be to designate as owners of the property anyone he chose, which could include himself and his estate. In either case, the result may be taxability.

An individual may be lulled into costly complacency by a lack of specific reference to the phrase "powers of appointment" in any papers. But all powers that are in substance and effect powers of appointment, regardless of the words used in creating the power and regardless of any definitions or usage under local property laws, *are* powers of appointment.

A common illustration of this is a trust agreement, where the trustee is given discretion in the designation of who is to get the trust properties or any portion of them. Nowhere in the agreement was anything said about a power of appointment, but the trustee nevertheless had been given one. This could be expensive to the trustee's estate if the power bestowed was a general one. But if a beneficiary or anyone else is given the authority to remove or to discharge a trustee, naming himself to fill the gap, this beneficiary holds a general power of appointment, even if he does not do anything with this authority.

The beneficiary does not hold a general power of appointment, however, if he can only appoint a successor, including himself, under limited conditions, and if these conditions did not exist at the time of his death. For example, perhaps he could name a successor trustee if the existing one died, but the trustee still was alive when the holder of the power of appointment died.

If the beneficiary of a life insurance policy has the continuing right to designate options during the life of the person insured, this beneficiary has a power of appointment. His subsequent choice of an option plan amounts to the exercise of a power of appointment.

A general power of appointment is held if a person is given the right to designate in his will the beneficiaries of an existing trust fund.

> An individual's will bequeathed his property to his wife, to be used, enjoyed, conveyed, or expended by her during her lifetime as she saw fit. Any property remaining at the time of her death was earmarked for designated persons. Even though the property going to the other designated parties went to them under her husband's will, up to the moment of her death she could have used it or sold it for her own benefit. So it was included in her gross estate when she died.

## POWER USED ACCORDING TO ASCERTAINABLE STANDARD

Even if the holder of a power of appointment could have designated himself to become the owner of property, its value will *not* be included in his gross estate when he dies if this authority was limited by an ascertainable standard relating to his health, education, support, or maintenance. This can be accomplished by limiting a holder's power to appropriate the property for himself, to use it for his "support," or his "support in reasonable comfort," or "accustomed manner of living," or to use it for his "health," his "medical, dental, hospital, and nursing expenses, as well as the expenses of invalidism."

> Even if a person had been named as the sole trustee of a trust and the sole recipient of its income, the trust principal was not included in his estate where he could appropriate trust property for an ascertainable standard relating to his maintenance and health.

> A wife's will made her husband the sole beneficiary and trustee of a trust she set up, with the right to use principal as needed for the four permissible purposes of health, education, support, or maintenance. it was provided that he could appropriate trust property for these purposes "with a high standard and quality of living." The trust property was not included in his gross estate when he died, for he had only a limited power of appointment. *A limited power is not restricted to the bare necessities of life.*

> A trust was set up for the benefit of the decedent, who could get

trust principal by submitting to the trustee a request for up to $50,000 to be used "for a business purpose." This could not be construed to mean if it were "necessary to generate business income to support the decedent. . ." Here the power to get at trust principal was not limited or restricted to needs for maintenance and support; in fact, use of principal was not expressed in terms of "need" but of "desire," which was unascertainable.

The holder of a power of appointment had the right to use property in accordance with ascertainable standards "or other expenses incidental to her comfort and well-being." This was regarded as being too vague a limitation to prevent the power of appointment from being a general one. Such also was the decision where the holder of a power could have appropriated property for his "use and benefit," a phrase that provided no ascertainable standard.

Whether or not an ascertainable standard limits a holder's power to take property may depend upon state law.

An individual possessed a power of appointment for "comfortable support, medical care, or other purposes which seem wise." Under Massachusetts law, there was an ascertainable standard: maintenance in accordance with his usual standard of living, a standard recognized by the state court.

But inasmuch as state laws and their interpretation by state and Federal courts varies, use of such imprecise language should be avoided in favor of words that undeniably provide as ascertainable standard.

In determining whether a power of appointment is limited by an ascertainable standard, it is immaterial whether the holder is required to exhaust his other income before the power can be exercised. If the holder of a power of appointment has the authority to take property to meet extraordinary medical expenses, the ascertainable standard exists, even if he had in his own bank account far more than was necessary to pay these bills.

Whether the holder of a power is limited by an ascertainable standard in taking property for himself is a matter of whether he *could* do so, rather than whether he *would*. The fact that the holder has not the slightest intention of taking property has no bearing on the matter.

In several cases, the executor argued that the decedent would not have taken property that he was empowered to acquire because he always had been such a frugal person that possessions had no great appeal to him. The answer was that the decedent had had the legal right to take property; hence, its value was includible in his gross estate, without reference to whether he might have taken it.

In another case, where the simple needs of parties was claimed as evidence that property covered by a power of appointment would not have been taken, the court observed: "It is interesting to note that they resisted until the end the urgings of their relatives that they buy themselves a television set, which fact may be regarded not only as evidence of their frugality but as a monument to their discretion." But the property still was included in the gross estate.

## POWER THAT CAN BE USED ONLY IN CONJUNCTION WITH ANOTHER PARTY

A power of appointment is not general if it cannot be exercised by the holder except with the consent of (1) the creator of the power, or (2) a person having a substantial interest in the property who is adverse to the exercise of the power in favor of the holder.

A co-holder of a power of appointment is considered as having an adverse interest when he may possess the power after the decedent's death and may exercise it at that time in favor of himself, his estate, his creditors, or the creditors of his estate.

An individual held a power of appointment with a bank as co-trustee. The bank was not regarded as a party with an adverse interest. The substantial adverse interest must be in the property itself, not an interest in continuing in the office of trustee.

## RELEASING THE POWER OF APPOINTMENT

A person who holds a general power of appointment and releases it, thus relinquishing any authority to transfer property to his own use, can help to assure that the property covered by this power will not be includible in his gross estate. This presupposes that relinquishment of the power was not within three years of his death.

But it is not so easy to disclaim or to renounce a power of appointment. A person cannot by his own acts alone declare that he no longer possesses the power.

Releasing a power of appointment calls for exercising it in someone else's favor, disclaiming it in the manner provided by the tax law, or having the power changed from general to special, an action that requires court approval in most instances. Transfer of the property covered by the power is not regarded as a release of the power if the holder has retained any degree of control over the property or revocation of its transfer. A disclaimer must be made by the holder of the power in writing within nine months after he acquired the power or, if later, within nine months of the date when he reached age twenty-one.

A power of appointment does not end merely because the holder could not have exercised it in his own favor or in another party's. If a decedent possessed a general power of appointment at the time of his death, it is immaterial whether he was physically or mentally incapable of exercising that power.

Where a power of appointment is given to someone who was not aware that it was given to him, he has a reasonable time after discovery to renounce it.

## SIMULTANEOUS DEATHS

An individual's will provided that a trust was to be set up for the benefit of his wife. She was to have the right to name in her will anyone at all to get the trust property. Both spouses were killed in an automobile accident in which it was impossible to determine who had died first. The Internal Revenue Service sought to include the value of the trust assets in the wife's gross estate, even though the assets never had been in her possession, because her husband's will had not been accepted at that time for probate by the appropriate state court. The Service won. Under state (Florida) law, the will became effective at the death of the person who made it. Even if both spouses died at the same instant, the husband's will became effective at that time. She had a general power of appointment because her will (if she had one) *could* have bequeathed the property to anyone, including her creditors. It mattered not that she could not have done anything about exercising the power in favor of her estate or her creditors, or that she lacked the time to renounce the power.

## ITEMS THAT SHOULD BE SUBMITTED WITH THE ESTATE TAX RETURN

In order to speed up the processing of estate tax returns, executors have been requested by the Internal Revenue Service to file with such returns a certified or verified copy of any document that grants a power of appointment, together with a certified or verified copy of any document by which the power was exercised or released.

The fact that there had been a power of appointment must be brought to the attention of the Service. This question is asked on the Federal estate tax return form: "Did the decedent, at the time of death, possess a general power of appointment created after October 21, 1942?"

## AVOIDING THE TRAPS

The power of appointment has a definite place in estate planning. It permits a person to ensure to a considerable extent that his property is allocated by a faithful, understanding, and sympathetic person in the light of circumstances as they appear after the death of the creator of this power. But if the creator of the power has any consideration for the tax situation of the estate of the person to whom he gives the power—and obviously he should have, especially since the holder of the power probably is a close relative or a dear friend—he should be very careful of the form that this power takes.

As this chapter has pointed out, possession of a general power of appointment can be very expensive. But a general power has this advantage over a special power: the holder can be given the right to take property for himself or for his purposes; and even though this can create estate tax liability, the estate tax rates do not go up to 100 percent. So what the holder applies to himself will not be subject to total erosion by taxes.

An individual may accept a general power of appointment because he does not realize the tax implications. As one court sadly declared, "Grace had difficulty grasping legal language and [her lawyer] doubts she had any idea what a power of appointment is, or that she had one."

Another trap is that the holder of a power forgets that he has it and hence never exercises it. Sometimes, by its nature, a power cannot be exercised for many years. For example, a person may be given the authority to say what is to be done with the decedent's stock in a family corporation when the youngest of the decedent's children attains age twenty-one. If the youngest child is four years old when the power becomes effective upon the decedent's death, the holder of the power cannot take steps to spare his estate from liability for another seventeen years. Meanwhile, he could well forget the power exists. Or he could become mentally incompetent so that he never can exercise the power and thus gets its value put on his estate.

## LIABILITY OF RECIPIENT OF PROPERTY

Unless a decedent directs otherwise in his will, if any part of his gross estate on which the tax has been paid consists of the value of property included in gross estate because it had been covered by a general power of appointment, the executor is entitled to recover from the person receiving the property by reason of the power of appointment that portion of the total tax paid as the value of this property bears to the taxable estate. If there is more than one such person, the executor is entitled to recover from these persons in the same ratio.

## POWERS OF ATTORNEY

The power of attorney is a legal document that designates one or more persons to perform designated acts, or any possible act, on behalf of the creator of this authorization. Its uses are many and are not restricted to estate planning. But such a power has some particular uses for estate planning purposes:

1. The power permits a named party to act on the creator's behalf should the latter be incapacitated or disabled. Without having a duly appointed party to act for him, a person would be unable to buy or to sell stock or other properties, or to borrow money—all functions that might have to be carried on for the purposes of personal or business finance.

2. A person might be given authorization to sign proxies or other statements that otherwise could not be handled.

3. Someone could be delegated to represent a taxpayer before the Internal Revenue Service. Forms or other documents must be filed by specific dates; elections must be made by set times or they are ineffectual. I.R.S. Form 2848, "Power of Attorney," empowers specified parties to

represent the taxpayer in matters and for periods described by the taxpayer on the form. Form 2848-D, "Authorization and Declaration," authorizes the named parties to receive from or to inspect confidential information in any office of the Service for the periods designated.

4. When an individual is to be away for an extended time on business, vacation, or for medical purposes, the Service may be instructed to send communications, or copies of communications addressed to the taxpayer, to his attorney for prompt attention.

5. Authorization may be given to an individual, a bank, a broker, or other party to purchase "flower bonds" for a person where it is anticipated that there will be estate tax liability in the predictable future. These are specified issues of United States Treasuries that must be accepted by the government at par for the payment of Federal estate tax. Inasmuch as these bonds have a very low rate of interest, they are selling far below face value. So there is an assured saving when the bonds are presented in payment of estate tax. But in order to qualify for this purpose, they must have been owned by the decedent at the time of his death.

A person can purchase flower bonds for himself when he is quite elderly or very ill and it is evident that the bonds will be needed. When an individual is unable to act for himself, such as when he has been in a serious accident or is in a coma, bonds can be purchased for him by a bank, broker, or an individual empowered to buy securities for his account.

In several cases, when the decedent-to-be was in a coma or was mentally incompetent, a party holding his power of attorney used the decedent's funds to purchase flower bonds. The government refused to accept them at par for payment of estate taxes on the ground that an individual's incompetency terminates the agency created by a power of attorney. But mental incompetency does not automatically void the authority to act under a power of attorney. This power, in fact, is intended to protect a person against inability to act because of such events as incompetency. If the acts of the holder of the power of attorney are detrimental to the principal, the principal when he regains consciousness, or his legal representative (such as the executor) if he does not, can void the transaction. Inasmuch as the purchase of flower bonds in such cases was not detrimental to the purchaser and in fact the executor tendered them in payment of the estate tax, purchases by the holder of the power of attorney were not void and the flower bonds could be presented at par.

# 13

## LIFE INSURANCE IS MORE THAN INSTANT ESTATE

Estate planning, of course, requires that there be an estate. There is no more rapid or certain way of creating an estate than the purchase of life insurance. With the payment of his first premium, the insured has created an estate that can be made available for the benefit of relatives or other designated parties. That may include the decedent-to-be himself if he chooses.

But the creation of instant estate is only one of the estate planning advantages of life insurance.

## ESTATE PLANNING USES OF LIFE INSURANCE

Life insurance can meet a variety of special estate planning purposes. The following list outlines sixteen of them:

1. Beneficiaries can be given a form of property that does not require expert business skills to manage, unlike an inheritance of a going business, oil wells, commercial real estate, or other operations. Beneficiaries receive a form of property that they are most likely to understand: *money.* If the beneficiaries are considered to be incapable of handling a lump-sum payment, the funds can be paid in the form of periodic payments, for stipulated periods or for life.

2. Flexibility is provided for meeting the changing requirements of beneficiaries. The insured is not likely to know today what his family's financial problems will be at the time of his death. But settlement options may be elected when death occurs.

3. The pay-out to the beneficiaries is virtually assured, as insurance companies must conform to reserve and to other requirements of state regulatory agencies.

4. The insured knows precisely how much his beneficiaries will receive if payment takes the usual form of the full face value of the policies, including cash increments. In the case of most forms of investment, the value of what the beneficiaries receive is subject to the vagaries of the marketplace.

5. Insurance payments are private. Heirs under a will and their own specific bequests, if in terms of dollars as usually is the case, are on the public record when a will is probated and published. Insurance settlements are known only to the insurance companies and the payees. It is not difficult to think of situations when this is highly desirable.

6. Insurance payments are not property subject to probate in most instances, so the delays and expenses of that process can be avoided.

7. Insurance provides a form of savings program by reason of the ever-increasing cash value of most forms of policy. This is a form of compulsory savings that many persons are unable to manage on a voluntary basis.

8. Where a policy has a cash value, there is in effect a reserve for emergency funding if absolutely necessary. Insurance loans customarily are made at an interest rate that is well below the figure charged by banks or other lending agencies.

9. A buy-sell agreement, funded by life insurance, can be set up so that the shares of a principal stockholder who dies will be purchased from his executors or estate by the corporation or its shareholders. The estate then will not be burdened with an asset that may not be convertible readily into cash, since the market for shares in a closely-held corporation usually is nonexistent.

10. Making life insurance proceeds available for the current living expenses of beneficiaries and to meet estate settlement costs avoids pressure on the executor that might force him to sell assets at a bad time. If the executor is able to devote all of his energies to administering the estate instead of arguing with needy beneficiaries or trying to raise cash, the savings in time and money could far offset the premiums on the insurance.

11. In some states, insurance provides funds to beneficiaries that are not subject to attachment by the decedent's creditors.

12. Funds can be provided for special purposes, such as the education of the decedent's children, who otherwise might not be able to go to college or to professional schools.

13. Insurance can provide for the liquidation of a decedent's major indebtedness, such as retirement of a mortgage on his home. This can be handled with declining-balance term insurance.

14. Insurance may be used to make available the funds that the decedent would like to have used so that his long-term gift objectives can be fulfilled. An example is annual payments to his hospital's building fund.

15. A person may wish to leave certain properties to a beneficiary net of taxes. If a beneficiary is given securities that will involve a built-in capi-

tal gains tax because they have appreciated greatly in value, or if stock is bequeathed and the testator believes that the shares will increase greatly in value, insurance may be taken out to pay the capital gains taxes that otherwise would erode the value of what the beneficiary will receive.

16. The receipt of life insurance proceeds in almost every situation is free from Federal income tax. Thus it is distinguishable from the conversion of other assets into cash, where investments or other properties that are sold at a gain result in taxable income.

## WHAT IS LIFE INSURANCE?

The preferential tax treatment of life insurance applies to *genuine* life insurance. If the so-called insurer is not exposed to financial loss in settling its obligations, the arrangement is not considered to be life insurance for this purpose. For example, a combination insurance-annuity package can be written involving the prepayment of premiums and the borrowing of money, where the insurer is so completely relieved of any possibility of a loss that the insured is not required even to take the usual physical examination.

If an insurance policy is the equivalent of life insurance, it does not matter that the policy is labelled something else or that a medical examination is not required. Thus, airport flight insurance is life insurance, there being no meaningful distinction between policies on the life of an individual that are payable in all events and those payable only if death comes in a certain way or within a specified time.

Where a person takes out an insurance policy on the life of an individual in whom he has no insurable interest, the policy is not a life insurance contract within the generally accepted meaning; it is a wagering agreement and the proceeds upon the death of the insured are taxed as ordinary income. An insurable interest is any reasonable expectation of monetary benefit or advantage from the continued life of another person.

The *type* of life insurance should be considered for estate planning purposes.

If all that the insured wants is protection, he can get the most for his money by purchasing *term insurance*. This may appeal to a young person with little property; he creates an instant estate of larger size than if he bought the package arrangement that is part of cash-value insurance (discussed below). Term insurance may be of interest also to a person who feels that his future wealth or the decreasing need to provide for his elderly parents or young children will only require insurance protection for a limited time.

Cash-value insurance provides continued coverage for as long as the insured lives (assuming that the premium payments are kept up), an increasing cash surrender value, borrowing capacity, compulsory savings, professional investment of part of his premiums, various settlement options, conversion options, and permanency of coverage at the rates applicable to his present age. This is not merely an indemnity contract for a limited period, but is property, with property values.

# WHEN INSURANCE PROCEEDS ARE SUBJECT TO ESTATE TAX

The proceeds of insurance on the life of a decedent are not subject to the Federal estate tax if they are not property rights passing from the decedent to his beneficiaries by reason of his death. The general rule that puts into gross estate all property passing to other persons upon death applies only where there has been a disposition under a will or similar *testamentary disposition.*

Under these circumstances, insurance proceeds are included in a decedent's gross estate:

☐ They are receivable by the executor or administrator, or are payable to the estate. This is the situation even if the estate is not named specifically as the beneficiary under the terms of the policy.

☐ The decedent still owned substantial rights in the insurance contract up to the moment of his death.

## INCIDENTS OF OWNERSHIP

The crucial test of whether a person owns economic interests in a policy—and thus runs the risk of having the insurance proceeds subject to estate tax—is existence of so-called incidents of ownership. Typically, they take one of the following forms:

☐ The right to borrow against the policy for the insured's own purposes.

☐ The right to obtain loans to pay premiums on the policy without the consent of the beneficiary.

☐ The right to change the name of the beneficiary, even if it is necessary to act in conjunction with the beneficiary. This incident of ownership, which a person may forget that he has, most commonly results in having insurance proceeds included in the gross estate of the insured. For example, a person reserves the right to change the name of an elderly beneficiary, such as a parent, believing that he will name another beneficiary when circumstances change, such as his marriage. An individual who names his new spouse as beneficiary on a policy he takes out when he gets married may reserve the right to change the name of the beneficiary, just in case the state of holy matrimony fails to survive. One individual gave all interests in a policy on his life to his spouse, who had been named the beneficiary. But, perhaps to prevent any rival from having an interest in his life (or his death), he reserved the right to prevent the change of beneficiary to anyone not having an insurable interest in his life. The policy proceeds were includible in his estate when he died.

☐ The right to receive payments under the policy if the insured sustains certain defined disabilities.

## CORPORATION-OWNED POLICIES

Even many thoroughly experienced insurance advisors are not always aware of the fact that when a life insurance policy is written for the sole or controlling shareholder of a corporation, and is owned by that corporation, any part of the proceeds not payable to the corporation will be included in the estate of the insured decedent. For instance, if the proceeds are payable to his wife alone, they all are included in his gross estate. If the proceeds are payable, say, 40 percent to his spouse and 60 percent to the corporation, only 40 percent will be included in his estate. He will not be deemed to be the controlling shareholder unless, at the time of his death, he owned stock possessing more than 50 percent of the total voting power. Needless to say, corporation-owned insurance on the life of an officer-stockholder is very common.

## FIDUCIARIES

An individual's estate will be taxed if he possessed an incident of ownership in a fiduciary capacity just the same as it will be if he held it in a personal capacity. So if an individual is the trustee of a trust that owns an insurance policy on his life, the rule applies.

## REVERSIONARY INTERESTS

If one's beneficiaries die before he does, insurance policies on his life can be taxed to his estate. That dangerous phrase "incidents of ownership" includes reversionary interests (the right to get back a policy now owned by somebody else) if the value of this reversionary interest exceeded 5 percent of the value of the policy immediately before his death. One way of avoiding this danger is to provide for contingent beneficiaries if the named individuals should die before the insured. The more beneficiaries are named, the less the arithmetical possibility is that the policy will revert to the insured.

## DIVORCE SETTLEMENT

Where an individual is required by the terms of a divorce decree to name his wife the beneficiary of an insurance policy on his life and to keep the policy in effect with premiums for as long as she lives and is unmarried, he has a reversionary interest in the policy. If the interest exceeds 5 percent of the value of the policy immediately before his death, the proceeds must be included in his gross estate.

## AVOIDING INCIDENTS OF OWNERSHIP

A decedent's estate is taxed if he possessed an incident of ownership, even if there was no way in which he could have exercised this incident of ownership. Thus, if an individual had the right to change the name of the beneficiary but the insurance company would make this change only when the policy was presented to the company for an endorsement, the practical fact that the policy was in the sole custody of the beneficiary does not change the situation.

> One individual took out $125,000 in flight insurance on his life at an airport, naming his wife as beneficiary. He gave her the policy, boarded his plane without her, and was killed in a crash. The proceeds were included in his gross estate, even though once he gave her the policy and was airborne, there was no possible way he could have changed the name of the beneficiary. He had not named the beneficiary *irrevocably.*

This very common trap could be avoided with a little forethought. The traveler could have taken out the flight insurance ahead of time, so that he would have time to notify the insurance company that he irrevocably renounced his right to change the name of the beneficiary. Or he could have studied the sample policy forms customarily displayed next to airport policy-vending machines. A few—a very few—forms of policy give the purchaser the right to indicate some person other than the insured as owner, with no provisions for changing the name of the beneficiary.

The insured may get rid of an incident of ownership by transferring it irrevocably to the beneficiary or to somebody else. Ordinarily, an insurance company will not honor a request such as changing the beneficiary's name unless an application is made on the insurance company's own specialized form. In most areas, transfers within three years of a person's death no longer are includible in a decedent's gross estate under the provisions of the Economic Recovery Tax Act of 1981. But insurance policies still are covered by the rule that transfers within three years of death are includible in gross estate.

## SPECIAL CONTROL CLAUSE

The question of incidents of ownership may be safeguarded by the inclusion in the policy of a "special control" clause. One example of such a clause: *"Third Party Ownership—It is agreed by the person to be insured that all right and title to the insurance applied for shall vest in and every incident of ownership thereof may be exercised and enjoyed irrevocably without the consent of any other person by* [the beneficiary], *whose insurable interest is* [spouse]."

## EMPLOYER-OWNED POLICIES

Sometimes an employee covered by his employer's group life insurance policy has an incident of ownership, such as the right to change the name of the beneficiary, even though he does not own the policy. Whether the employee has the right to transfer his incidents of ownership in such a policy, so that the proceeds will not be includible in his gross estate, is a matter of state law. For example, New York State specifically permits such an arrangement.

## FULL DISCLOSURE

The preparer of an estate tax return has the responsibility of disclosing certain properties on the return, even though he and the executor might consider this property not includible in gross estate. One such item is insurance on the decedent's life, payable to a beneficiary other than the estate, in which the decedent was believed not to have possessed incidents of ownership. Failure to disclose this situation on the Federal estate tax return can result in the assertion of penalties against all persons who caused the filing of a false return.

# SIMULTANEOUS DEATHS OF INSURED AND BENEFICIARY

If an insured person and his beneficiary both are killed in an accident where it is not possible to determine who died first, a question arises: Are the insurance proceeds includible in the gross estate of the beneficiary?

In one such case, the husband was the insured and his wife was the beneficiary. They died in an airplane crash. It was held that the face value ($100,000) of the insurance proceeds was not includible in her estate because she could not have claimed that sum from the insurance company up to the moment of her death. All that could be included in her estate was the value of the policy immediately prior to his death, its $8,000 cash surrender value, for that was all the policy was worth until the husband died.

Most states have adopted some version of the Uniform Simultaneous Death Act to solve the problem of the proper passage of property when distribution depends on the order of death and the circumstances are such that the order of death is not ascertainable. Under such an act, where the sequence of death cannot be ascertained, the insured is presumed to have survived the beneficiary. *Here is another strong reason why a person should name a contingent beneficiary should the named person not survive him.*

A husband's will provided that insurance on his life would be payable to a trust in which his wife would have a life interest should she survive him; that is, she would receive the trust's income for life if he died first. It was further provided that if it were impossible to determine which spouse had died first in a common disaster, she would be presumed to be the survivor. Both spouses died in a simultaneous disaster. It was held that the life estate created by his will had no value in her estate under the circumstances. She could have no interest in a trust that was created at the moment of her own death.

Where husband and wife were killed simultaneously in an accident and the wife was the owner and beneficiary of the insurance on him, this insurance was valued in her estate at the interpolated terminal reserve (akin to cash surrender value) and not at face value. Under the Uniform Simultaneous Death Act, the insured was deemed to have survived the beneficiary, and the proceeds were payable not to the wife but to the secondary beneficiaries.

## INSURANCE TRUSTS

The insurance trust is another device to achieve a frequent aim of estate planning: to empower somebody to make discretionary decisions as to how the wealth of a decedent is to be apportioned after his death. It has been recognized as a tool of estate planning for many years.

Typically, the person who is insured transfers policies on his life to trustees irrevocably. The trustees then have the power to designate beneficiaries of the insurance proceeds from within a limited group of persons. The trustees also may be given power to determine the terms of the various option settlements that are available under these policies.

An insurance trust can provide financial security for the beneficiaries. It also protects the policies from the creditors of the insured and of the beneficiaries because the policies belong to the trust. It prevents the insured and the beneficiaries from getting and wasting the cash surrender values of the policies.

With all of these advantages to cite, it is immaterial that the trust also may be utilized to obtain an estate tax saving: the decedent's estate does not include the value of policies he validly and irrevocably had assigned to the trust.

A trust also can be used in such a manner that the proceeds are kept out of the estates of those beneficiaries who will receive incomes for life but no payments of principal. How long this may be carried on depends upon state laws against perpetuities—laws that limit the length of time that property may be tied up in a trust. Typically, a trust is limited to the life or lives of persons now living, plus twenty-one years.

## ALIMONY

During the negotiation of a divorce settlement, the wife may insist that the annual payments called for in a property settlement be completed, even if the husband dies. One way to secure the arrangement is for the husband to give her an insurance policy on his life.

> A husband gave his wife a decreasing term policy on his life for the twelve-year period he was obliged to pay off the divorce settlement. The face amount of the policy was reduced each year by the amount of the payments made to her, for he now was indebted to her for a smaller amount. He sought to deduct the insurance premiums annually, on the ground that they constituted alimony income to her and thus were tax deductions to him, being economic benefits to her. The court held, however, that the insurance policy merely provided security for his required payments and did not qualify as an economic benefit to her sufficient to create taxable income.

The result could have been different if he had given his wife a whole life policy instead of the decreasing term policy. As owner of a whole life policy, she would have been entitled to surrender it for its cash value, to borrow on it, etc., thereby obtaining an additional economic benefit over and above any agreed-upon alimony payments. Her receipt of additional alimony under this arrangement would provide him with an income tax deduction. Of course, a whole life policy would be more expensive than a decreasing term policy. The income tax advantage obtainable would have to be weighed against this additional cost.

## TAXABILITY OF INSURANCE PROCEEDS

Payments made by the insurance company by reason of the death of the insured are excluded from the gross income of an estate, a beneficiary, a transferee who receives the right to the proceeds that had been assigned by the designated person, or anyone else, with these three exceptions:

1. Death benefit payments under a Workmen's Compensation contract or an accident and health policy having the characterization of life insurance proceeds payable by reason of death.

2. The interest element contained in life insurance proceeds that are payable at a later date (in installments, as an annuity, or in any other manner) will be taxed to the beneficiary, except that the surviving spouse of the insured is entitled to an annual exclusion of $1,000 of that interest. For example, an insurance company may agree to pay annual or other regular amounts over a period of time. These pay-outs include interest for the period the insurer is holding the money; this represents the interest element.

3. Where a life insurance policy is assigned for a valuable consideration, the nontaxable proceeds when the policy matures by reason of the death of the insured cannot exceed what the new owner paid for the transfer and in premiums to keep it in force.

One corporation held a policy on the life of an executive. He had an option to purchase the policy if the corporation ever decided to discontinue it. When the corporation was taken over by another company, decision was made to discontinue the policy. The executive notified the company that he was assigning his option to his wife, who bought the policy. Upon his death, the proceeds were taxable to her to the extent that they exceeded the amount she paid to the employer corporation and the annual premiums subsequently paid. Had the husband acquired the policy from his employer under his option and then had given it to her, she would not have acquired the policy *for a valuable consideration*. But, as the court noted sadly, "We cannot make a contract for him."

## EMPLOYEE DEATH BENEFITS

Only the first $5,000 of an employee death benefits are excluded from the beneficiary's gross income. Thus, amounts passing to beneficiaries of employees who die get a far better tax break if they can qualify as life insurance proceeds rather than an employee death benefits.

## CLOSELY-HELD CORPORATIONS

Proceeds of insurance on the life of an officer of a closely-held corporation, when paid upon his death directly to the stockholders of the corporation, are regarded by the Internal Revenue Service as taxable dividends if there are earnings and profits large enough to pay such dividends.

# MAKING A GIFT OF LIFE INSURANCE

The gift of an insurance policy on the life of the donor can have various advantages for both donor and recipient. As a person gets older, frequently his needs for insurance coverage are lessened. In fact, he may not need any coverage, for his older dependents may have died, his children may have ceased to require his assistance, and his income may have reached a point where insurance no longer is indicated.

When a donor makes a gift of life insurance, he reduces his ultimate gross estate, saves premium payments, benefits the recipient, qualifies for annual gift tax exclusions—all without the loss of any income to himself, such as would occur if he made gifts of income-yielding securities or real estate. No income is given up on the gift of insurance, except, in the case of certain policies, he may give up a modest amount of dividends.

The donor also provides the recipient with something of value, namely, the equivalent of the policy's cash surrender value, known as interpolated terminal reserve.

Where some or all of the annual $10,000 per donee gift tax exclusion would be wasted because there is nothing available to give, consideration should be given to policy gifts. Gifts within three years of the donor's death, however, are includible in his gross estate, although in the case of persons dying after December 31, 1981, such is not the situation for most other forms of gift.

A gift of life insurance requires the endorsement of the insurance company to be effective.

Many states include insurance policies in the type of property that may be given to a minor child under the Uniform Gifts to Minors Act.

## MAKING A CONTRIBUTION OF AN INSURANCE POLICY

An individual who no longer needs his full insurance protection can contribute a policy to an approved charitable, religious, educational, or other organization in that category. He will get an income tax deduction for the amount of the contribution, that is, the cash value of the policy. He can save the cost of making further premium payments. Or he can continue to pay the premiums for the benefit of the charitable organization each year and thus obtain additional tax deductions for such payments. In addition, he will reduce the amount of his ultimate gross estate.

## PREMIUM DEDUCTABILITY

Premiums paid on any insurance policy covering the life of any person financially interested in any trade or business carried on by a person is not deductible, if he is directly or indirectly a beneficiary under the policy.

## USE OF INSURANCE TO PURCHASE A DECEDENT'S STOCK

When a shareholder in a closely-held corporation dies, the disposition of his stock is a problem. A valuation will have to be placed upon it for Federal estate tax purposes, an extremely difficult matter where the shares never have been sold in an arm's length transaction. In the absence of actual sales, the Internal Revenue Service may place an exceedingly high value on the shares. The lack of a market also creates a problem for the estate or family of the deceased shareholder that needs cash for the payment of taxes and living expenses.

Ordinarily, the best solution for such problems is to have the shareholders of a closely-held corporation enter into an agreement that calls for the purchase of a decedent's shares at a predetermined formula price. Commonly used yardsticks include: the per share value of net worth; average earnings for a specified number of years capitalized at a stipulated percentage rate; value of the underlying assets; comparison with market quotations of active stocks where there seems to be a basis for comparability. Usually an estate can get a better price for the stock it holds under such an arrangement than it could by forcing the liquidation, which it might not have sufficient votes to compel anyway. Most companies are worth more as going entities than when they are liquidated.

The buy-sell agreement can take either of two principal forms:

1.  The shareholders can agree to buy the shares of any other stockholder who dies.

2.  The corporation and the shareholders agree that if a shareholder dies, the corporation will buy his shares and retire them.

The big problem that often remains, however, is finding the money for this purpose. Life insurance is an excellent way to finance the arrangement.

When the shareholders agree to buy the shares, each stockholder can take out insurance on his own life. Usually it is advisable to have all of the participating shareholders transfer these policies to a trustee who will administer them. This procedure assures that all of the policies will remain in force.

When the corporation is to buy the shares, the corporation takes out the insurance.

Insurance is such a desirable method to fund a buy-sell agreement that some agreements specifically contain language such as this: *"The parties mutually desire that life insurance be used as a means of providing all or a portion of the funds with which to finance the obligations arising under such sale-and-purchase agreement."*

A buy-sell agreement funded by life insurance may become void if any of the policies lapse, so it is important that someone be delegated to ensure that this does not happen.

Inasmuch as the parties to a buy-sell agreement do not know who is going to die first, regardless of the age or health of the parties, this is regarded as an arm's length transaction in which a generally accepted valuation formula is used. That means an actual sale of stock in the closely-held corporation has taken place and this figure will be used to value the stock for estate tax purposes. In the absence of such a figure, the Internal Revenue Service has a virtually free hand to use any value it chooses. The executor then is left to disprove this figure if he can, a troublesome problem in the absence of an actual sale.

## LIENS UPON INSURANCE

An individual is very likely to believe that if he suffers business reverses or lawsuits, even if he loses everything else, he still has insurance protection for his family. This is a dangerous trap.

If a person owes taxes to the Internal Revenue Service, the Service can impose a lien against any property that he owns. This includes the cash surrender value of any insurance on his life that he owns.

Some policies can be endorsed to provide, however, that if there is a default in premium payments for a specified period, such as thirty-one days, the policy automatically will be converted to paid-up insurance, effective on the due date of the premium. In such a case, by the time the I.R.S. notifies the insurance company of the lien, there is nothing to attach, the policy having been converted automatically to a form of insurance that has no cash value. Who would think that a person could benefit from failing to pay an insurance premium?

Inasmuch as the government can put a lien on the cash surrender value of any life insurance in which a person has an interest, term insurance with no cash surrender value offers attractions to any individual with impending tax troubles.

A lien also can be imposed on the cash surrender value of a life insurance policy the taxpayer no longer owns, for example, one that he validly had assigned to someone else, if he retains any significant incident of ownership of the policy, such as the right to change the name of the beneficiary.

## SPOUSE INSURANCE

A married person, here called the husband for convenience, should consider taking out life insurance on his nonworking wife to compensate himself for measurable dollar losses should she die before he does. He will lose the tax advantage of filing a joint Federal income tax return. If there are minor children, elderly relatives, or other persons to take care of, he now will have to hire somebody to take care of chores formerly handled by his wife. The marital deduction will be lost for Federal gift and estate tax purposes, as will be the advantage of making split-gifts with his wife.

## PERIODIC REVIEW

Estate planning should include a regular review of one's life insurance policies. On those policies where the power to make changes still exists, have names of beneficiaries been changed to reflect deaths, marriages, additional children, changes of circumstances? A widow may be startled to learn, for instance, that the beneficiary of her husband is his sister, long since married to a very wealthy man, because the decedent never had gotten around to renaming the beneficiary when he himself got married.

# 14

## ANNUITIES, COMMERCIAL AND PRIVATE

This chapter deals with a useful tool of estate planning. Annuities are a form of capital that a person cannot outlive. To the extent that a person retains an asset that produces annual income, he may make dispositions of much of his wealth in order to have the pleasure of seeing the results of his generosity while he still is alive. Even in the case of larger estates, estate taxes can be reduced drastically if not eliminated entirely, with the result that there is more available to give away. The use of an annuity can cut down the expense and delay of probate, for the contract can be structured so that it is not part of one's gross estate where value is extinguished by death.

## WHAT IS AN ANNUITY?

Basically, an annuity is a periodic fixed payment for life, or for a specified period, made to an individual by another party, which will be paid absolutely and without contingency. The most common form of annuity provides the annuitant with a fixed amount of income for the remainder of his life. But the *variable annuity*, a relatively recent version, provides for periodic payments of fluctuating amounts from the income of stipulated securities in a fund upon which this annuity is based.

A person may be disinclined to pay money to an insurance company for an annuity that actually might produce little or no income for the annuitant because he dies too quickly. He may prefer to purchase a contract that guarantees a certain number of payments—for example, twenty—so that even if the annuitant dies before he receives that many payments, the remainder will be paid to designated beneficiaries.

Lord Byron wrote in *Don Juan:*

*'Tis said that persons living on Annuities*
*Are longer lived than others—God knows why,*
*Unless to plague the grantors....*

Although he was talking specifically of people who were given annuities by others, Byron has a point. The experience of insurance companies demonstrates, declared one court, "that persons who purchase life annuities from insurance companies are a self-selected group who live longer than the general population." One reason perhaps is that elderly annuitants are not disturbed by worries that they will outlive their investments, as are many persons living on capital. Annuitants are not so apt to be concerned that they will do something foolish with their capital as they grow older or that they will be subjected to pressures from relatives.

If an individual has relatives, friends, former employees, or anybody else for whom he wishes to have provisions for continued financial support after he dies, he can purchase annuities for these persons, thereby avoiding the diversion of principal sums to them at the expense of primary beneficiaries. He also can make provisions for the purchase of such annuities in his will.

## ESTATE TAX TREATMENT

If an individual has an annuity solely for the duration of his own life, with no minimum number of guaranteed payments, nothing is included in his gross estate when he dies, for there is nothing of value to pass to anyone else. Generally, the value of any payment or payments receivable by a beneficiary by reason of surviving a decedent, if under the contract an amount was payable to the decedent, does go into gross estate. But gross estate does not include the value of an annuity receivable under a qualified employee benefit plan, as where a corporate employee is entitled to a retirement annuity and he has chosen to receive a lesser amount so that his spouse and he are covered by a survivorship annuity. There also is excluded from gross estate the value of an annuity receivable by a beneficiary under an Individual Retirement Account, provided the retirement payment had not been made as a lump-sum payment.

There is a $100,000 aggregate limit on the exclusion from a decedent's gross estate for certain amounts received by any beneficiary other than the executor in the case of tax-sheltered annuities, Individual Retirement Accounts, qualified (Treasury-approved) pension plans, and certain military retirement plans. This applies in the case of persons dying after December 31, 1982. Before enactment of the Tax Equity and Fiscal

Responsibility Act of 1982, there had been no limitation on the amount that could be excluded from an estate.

For purposes of the estate tax, a distinction is made between contributions made by the employee and contributions made by the employer. If both employer and employee contribute to the purchase of a qualified retirement annuity, and a designated beneficiary of the employee receives a payment attributable to contributions made by *both, only the part of the total payment proportionate to the employee's contribution is includible in his estate.*

# VALUATION OF ANNUITIES

The valuation of an annuity in the decedent's gross estate depends on the number of payments that surviving annuitants or beneficiaries will receive. *The decedent had property interests to the extent that other persons were entitled to receive payments attributable to his contributions in cash or services.* Inasmuch as no one knows how long the surviving annuitant or other beneficiary will live, the present worth of an annuity is determined by using actuarial tables and a 6 percent interest factor. The present worth of an annuity is shown in tables contained in Treasury Regulations Section 20.2031-7(f). Competent medical testimony can be introduced when there are facts to suggest a shorter life expectancy than indicated by the tables.

# INCOME TAX

A part of each payment received by an individual who purchases an annuity is considered to be a return on his investment and is excluded from his gross income. The amount of this exclusion from gross income is determined by the *ratio of his investment* to the total expected return under the contract. The *return* is the amount of each annual payment times his years of life expectancy. This "exclusion ratio" remains fixed, despite the fact that the annuitant may die before or after his normal life expectancy.

For example, an individual purchased an annuity contract providing for payments of $100 per month for a consideration of $12,650. Assuming that the expected return under this contract is $16,000, the exclusion ratio to be used by him is:

$$\frac{\$12,650 \, [\text{cost}]}{\$16,000 \, [\text{expected return}]}$$

or 79.1 percent (that is, 79.06 rounded to the nearest tenth). If twelve such monthly payments are received by him during his taxable year, the total amount he may exclude from his gross income in that year is $949.20 ($1,200 times 79.1 percent). The balance of $250.80 ($1,200 less $949.20) is the amount to be included in gross income. If he instead received only five payments during the year, he should exclude $395.50 ($500 times 79.1 percent) of the total amounts received.

Where a single consideration is given for a particular contract that provides for two or more annuity elements, as where there is a survivorship annuity covering husband and wife, an exclusion ratio is determined for the contract as a whole by dividing the investment in the contract by the aggregate of the expected returns under all the annuity elements provided thereunder.

Sale of an annuity contract shortly before it matures is treated as ordinary income rather than capital gain.

No loss is recognized on the purchase of an annuity because a person's primary motive was not to make a profit but to obtain a life income.

## GIFT TAX

Except in the case of a qualified employee benefit plan, an irrevocable election by a father to accept reduced annuity payments under a retirement system so that his son, as survivor annuitant, would also receive amounts as annuities commencing with his father's death is treated as a taxable gift.

## PRIVATE ANNUITIES

Most annuities are purchased from commercial sources such as insurance companies, and the annuitant is virtually certain of receiving the stipulated amounts for life. Insurance companies are required by law to maintain certain reserves, and all activities are under constant supervision of state regulatory agencies. A different situation exists in the case of annuity arrangements with private parties.

If an individual transfers property to a private party (such as a relative) in return for a promise of payment of a stipulated annual amount for life, the annuitant *may be parting with property worth more than the value of the annuity*. In that case he has made *a taxable gift*.

It is also conceivable that a person might turn a tax loss into a tax liability inadvertently as a result of setting up a private annuity. Suppose he has an indicated capital loss on securities. If he uses these securities to fund an annuity, and the value of the annuity turns out to be higher than that of the property he has transferred, he has realized a gain on the transfer of property. This gain is reportable over the period of years measured by his life expectancy. Thus, the annuitant's investment in the annuity for exclusion ratio purposes does not reflect the cost of the property he transferred in order to get the annuity.

But tax rulings have not been consistent as to whether an individual really has taxable gain or loss when he transfers property to a private party in return for a promise of stipulated annual payments for life.

In some cases, the annuitant has been judged to have no gain or loss when he transfers his property, because he has received in return something without ascertainable market value, namely, a promise to pay made by someone who may not be able or willing to honor that promise. Under this line of decisions, gain is recognized only when the annuitant has received income in excess of the value of his property.

Other decisions have recognized gain or loss in the belief that the private persons agreeing to make payment were subject to an enforceable obligation that they were in a position to honor.

In one case, an individual argued that inasmuch as the persons to whom he had transferred property were not in the impregnably strong financial condition that an insurance company is presumed to be, he could not be sure of getting back what his property had cost him until he actually received annuity payments that totalled this sum, which might take many years. To the contrary, ruled the court, for this was not an unsecured and dubious promise to pay by the transferees. The property he had transferred produced rentals sufficient to pay the annuity each year, and the transferees were not permitted under the arrangement to sell this property without the consent of the transferor-annuitant, who was scarcely likely to permit any modification that would jeopardize the security of his annuity income. Inasmuch as the annuitant got back something with an actuarial value that was more than the basis of the property transferred, he was taxed on the difference when he received the promise to pay the annuity.

The sole stockholder of a corporation wished to retire with a satisfactory income, while leaving his business "in the family." He gave his shares to his adult children. In return, they agreed to provide him with an annual income of the same amount that he would have received had he transferred consideration with the value of his shares to an insurance company for its annuity contract. But what he received from his children as a private annuity was worth less than a commercial annuity with the same agreed pay-out to him. A commercial annuity is subject to strict state insurance department controls as to permissible types of investment, reserves, and the like. The private annuity, lacking the built-in protection features of a commercial annuity, has a lower value in most instances. As the retiring shareholder was getting from his children something which was worth less than the property he had transferred, he was deemed to have made taxable gifts to the extent of the difference.

Where a husband and wife transferred cash and securities to their children in return for a promise of income for life, it was found that no gift tax was due for there had been no intent to make a gift, the value of the cash and securities being substantially equivalent to the value of the annuity.

The Internal Revenue Service has published tables for valuing private annuities, for there is not the same assurance that the private annuities will be paid.

Where an annuitant transfers properties now worth less than his cost in return for a private annuity, his loss automatically is disallowed for Federal income tax purposes where the other party is his spouse, ancestor, brother, sister, or lineal descendant. Various fiduciary relationships between the parties also can result in automatic disallowance of any loss.

## PURCHASE OF ANNUITY
## FROM CHARITABLE ORGANIZATION

Where an annuity is purchased from a charitable organization at a cost that is higher than the going rate for comparable annuities, the annuity cost that may be recovered tax-free over the annuitant's life expectancy is limited to fair market value. The excess cost is deductible within the permissible limits as a charitable contribution.

# 15

## SIMULTANEOUS DEATHS

Estate planning is concerned to a considerable degree with arranging for what a person wants to transmit to his beneficiary or beneficiaries. Inasmuch as the disposition of his property should be in accordance with his wishes, provision must be made as to contingent or successor beneficiaries in case the parties he has selected die before he does. Transmission of his wealth, including interests in property and proceeds of insurance upon his life, depends frequently upon establishment of whether he dies before a beneficiary or whether the beneficiary predeceases him. At times, however, the sequence of deaths cannot be determined because the parties die in a common disaster where the order of dying is not determinable. Usually the common disaster is an airplane, car, or railroad crash. It can come about less spectacularly where two parties each eat soup that came from a botulism-containing can or where there had been a suicide pact.

Aspects of the simultaneous deaths problem have appeared elsewhere in the book in conjunction with discussion on such matters as the marital deduction and life insurance. Now the entire concept will be considered, with the available alternatives.

## THE UNIFORM SIMULTANEOUS DEATH ACT

Even for Federal tax purposes, property rights customarily are determined under the laws of the state where the property is situated. For the purpose of solving the problem of the proper passage of property when distribution depends upon the order of deaths and the circumstances are such that this sequence is not ascertainable, the states have adopted their own versions of the Uniform Simultaneous Death Act as written by a national conference of state officials. With some variations, this is what such laws provide:

☐ Where title to or disposition of property depends upon the priority

155

of death, and there is no evidence that the parties have died other than simultaneously, the property of each person is disposed of as if he or she had survived, except as provided elsewhere in the act.

☐ Where two or more beneficiaries are designated to get property successively or alternatively under another person's disposition of property (as by will) and there is no evidence that deaths were not simultaneous, the property thus disposed of is divided into as many equal portions as there are successive or alternative beneficiaries, and the portion allocable to each beneficiary will be distributed as if he had survived all other beneficiaries.

☐ When there is no sufficient evidence that two joint tenants, or tenants by the entirety, have died other than simultaneously, the property so held will be distributed one-half as if one had survived and the other one-half as if the other person had survived. Where more than two joint tenants died under these circumstances and there is no evidence that deaths were other than simultaneous, the property will be divided into as many equal shares as there were joint tenants, and the share allocable to each will be distributed as if he had survived all of the others.

☐ Where the insured and the beneficiary in an insurance contract (life or accident) have died, and there is no evidence that the deaths were other than simultaneous, the proceeds are payable as if the insured had survived the beneficiary.

If a person is not satisfied to have these provisions govern the distribution of his property interests should there be a common disaster, he can make other arrangements. The Uniform Simultaneous Death Act does not apply to a will, living trust, or deed where provision has been made for a different distribution, or to an insurance contract where different provisions had been made.

By means of a *reverse simultaneous death clause*, provision can be made so that if the order of deaths is not determinable, the testator (the one making a will), or the spouse, or other named party is to be presumed to have died first.

A reverse simultaneous death clause may be desirable where one spouse believes that the other spouse has sufficient wealth so that provision need not be made for the latter (here called the wife). If provision is made that he is considered to be the survivor, even where this is for a matter of seconds, his property will be channeled to his children by a prior marriage or to other named parties.

Husband and wife may each make a will at the same time, with a corresponding clause in each will that states that if deaths occur in a common disaster, the other party will be presumed to be the survivor. In that way, property of each spouse that goes to the other will qualify for the marital deduction.

In choosing whether to go along with the Uniform Simultaneous Death Act or to set up an alternative arrangement, these facts should be considered:

□ Is it desirable to have property go to another party who, as the result of a common disaster or simply by reason of advanced age or poor health, is likely to die very soon without being able to enjoy the property?

□ Property that goes to a spouse or to a joint owner, even if momentarily, will be distributed in accordance with that person's will or other arrangements. For example, if husband and wife are involved in a common disaster, any of his property passing briefly to her is apt to end up in the hands of her relatives and friends, with no provision for persons preferred by him.

□ Successive ownerships of property within a short period of time make for generally unnecessary additional state death taxes, administration expense, and disputes among would-be beneficiaries.

□ Where husband and wife are involved, it might be advisable to provide that the wealthier spouse, for example the wife, is to be presumed to have died first, so that there will be a more significant marital deduction for property passing to the other spouse.

□ Ordinarily, no marital deduction is allowed if the interest that passes to the surviving spouse is only for a limited period of time. (But see the discussion in Chapter 8 on *qualified terminable interests* that are eligible for deduction in the case of decedents dying after December 31, 1981.) The marital deduction is available, however, if the will states that the surviving spouse (here presumed to be the wife) will get property unless she dies within six months of her husband and, in fact, she does not die within that time.

□ In the case of persons dying after December 31, 1981, where property is held by spouses in joint tenancy with the right of survivorship, the estate of the first spouse to die includes one-half of the value of the property regardless of which spouse had furnished the consideration.

□ In the case of assets jointly held, the "disposing instrument" is not the decedent's will. The parties may provide jointly for a disposition or a presumption as to survivorship in case of simultaneous deaths, for example, in a deed for joint property signed and agreed to by both parties. But neither party unilaterally may provide by will for a disposition or presumption as to that joint property. Despite a provision in a decedent's will stating a presumption as to his survivorship in case of simultaneous deaths, one-half of the joint property continued to be distributed as if the wife survived.

□ A presumption in a decedent's will is operative only with respect to property over which he had the power of disposition.

## EFFECT OF SIMULTANEOUS DEATHS
## ON A POWER OF APPOINTMENT

Gross estate includes property subject to a testamentary general power of appointment where the designated holder of the power died prior to the probate of the will creating this power and the will contained a provision that in the event of simultaneous deaths, the wife would be deemed to be the survivor. The wife's will, which had been executed on the same day, made no reference to any effort to exercise the power of appointment. State law may govern as to whether a power of appointment created by will is postponed until probate of the will or until any other time later than death.

## EFFECT OF SIMULTANEOUS DEATHS
## ON LIFE INSURANCE POLICIES

As mentioned previously, the Uniform Simultaneous Death Act provides that where deaths occur in a common disaster where there is no evidence as to the sequence of deaths, the insured is deemed to have survived the beneficiary.

In one case, the beneficiary was the owner of a policy on the life of her husband. They died in a plane crash where there was no evidence that the deaths had been other than simultaneous. The proceeds of the policy on her husband were not includible in the wife's estate. The value of any asset is what can be gotten for it, and until the crash, the policy had no value except the interpolated terminal reserve, that is, what the insurance company was putting in reserve to cover the cash surrender value. Dividend accumulations also were added in.

The provision that an ordinary insurance policy is to be valued at the interpolated terminal reserve applies both to the customary situation where the owner dies leaving the insured surviving and in the unusual situation where the insured and the beneficiary perish in a common disaster.

## SIMULTANEOUS DEATHS MAY CREATE ORPHANS

Although the orphans' exclusion was terminated by the Economic Recovery Tax Act of 1981, estate planning should consider the possibility that simultaneous deaths of both parents will create problems for which there may be solutions if the situation is addressed in advance.

The parents' wills can make provision for specific guardians if minor children should be left without parents.

Bequests and life insurance proceeds may have been provided for children. But if they are too young or financially inexperienced at the unforeseeable time of the parents' deaths, due care for the children's interest can be provided by leaving their entitlements in trust, which would be arranged to terminate when a child is twenty-one years old or at any other time deemed to be appropriate.

# 16

## PROBLEMS WHEN A MAJOR STOCKHOLDER DIES

Estate planning should consider the perplexities that will be raised upon the death of a major stockholder in a closely-held corporation. Problems involve the estate of the decedent-to-be, the surviving shareholders, the corporation itself, its employees, its suppliers and creditors.

## THE CHOICES

When such a shareholder dies, the executor of his estate has these principal options.

1. *Keep the stock.* It may be desired to have the children of the decedent step into his managerial shoes, although many years could elapse before the children are old or experienced enough to do so.

2. *Sell the shares.* But in the case of a closely-held corporation, generally there is no available market. A value for the stock rarely is known, for never has there been an arm's length sale. A logical buyer, such as family members or employees, may lack the funds.

3. *Liquidate the corporation.* But the estate may not own enough shares to force dissolution. Under the laws of some states, 80 percent of the stock must be voted for liquidation to make it effective. And most corporations, unlike people, are worth more alive than dead because of good will, going-concern value, and the existence of nontransferable rights or franchises that would be useless if the corporation were dissolved.

The executor may prefer to sell the shares or to liquidate the corporation. He may be unfamiliar with its problems and personalities, and he might be disinclined to remain involved in the conduct of a business for what could be many years. His anxiety to "get out from under" may result in realization of far less than the business interest actually is worth. He has the problem of raising cash to pay the Federal estate tax, if any. The amount needed to pay such a tax, if required, is extremely difficult to estimate, for valuation of stock in a closely-held corporation may require lengthy litigation to settle. The executor's compulsion to raise cash quickly may be aggravated by demands of the family or other beneficiaries for immediate implementation of their entitlements.

Desires of family members or other beneficiaries are difficult to predict. Many persons are not interested in the responsibilities and duties of management, merely wanting to be paid off promptly. Other persons may prefer to keep the business going and to step into the decedent's place, especially on pay day, regardless of their competency and experience.

The surviving shareholders have the problem of continuing the enterprise without the presence and involvement of members of the decedent's family, who may bring little to the corporation except interference with management and unjustifiable demands for compensation or dividends. If the beneficiaries sell their stock to outsiders, the surviving shareholders will have the unwelcome problem of working with associates not of their own choice, whose business objectives and philosophies may be irreconcilable with those of the surviving shareholders. As a court noted in one case, "the injection of a new owner of [the decedent's] half of the stock would certainly complicate matters."

Employees of a closely-held corporation may realize that their own jobs are at risk if a principal shareholder dies and the corporation has to be liquidated in order to raise cash for the estate. Alternatively, beneficiaries or purchasers of the decedent's stock may insist upon being employed as executives, to the detriment of the careers of the existing work force. Farsighted persons might not be willing to work for a corporation where the company's life or their own careers are so dependent upon the life of an important shareholder.

Suppliers, banks and other creditors, and franchisors predictably will be disinclined to deal with a closely-held corporation that lacks a realistic plan for what will happen upon the death of an active stockholder. The *New York Times* of July 6, 1969, quoted a banker as saying, "Our primary concern with private companies is management structure and depth. Sometimes there is a severe problem of management succession." On occasion the grantor of a franchise may "suggest" to a distributor that there be a plan for the latter to reacquire the shares of a principal shareholder who dies.

Plans to have the corporation reacquire the shares of deceased stockholders sometimes are necessary in order to prevent intrafamily or interfamily feuds. It cannot be assumed that blood is thicker than water in closely-held corporations.

Under certain circumstances, to be discussed in Chapter 19, a corporation can avoid Federal income tax if Subchapter S status is voted by all of the shareholders, who may not exceed twenty-five in number in taxable years ending after December 31, 1981. If any of a decedent's stock in such a corporation gets into the hands of another person, he may refuse to make the necessary election. This will terminate the advantages of Subchapter S status for *all* of the shareholders.

These problems exist not only in the case of a major stockholder in a closely-held corporation. Even if the decedent had held only a small minority interest, his beneficiaries may demand responsible positions (and compensation to match), as well as a dividend policy, which in the opinion of management, would cripple the corporation's expansion and growth program. The beneficiary of a minority interest also has a difficult problem determining the value of his shares. A substantial discount usually is applied to fair market value, for without that discount, few persons would be interested in purchasing a minority interest that would not enable a buyer to have any say in the running of the business or the setting of its policies. (See Chapter 4, "Where Estate Planning Starts: The Valuation of Assets.")

# BUY-OUT AGREEMENTS

As mentioned earlier in the chapter, the death of a major shareholder in a closely-held corporation creates many problems: finding a market for his shares, keeping out persons not competent to run the company, enabling the business to be continued despite the reluctance of an inexperienced executor, setting a value of the stock for estate purposes, assuring employees and creditors that the company will not go out of existence simply because somebody dies.

In the words of one court, "Many businessmen now anticipate such problems and provide solutions through agreements, and implementing devices, to take out of the estates of a co-venturer, who dies, on a basis designed to be fair to the estate, to the enterprise, and to the surviving co-venturers."

In order to make provision at the present time for a reconciliation of the frequently divergent views of the executor or beneficiaries and the surviving shareholders, and to make associations with a corporation more attractive to employees and to creditors, a buy-out agreement may be entered upon. Such agreements customarily take the form of either a buy-and-sell agreement or a stock retirement agreement. Both are discussed here with their characteristics.

## BUY-AND-SELL AGREEMENT
In this kind of an agreement, the stockholders are bound to purchase a decedent's shares.

☐ A surviving shareholder might be unable or unwilling to buy the stock. An unwilling person, however, is bound to the agreement, for he had acquired the shares subject to it.

☐ Where a plan is financed by insurance taken out by each shareholder on his own life, he might fail to keep up with his premium payments.

☐ Sale of stock to a shareholder can be regarded only as a capital transaction. Sale of stock to the corporation, under circumstances to be discussed later in this chapter, might be treated by the Internal Revenue Service as a dividend.

## STOCK RETIREMENT (OR REDEMPTION) AGREEMENT

This second kind of agreement provides that the corporation itself will purchase the shares of any stockholder who dies if he is a party to the agreement.

☐ If the corporation retains earnings for the purpose of buying up a decedent's stock the company may be subjected to the accumulated earnings tax for having retained earnings beyond the reasonable needs of the business. Such is not the case, however, where earnings were retained for a redemption of stock to pay death taxes, which will be discussed later in this chapter. Earnings legitimately may be retained in order to buy a decedent's stock if it can be demonstrated that the corporation would be injured if this stock got into the hands of a person whose views were contrary to corporate policy and philosophy.

☐ If the plan is funded with life insurance, an alternative to be discussed later in this chapter, premium payments are less likely to be missed than if each shareholder took out his own insurance.

☐ If the surviving stockholders get the insurance and use the proceeds to buy up the decedent's stock, they will have additional basis for their investment, whereas if the corporation purchased the shares and cancelled them, the basis of the shares of the surviving shareholders would remain unchanged. This may not be a factor of importance in the case of a closely-held corporation, for a holder of such shares usually has no intention of selling them. They are by way of being a permanent investment. Intentions do change, however.

# THE PRICE FORMULA

In order to be fair to all of the parties, the price that the surviving shareholders or the corporation are to pay for the decedent's stock must be a self-adjusting one. Usually it is not known which shareholder will die first, or when, and a price set today could be meaningless when the settlement time arrives.

Consequently, the agreement should set the consideration according to some standard formula. Examples are net worth per share, net asset value; earnings for a specified period, capitalized at a stipulated percentage rate. It may be provided that good will is to be valued separately by arbitration.

If book value is to be used, there should be spelled out such points as what depreciation method is to be followed and what inventory method. How are investments to be valued? Are repairs to be capitalized?

Post-death valuation of assets or of the stock is a possibility. But it is just about impossible to know how much funding this would require.

A formula clause should not be used where the estate or beneficiaries could require a court's interpretation. This might take years.

The price could be paid out of the general funds of the buyer, corporate or individual. Money may be borrowed for the purpose. Amounts can be accumulated in a sinking fund for this purpose.

If a valid buy-out agreement requires the estate or the beneficiaries to sell the stock at a formula price, or if the corporation or the surviving shareholders have an option to buy at that price if they desire, *this sets the valuation of the stock for Federal estate tax purposes*. This can be very important because, in the absence of an arm's length sale of the stock, valuation of shares of a closely-held corporation is an extremely difficult problem, with the burden of proof being on the taxpayer.

## LIFE INSURANCE AS A FUNDING MECHANISM

In order to ensure that there will be funds to purchase a decedent's shares, life insurance may be obtained or specially earmarked for the purpose. The corporation's accountant periodically should quantify the formula in order to determine how much insurance coverage is required. Where, because of inflation or the corporation's mounting profitability, the existing coverage no longer is sufficient to buy up the stock, additional insurance should be taken out. If a stockholder no longer is insurable, or if premiums have become excessively expensive by reason of higher ages or risk factors, the value of the stock to be purchased could be brought down. For example, a closely-held corporation is capitalized with one-class stock. By means of a tax-free recapitalization into nonvoting preferred or nonvoting common and voting common stock, the value of the stock could be spread between nonvoting and voting stock. It really is *essential* only to purchase the *voting* stock. See Chapter 17, "The Uses of Tax-Free Reorganizations."

A buy-out agreement may be funded by life insurance even if one or more shareholders is uninsurable. An uninsurable shareholder may set aside policies of insurance on his life that he owns, which had been taken out previously when he still had been insurable. Where a person ordinarily would be classified as uninsurable by an insurance company, there are "high risk" policies available from many companies. The policies will cover persons regardless of age, health, or hazardous employment, the premiums being high enough to compensate the insurance company for its greater risks.

If the life insurance proceeds prove to be insufficient to purchase a decedent's stock, at least part of the cost has been financed. And the value for Federal estate tax purposes has been set conclusively. Other shares can be purchased at the formula price through alternative funding or borrowing. If the insurance coverage is excessive, the corporation doubtless has other uses for the money.

## TAX TREATMENT OF PREMIUMS

A corporation cannot deduct premiums on life insurance purchased in order to fund a buy-out agreement. Neither can a shareholder. But even though shareholders may benefit from such an insurance arrangement, the premiums when paid by the corporation do not represent taxable income to them.

Even where a corporation redeems and retires a decedent's stock, thereby increasing the proportionate equities of the surviving shareholders, this does not represent a taxable dividend to them. They are taxed only when, by selling the stock, they cash in on the greater value.

Where the stockholders have entered upon an agreement with each other to purchase the shares of a person who dies, but the corporation actually pays for this stock, the use of corporate funds to discharge shareholder obligations is taxed as dividends. Thus it may be necessary to be able to prove who the buyer actually was.

Ordinarily, when a corporation with earnings and profits large enough to pay dividends purchases a shareholder's stock, this is taxed as a dividend to him, for corporate earnings have or might have flowed to him. There is no dividend, however, if a corporation *completely* redeems the shares of a stockholder, including those owned by his spouse, parents, children, and grandchildren. Even where any of these persons continues to hold stock, the corporation's purchase of a shareholder's stock is not treated as a dividend if these ground rules are met:

☐ No interest may be retained by him as employee, officer, director, or anything else except as a creditor.

☐ He may not reacquire any stock within ten years except by inheritance.

☐ He must agree in writing to notify the Internal Revenue Service of any reacquisition of stock within ten years, at which time the "sale" will be taxed as a dividend.

☐ None of the redeemed shares may have been acquired from a close relative within the past ten years.

☐ Any stock that had been transferred to a relative within ten years must be redeemed by the corporation at the same time as his shares.

## REDEMPTION OF STOCK TO PAY DEATH TAXES

Even if a decedent's immediate relatives continue to own stock in the corporation, purchase of his shares will have no dividend implications if the transaction qualifies as a redemption of stock to pay death taxes. This opportunity is available where:

☐ The decedent owned stock in the corporation that, in the case of death occurring after December 31, 1981, exceeds 35 percent of his adjusted gross estate. Stock of two or more corporations is treated as stock of a single corporation for the purpose of meeting the 35 percent requirement if, in the case of decedents dying after December 31, 1981, more than 20 percent in value of the outstanding stock of each corporation is included in the determination of the decedent's adjusted gross estate.

☐ The stock being redeemed is to produce funds solely to pay the decedent's death taxes (including state), funeral expenses, and administration expenses. Redemptions of stock involving any larger amounts may, to the extent of any excess over the permissible uses, be treated as dividends.

"Redemption" for this purpose refers to a purchase by a corporation of its own shares, regardless of whether or not they actually are retired.

Careful estate planning can reduce the size of what will be a decedent's adjusted gross estate, so that his stock interest will exceed 35 percent of the value. For example, he may make gifts or charitable contributions. Alternatively, his stock interest may be brought up to more than 35 percent of his adjusted gross estate if he acquires additional stock before he dies.

Ordinarily, if a corporation retains earnings in order to purchase a shareholder's stock, accumulated earnings tax will be imposed unless it can be shown that the redemption will benefit the corporation rather than a shareholder. But a corporation is authorized by the tax law to retain earnings for the purpose of a redemption to pay death taxes which meets the tests contained in the present section.

## BUSINESS TRUST

As mentioned previously, an executor may be inclined to liquidate or to dispose of the decedent's business as rapidly as possible in order to save himself the time commitments and headaches of running the business. But a decedent-to-be might want to have the business continued, so that his family may keep on benefitting from it, because he believes the enterprise has attractive profit potential, or because he wants the business to be there when his children are in position to participate in management.

*His* wishes rather than the executor's could be implemented if his will sets up a testamentary trust, to which his business interest is transferred. The trustees named would be persons ready, willing, and able to operate the business, such as professional associates, his lawyer and his accountant, perhaps a business consultant or a university business school professor. A "safety valve" could be provided by authorizing the trustees to dispose of or to liquidate the corporation, at their discretion, if there are losses in a specified number of years.

## KEY MAN INSURANCE

A closely-held corporation is likely to suffer losses when an executive dies. The corporation could take out key man insurance as indemnification.

Sometimes a lending institution suggests to the management of a corporate borrower that insurance be taken out on the life of the chief executive, so that if anything happens to him, the company will have funds to reorganize or to put someone else in his place.

## BUY-OUT AGREEMENT NEED NOT BE CONFINED TO VOTING STOCK

Ordinarily, a buy-out agreement is tailored for the purchase of voting stock, so that no member of the decedent's family or outsiders has a license to "interfere" with management.

It may be desirable to make plans to acquire a decedent's preferred or other nonvoting stock as well. In this manner, the decedent's family or nominees can be eliminated completely from any possibility of unpleasant associations or potential blackmail.

## STOCK PURCHASE PLAN MAY BENEFIT PUBLICLY-HELD CORPORATION

It is uncommon for a publicly-held corporation to take out insurance on an executive's life in order to purchase stock should he die. The corporation's existence is not likely to be endangered by succession problems, such as funding or the lack of seasoned back-up personnel. And the stock will have ascertainable value without such an arrangement.

But on occasion, a publicly-held corporation will take out insurance on the life of a chief executive, the proceeds to be used to buy stock of the corporation in the open market should he die. The purpose is to "peg" the market until the public at large can realize that the corporation will not be hurt irreparably by his loss. At that time, it is hoped, market prices will have been stabilized.

## COMPLETE DISABILITY OF STOCKHOLDER

Almost invariably, a buy-out agreement is drawn up to cover the deaths of shareholders. But such a plan could be used to buy up the shares of an officer-stockholder who is permanently disabled. It is unlikely that he can continue to participate in management, and his shares could be utilized to attract another executive who might insist upon "a piece of the action."

## PARTNERSHIPS

A buy-out agreement can be used satisfactorily in the case of partners and partnerships.

## SIMULTANEOUS DEATHS

Where husband and wife are the principal shareholders of a corporation, they may worry about the continuance of the company should they die in a common disaster. Some mechanism to perpetuate the corporation's management and existence may be desired, as well as the keeping of their stock within the family. A voting trust may be used to hold all of the shares. This could keep stock out of the hands of outsiders.

## STOCK RETIREMENT RESTRICTIONS SHOULD NOT BE KEPT SECRET

When there is a buy-out agreement, the parties should agree in writing that they will not pledge, mortgage, or otherwise encumber the stock. Certain practical difficulties can be avoided by stamping the restrictions on the stock certificates. For example, a third party purchaser of stock may claim that he is not bound by restrictions that he could have known nothing about. State laws vary as to whether such a buyer would be bound by the restrictions. Avoid this problem by stock inscriptions or other means.

## THE PERSONAL HOLDING COMPANY DANGER

If a stockholder's shares are purchased by the other stockholders, or if his shares are acquired by the corporation and retired, there could be an unsuspected, personal holding company problem. A personal holding company is a corporation where (1) at least 60 percent of its adjusted gross income is from nonoperating sources, and (2) at any time during the last half of the taxable year, more than 50 percent in value of its outstanding stock is owned, directly or indirectly, by or for not more than five individuals. Reduction of the number of shareholders by a buy-out agreement could well create this situation. Even if a corporation's income ordinarily is from active operations, such as manufacturing, a fire or a lengthy strike could result in income being solely from nonoperating sources, such as investments. Then the buy-out agreement may trigger the personal holding company tax because of the reduced number of shareholders.

# 17

## THE USES OF TAX-FREE REORGANIZATIONS

In the planning of one's estate, many benefits may be made available through a tax-free corporate reorganization. Several forms of these reorganizations that lend themselves to estate planning will be discussed in this chapter.

## RECAPITALIZATIONS

A recapitalization is not necessarily tax-free, but one may be structured by an experienced tax advisor so that it is tax-free. Here are some practical uses of recapitalizations:

☐ A sizeable portion of one's estate may consist of his interest in a corporation. He is disinclined to reduce what will be his ultimate gross estate by giving away any of his stock to his intended beneficiaries or to charity at this time because he does not want to dilute his interest in the corporation. This would interfere with his ability to control the operation of the business, to set his own compensation, to name his successor. But a recapitalization could replace the one-class stock that serves as the capitalization of most closely-held corporations with nonvoting stock (preferred or common) and with voting stock (almost invariably this would be common shares). The value of the former stock would be apportioned between the voting and the nonvoting shares. He then would give away or donate to charity the nonvoting shares, retaining his original degree of control of the corporation, but with a reduced portion of the value of the stock remaining to be included in his gross estate.

☐ This reduced value for the voting stock would make it more affordable for purchases by company executives or employees who might be desirable purchasers of stock when he dies.

☐ The lowered value of the voting stock would make it more practical for shares to be purchased by executives invited to accept employment with the corporation in order to provide additional strength now or at the time of the decedent's death.

☐ Some of a decedent's children or other beneficiaries might be interested in management of the corporation and in sharing in the financial success of their work endeavors. Other beneficiaries might prefer not to work for the corporation or to participate in management; they would be interested in a relatively safe and steady income. A recapitalization into voting common and nonvoting preferred stock would enable a person to provide voting stock to beneficiaries who would participate in management and thus participate in the profits they help to generate, while the preferred would go to persons who would not be part of management and thus should not have the power to vote.

☐ A recapitalization can enable a person to leave shares to his surviving spouse without loss of the marital deduction, even though the stock she will receive after his death is not the same as he had owned when he dies. In one case, a decedent had provided in his will that common shares that were bequeathed to his widow would be replaced with new preferred stock of equal par value, the preferred to be issued under the terms of a recapitalization that would be effectuated at the time of his death. The remaining common shares were willed to his children. The preferred stock received by his widow after his death qualified for the marital deduction, even though the shares did not exist when the decedent died, the recapitalization not taking place until after his death. The widow's stock interest had been created by his will and therefore passed from the decedent to her, as required for the marital deduction.

☐ Often an enterprise is owned by several persons who had started the business or who had worked for it for years. As these persons grow older, they are apt to be less anxious to spend the same time and effort in this role. But younger people would be interested in taking over major responsibilities only if this were accompanied by voting power and the potential of unlimited earnings ("a piece of the action"). Older persons could be given preferred stock so that their voting shares could be used to bring new management into the corporation.

☐ Bankers, other creditors, and franchisors are likely to become less interested in continuing to do business with a corporation that is run through the stock control of aging persons with declining capacity to be effective, even though in fact these persons continue to have their former vigor and enthusiasm. The bankers, etc., might even insist as a condition to continued association that new talent be brought into the executive suite. A recapitalization could accomplish this survival measure.

☐ Gross estate includes stock transferred to a trust where the transferor continues to own, directly, or indirectly, at least 20 percent of the voting rights. So if a person wishes to transfer stock of a corporation to a trust for the benefit of his beneficiaries, he should first make certain that he does not retain 20 percent of the voting rights. The solution to any problem in this area is to have a recapitalization, so that enough of the shares that he does retain are of the nonvoting variety.

□ A person wishes to make contributions to approved charitable organizations but he is short of cash or the equivalent. His wealth is largely tied up in his business. By means of a recapitalization into voting and nonvoting stock, he could give away the latter and obtain Federal income tax deductions without diluting his degree of control of the corporation.

## MERGERS

Merger with or into another corporation may solve some problems concerning what will happen upon the death of a shareholder in a closely-held corporation.

□ As a person gets older or his health becomes less robust, he has cause to worry about how his stock in a closely-held corporation will be valued for Federal estate tax or for state death tax purposes, at the generally unpredictable time of his death. In such a situation, it is unlikely that there ever will have been an arm's length sale of the stock that would establish a value for tax purposes. In consequence, the taxing authorities may set an astronomical figure in the absence of proof to the contrary. A solution is to merge the corporation with another corporation, the shares of which are traded on an exchange or active over-the-counter basis. Shares of the latter corporation received in exchange will have a far more satisfactory basis for estate tax valuation purposes or for estate planning purposes.

□ If the corporation does not have a strong back-up team, a major shareholder's death is apt to mean the end of the enterprise. But a merger into a well-endowed corporation would provide the experienced management and the expertise to enable the business to survive and perhaps even to do better than previously.

□ A closely-held corporation often suffers a severe capital drain when a principal stockholder dies. For example, the corporation may have to purchase his shares, as under a stock redemption agreement. Merger into a corporation with abundant capital can obviate this situation.

## SPIN-OFFS

An individual may realize that his children or other beneficiaries should not be provided for in identical manner because of their different capabilities and objectives. For example, a person may own the stock of a corporation that operates a factory on its own real estate. His son is a capable, experienced businessman who has worked in the business for many years. His daughter has no business experience or interest. The father may effect a tax-free spin-off of the corporation's realty to a company formed for the purpose. The real estate is leased at a fair rental to the corporation, which henceforth engages only in manufacturing. The father's will leaves his manufacturing company stock to his business-oriented son, while the stock of the realty company, the income of which comes from a steady lease with the manufacturing company, the income of which comes from a steady lease with the manufacturing company, goes to his daughter. Neither she nor her husband is able to interfere in the operation of the manufacturing business.

## TRANSFER TO A CONTROLLED CORPORATION

An individual's assets may be of various natures, some of which require technical skill of a high level to operate or dispose of. Some of the properties are worth far more as a single unit than they would if fragmented. He transfers those assets he chooses to a newly formed corporation in return for all of its stock in a transaction that can be structured to be tax-free under Section 351 of the Internal Revenue Code. By bequest and/or by gift, he transfers varying amount of stock in the corporation to his beneficiaries. Management of the corporation and of its properties is vested in experienced persons, and a sale by the corporation of assets will be as a single unit, so that realty, a collection of British first editions, or a block of stock will not lose in value because it is sold in fractional pieces by individuals with different ideas of values, needs for cash, or business judgment. Such a procedure could take into account the fact that on the market place, the whole frequently is worth more than the sum of its parts.

## REDEMPTION OF STOCK TO PAY TAXES

The tax advantages of having a corporation buy back its own shares in a transaction that will qualify as a *redemption of stock to pay death taxes* was discussed in Chapter 16, "Problems When a Major Stockholder Dies." But this treatment is available only if the decedent at the time of his death had owned stock in the corporation that, under the Economic Recovery Tax Act of 1981, amounted to more than 35 percent of his adjusted gross estate. By means of a tax-free reorganization, a person could transfer assets to a corporation that could qualify for this treatment.

## BUY-OUT AGREEMENTS

A corporation may be required to purchase and to retire the shares of a shareholder who dies. The subject of stock redemptions, which are a form of tax-free reorganization in that there is a reduction in capitalization, is treated in Chapter 16.

# 18

CHARITABLE DISTRIBUTIONS
AND BEQUESTS

With the greatly lessened impact to Federal estate tax resulting from the Economic Recovery Tax Act of 1981, it might appear that there now is less of an incentive for charitable dispositions. Bequests of this nature long have been regarded as a means of reducing estate tax. But, as has been stressed at the outset of this book, the real objective of estate planning is not saving taxes but the effectuation of one's desires and objectives. The wish to assist charitable, religious, educational, and scientific undertakings remains regardless of lessened tax incentive.

The justification for the tax deduction of charitable bequests is that the government is able to relieve itself of the burden of meeting public needs that would fall on governmental shoulders in the absence of charitable activity. In one decision, the United States Supreme Court explained: "Congress was in reality dealing with the testator before his death. It said to him, 'If you make such gifts, we'll reduce your death duties and measure them not by your whole estate but by that amount, less what you give.' "[1]

A noble charitable impulse is not a requirement for a deductible charitable bequest. In the language of one court,

> Community good will, the desire to avoid community bad will, public pressures of other kinds, tax avoidance, prestige, conscience-salving, a vindictive desire to prevent relatives from inheriting family wealth—these are only some of the motives which may lie close to the heart, or so-called heart, of one who gives to a charity. If the policy of the . . . tax laws favoring charitable contributions is to be effectively carried out, there is good reason to avoid unnecessary intrusions of subjective judgments as to what prompts the financial support of the organized but non-governmental good works of society."[2]

[1] Y.M.C.A. v. Davis, 264 U.S. 47 (1924).
[2] Crosby Valve & Gage Company v. Commissioner, 380 F. 2d 146 (1st Cir. 1967).

177

The fact that a charitable bequest was tax-inspired is irrelevant. Common noncharitable reasons for bequests are:

1. Avoidance of Federal estate tax by reducing the size of the estate.

2. Reduction of income tax by disposing of income-producing properties.

3. Provision of a memorial to the decedent or a member of his family.

Bequests to approved charitable organizations qualify for the deduction even though the decedent had expected a personal benefit. One individual's will left a sum to a specified church, to say masses for members of the family who had died. Masses could have been said even without this bequest. The Internal Revenue Service ruled that deduction was proper, for the church was able to use the money for any of its functions.

## QUALIFYING FOR A CHARITABLE PURPOSE

The amount of all bequests, legacies, devises of realty, or transfers to be used exclusively for religious, charitable, scientific, literary, or educational purposes is deductible from the value of one's gross estate.

The common element that defines a charitable purpose is that it is designed to accomplish objectives that are beneficial to the community or area. Usually recognized as charitable purposes, where not otherwise limited by some provision of the law, are:

☐ The relief of poverty.

☐ The advancement of religion.

☐ The advancement of education.

☐ The protection of health.

☐ Governmental or municipal purposes.

☐ Other purposes, the accomplishment of which is beneficial to the community.

A charitable deduction is allowed for a bequest to or for the use of the United States, or any state, territory, or political subdivision of one of these, for public purposes exclusively. "Political subdivisions" means for this purpose political units, such as municipal corporations, and governmental instrumentalities exercising the powers associated with their purposes, such as a county park system. Separate governmental instrumentalities that are the equivalent of private charitable corporations, such as separately organized state colleges, could qualify as charitable organizations for this purpose. A charitable bequest may be made to or for the use of any veterans' organization incorporated by Act of Congress, or of its departments or local chapters or posts, if the tax law's guidelines for deductibility (to be mentioned later in this chapter) are met.

If properly structured, a charitable bequest can serve a person's estate planning objectives by making provision for the assistance of members of his own family. If the recipient organization is a *bona fide* religious, charitable, etc., body, a charitable bequest is deductible even though preference is to be given in the selection of ultimate beneficiaries to relatives of the testator, provided that they qualify as objects of legitimate charitable purposes.

Deduction was allowed for a bequest to set up an educational loan fund to provide scholarships "first to relatives or other boys or girls," who lacked funds.

Recognition was given to a decedent's bequest to pay the annual income of a trust to persons in need of financial assistance, despite this language in the will: "It is my wish that in carrying out the objects in this trust fund preference be given to my relatives and friends that are in need of such aid and assistance."

Bequests were deemed to be charitable when university scholarships were funded for high school graduates "in need of funds." Preference was to be given to applicants with the same surname as the grantor, who were related to him; but the scholarships could be awarded to other qualified persons if no applicant met the special qualification. Although the testator plainly expressed a preference that properly qualified persons with his surname who were relatives should have the opportunity to benefit from the scholarships, his charity was not confined to such persons.

One decedent's will set up a trust to provide scholarships for students who wanted education in vocational or agricultural studies. The trustee was first to award scholarships to students who had been the decedent's employees or their descendants, a requirement that could be waived in favor of any students only if insufficient employees made applications. This bequest qualified for deduction, being for the benefit of a general class as distinguished from mere benevolence to employees, so long as the general class to be benefitted (nonemployees) was not so small that the community did not benefit from the aid given to students.

A bequest to trustees for the care of neglected animals is deductible.

A charitable bequest is not subject to percentage limitations for Federal estate tax purposes, although there are such limitations in the case of charitable contributions for Federal income tax purposes.

In the case of estates of citizens or residents of the United States, the definition is not limited to transfers to domestic corporations, or to trustees for use within the United States.

## THE MEANING OF "EXCLUSIVELY"

A deductible bequest must be used exclusively for religious, charitable, literary, educational, or similar purposes. But the word "exclusively" has not been interpreted to mean "solely" or "absolutely without exception." The primary activity of the recipient organization must be devoted to the religious, charitable, etc., purpose. Activity that is not religious, etc., will not result in loss of deductibility if that activity is only incidental and less than substantial. A slight and comparatively unimportant deviation from the narrow line of approved activity is not fatal to the tax benefit.

Where 5 percent of one charitable organization's efforts was devoted to noncharitable activity, this was regarded as relatively insubstantial and the requirement that the organization be devoted exclusively to charitable purposes was not violated.

A charitable bequest to a county medical association was not deductible. Much of the association's activity qualified as charitable; but there also were noncharitable aspects. Thus, scientific meetings qualified as educational activities; but some meetings dealt with the personal, social, and economic problems of physicians. The association's bulletin contained educational material, but it also contained political philosophy and requests to members to communicate with congressmen about legislation. There was a doctor referral service and a telephone answering service, which could be characterized as personal rather than public.

A similar society, which had a group insurance program for members, published advice on tax matters, and rendered counsel on office management and economic practices, also was ruled to be ineligible.

## TRUSTS

No deduction is allowed if a will provides that bequests are to be for any charitable organization selected by the trustees who are named to administer the funds. The recipients selected by the trustees might *not* be organizations characterized as charitable according to Federal tax standards.

A deduction was denied also where a will made provision for contributions by trustees to any organization that qualified as tax-exempt under the laws of the United States *or* any state having supervision of the trust. It was not clearly evident from the will that the decedent had intended to limit distributions to organizations coming within the scope of the Federal tax laws. (The definitive list of tax-deductible contributions is published by the Federal Government in its Publication No. 78, "Organizations Contributions to Which Are Deductible.")

No deduction is allowed where a trust is created or property is transferred for both a charitable and a private purpose if the value of the charitable interest is not ascertainable at the time. The charitable interest must be capable of being separated from the noncharitable interest. If the donee or trustee has the power to cut off the charity's interest by diverting the property to noncharitable use, that portion of the property over which the power can be exercised does not qualify for the deduction.

## INFLUENCING LEGISLATION

Charitable bequests are not deductible if a substantial part of the activities of the recipient organization, or of a trustee, involves carrying on propaganda programs or otherwise seeking to attempt to influence legislation.

## PRIVATE USE OF FUNDS

Bequests to an organization are not deductible if any part of the organization's earning are used for the benefit of any private stockholder or individual.

## NOTHING MAY BE RECEIVED IN RETURN

A charitable bequest is not deductible if anything is given or is made available in return.

Money was given to a hospital "for the establishment of free room or rooms, first, for the persons named as beneficiaries of this trust and then, for such other persons as the Board of Directors of said hospital may from time to time direct." The deduction was not allowed, for relatives of the decedent were to be eligible before other persons, without regard to financial need.

Sometimes an unrestricted bequest is made to a hospital or other eligible organization. The grateful trustees of the recipient organization write to the executor or trustee that any time a member of the decedent's family requires medical care, he will be given first priority as to facilities, without charge. Here the executor or trustee should immediately renounce this unsolicited offer, in writing, with a statement that no *quid pro quo* had been intended nor would be accepted.

## DISCRIMINATION

A deduction is not allowed if it is made to an organization that practices racial, religious, or other discrimination. To be characterized as a tax-exempt organization, contributions to which are deductible, it is not enough that an educational institution refrain from discriminatory practices; a school not having a racially nondiscriminatory policy concerning students is not characterized as "charitable" under the Federal tax laws. Deduction was denied to an organization that excluded nonwhites from membership. And any interested party can bring suit to prevent the Secretary of the Treasury from approving or continuing on the approved list an organization that practices racial discrimination.

An individual who intends to make charitable bequests should find out directly from each organization he had in mind what its practices and policies are with respect to discrimination. If he fails to do so, the result may be loss of deductions on the estate tax return, with resultant increased taxes. The organization may not be one to which he would have wanted to leave money had he known all of the facts. It is not enough for officials of an organization to say, "We've never turned down an applicant because of his color." That may be quite correct. But it may be that because of the institution's well-known prejudices, no member of a minority group may ever have made application.

An individual or his representative should seek an affirmative statement from a charitable organization to which he intends making a bequest. Some organizations make known their eligibility for charitable bequests through public advertisements, such as this advertisement that appeared in the *New York Times* of June 10, 1979:

Notice Of Nondiscriminatory Policy As To Students. The Lincoln Institute of Land Policy...admits students of any race, color, national or ethnic origin to all of the rights, privileges, programs and activities generally accorded to or made available to students at the school; it does not discriminate on the basis of race, color, national and ethnic origin in administration of its educational policies, admissions policies, scholarship and loan programs, and athletic and other school-administered programs.

## CONDITIONAL BEQUESTS

Only charitable bequests capable of being stated in terms of money are deductible. Normally, no charitable deduction is allowed for a conditional bequest because the determination as to whether a charitable deduction is allowable is made as of the date of the decedent's death, at which time it may not be known whether the condition will be met.

In her will, an individual left a portion of her estate to named trustees for the purpose of assisting in the establishing of a denominational hospital in a certain South Carolina county. No deduction was permitted because there was no indication that this particular denomination ever intended to establish a hospital in that community. If it did not, the bequest would *come back* to the decedent's estate.

A deduction was disallowed for a contribution to a charity that would take effect only if the decedent's twenty-seven-year-old childless daughter died without any surviving descendants. The mathematical possibility of this contingency was complicated by the matter of volition, inasmuch as the opportunity of obtaining the bequest provided the daughter with a substantial inducement to marry and to have children.

An individual's will provided for a bequest to the Michigan College of Mining and Technology at such time as that institution established a tax-exempt foundation in Canada to the satisfaction of the testator's trustees. The Internal Revenue Service argued that no charitable deduction was allowable because these conditions made it uncertain whether the bequest ever would be implemented. But the court held that the possibility that the terms of the bequest would not be met was so remote as to be negligible. It could be presumed that the offer of a $325,160 bequest would be enough inducement to assure that the college would take the proper steps to qualify for the money.

## HOW MUCH OF THE BEQUEST IS DEDUCTIBLE?

If a charitable organization assigns or surrenders part of a transfer to it in order to reach a compromise agreement with contesting heirs, the amount assigned or surrendered is *not* deductible as a transfer to the charitable organization.

A decedent's will provided that after payment of debts, expenses, and specific bequests, the remainder of his estate was to go to specified charities. Several heirs contested the will on the ground that the decedent had been mentally incompetent at the time he made the will. In order to obtain a dismissal of the contest so that the estate could be settled, the executor paid $100,000 of the estate's assets to the claimants, which left $100,000 less for the charities. The estate's charitable deduction was limited to what the charities actually received, rather than the amount of the estate that the charities were to get according to the will, even though that was what the decedent had wanted the charities to receive.

If nothing is left in an estate to honor a charitable bequest that the decedent had made, or if the will is for any reason void, payments made by heirs of anybody else to fulfill the decedent's intentions do not represent money flowing from the estate to the charitable organization. The donation is a gift from the heir to the charity, and the estate is entitled to no deduction, even though the end result as far as the charity is concerned is exactly what the decedent had had in mind.

## CHARITABLE EXECUTOR DOES NOT CREATE ESTATE TAX DEDUCTION

An executor was directed by a decedent's will to spend $25,000 for the erection of a monument in Israel in the names of specified relatives of the decedent. Instead, the executor transferred $25,000 irrevocably to a bank in Israel to establish an endowment scholarship fund for Jewish students. The estate was not entitled to a deduction for a charitable bequest. Even though the legacy went to an organization meeting the definition of a charitable organization, this was not the result of any direction or requirement of the will. The purpose of allowing charitable deductions, said the court, is to encourage persons who are writing their wills to make charitable bequests, not to permit executors to rewrite a will so as to achieve tax savings or anything other than what the decedent had provided. The decedent-to-be must show the charitable motivation or at least direct the charitable bequest.

> One decedent's will provided for certain charitable bequests, subject to his wife's consent. (Old habits die hard.) No deduction was allowed, for this contest was outside of the legal reach or mandate of the will.

> Deduction was not permitted where a will gave the decedent's executor instructions to take care of charities to which he knew the decedent had been devoted.

> A decedent had not made a charitable distribution when he leaves all of his wealth to named relatives, stating that he knows that they will give substantial amounts of what had been his money to his favorite charities in his name.

## BEQUESTS TO EMPLOYEE BENEFIT PLANS

A person might think that a donation toward the welfare of his company's employees is a charitable gesture. But a bequest made to the trustees of a qualified corporate profit-sharing plan was not deductible. It was irrelevant that the trust benefitted the government by sharing the burden of caring for company employees in their old age. The stated purpose in setting up the plan was to provide "a reward for all of [the company's] employees." So the trust, although valid under the law of the state where it was created, was not exclusively for charitable purposes.

A bequest to an employees' retirement plan does not create a charitable deduction if pay-outs by the fund are not geared to the needs of the individual employees involved.

## WHAT CONSTITUTES A CHARITABLE BEQUEST?

A charitable bequest can be deductible even if it is not made in the form of cash or other property.

A deduction is allowed for the value of property passing to or for the use of a charitable organization because a power of appointment is exercised, fails to be exercised, is released, or lapses and the result is that the property is includible in the decedent's gross estate as a general power of appointment held at the time of his death. See the discussion of powers of appointment in Chapter 12.

## FOREIGN CHARITABLE ORGANIZATIONS

A charitable bequest to a government must be made to the United States or a political subdivision in order to qualify as a deduction. But a gift in trust may be made to a foreign political unit when the gift is restricted to charitable purposes.

> An alien resident in the United States made a bequest to a trust for the benefit of a home for the aged in a German community. The deduction was allowed because the gift was restricted to charitable purposes. A deduction is not allowed where the bequest is for all practical purposes unrestricted and may be used for such noncharitable purposes as the payment of salaries to a community's policemen or the construction of a new sewer.

> The bequest of a coin collection to Israel was deductible, when the nation agreed to keep the collection in perpetuity, never to be sold or otherwise disposed of. This was regarded as a bequest to trustees that could be used only for exclusively religious, scientific, literary, educational, etc., purposes. The court noted that in agreeing to accept and to perform the conditions of the trust, the state indicated no likelihood that it would deviate from its pledged responsibilities.

## CHARITABLE REMAINDERS

A person may desire to set up a trust for the ultimate benefit of a charitable organization, with his spouse to receive the income for as long as she lives. Inasmuch as the income interest that he provides for her is to end when she dies, without her having the ability to say what is to happen to the trust principal at this time, this amounts to a terminable interest, and there is no marital deduction. Such an arrangement, despite any tax benefit, might still be attractive to a person, however, for it provides a life income to his spouse. Then the principal will go automatically to his alma mater or other designated eligible organization without the possibility of contrary action by his spouse.

But in the case of transfers of interests in the same property to one's spouse and to an approved charitable organization made after December 31, 1981, tax benefits may be available. If a person creates a qualified charitable remainder annuity trust or a charitable remainder unitrust, and the only noncharitable beneficiaries are the donor and his spouse, the disallowance rule for terminable interests does not apply. Therefore, the individual receives a charitable deduction for the amount of the remainder interest that will go to the charitable organization and a marital deduction for the value of the annuity or unitrust interest. No tax is imposed on the transfer.

An annuity trust is one that specifies in dollar terms the amount of the annuity that is to be paid to the income beneficiary, such as one's spouse. This must be at least 5 percent of the principal transferred to the trust when it is created. Income payments must be made at least annually.

A unitrust is a trust that specifies that the income beneficiary is to receive annual payments of not less than 5 percent of the net fair market value of the trust's assets, as determined each year. Provision *may* be made to have the trustee pay the income beneficiary the lesser of the stated pay-out or the trust income for that year. But the trustee may not be given discretion as to which alternative to use. This means that trust principal cannot be used to make up for an income deficiency. Provision may be made that when less than 5 percent is paid out by the unitrust, because of insufficient income, this diminution will be restored in subsequent years when income is larger than the required pay-out.

The allowable charitable deduction is computed actuarially on the present value of the charity's remainder interest.

## ONE'S RESIDENCE IS AN EXCEPTION TO THE REMAINDER INTEREST RULE

A charitable contribution deduction is allowed where an individual makes a gift of his personal residence to a charity and retains the right to live in the residence for the balance of his life.

In determining the value of a remainder interest in real property that is given to charity, straight line depreciation and cost depletion are taken into account. Thus, in valuing the charitable gift, the property is decreased by an amount that reflects the depreciation or depletion of the property. In addition, in valuing this type of charitable gift, the present value of the gift is determined on the basis of an interest rate that is set by the Internal Revenue Service.

# 19

## THE INCOME TAX ASPECTS OF ESTATE PLANNING

The Federal taxes usually thought of in connection with estate planning are the gift and estate taxes. This chapter deals with the interplay between estate planning and the Federal income tax.

## AVOIDANCE OF TRANSFEROR'S INCOME TAXES

Earlier in this book, we discussed how a person can reduce his Federal income taxes through:

☐ Transfer of income-producing properties to his beneficiaries during his lifetime by gift. Proper utilization of the annual exclusion, split-gifts, and the gift tax marital deduction can reduce or even offset any transfer taxes.

☐ Transfer of such properties in trust for the benefit of individuals or charitable organizations for a period of more than ten years, at the end of which time the property, its income, and the taxes on that income again become the transferor's.

☐ Holding of income-producing properties in joint ownership, which will spread income tax liability between two or more parties.

## CONSIDERATION OF BENEFICIARIES' INCOME TAX LIABILITY

A person may believe that he has done all that he needs to do for his beneficiaries by transmitting property to them. Estate planning also may consider *how* this property is transmitted. It is likely in the case of most properties that a beneficiary at some future time will want to sell what he has received. In inflationary times, when the beneficiary sells, he may have Federal income tax liability upon the excess of the realization over the tax basis for the property in his hands. The tax basis depends upon how he had received that property.

DEATHTIME TRANSFERS

The basis of inherited property in the hands of a beneficiary is the value used by the executor on the Federal estate tax return, subject to modifications made by the Internal Revenue Service or a court. In almost all instances, this is the value at the date of death or, if the executor makes a property election, the value six months later. Where a valid election is made, the basis of any assets sold between these two dates is the price realized. If, as will increasingly be the case because of changes being phased in by the Economic Recovery Tax Act of 1981, an estate is not required to file a Federal estate tax return because the estate is not of the required size, the appropriate value for state inheritance tax purposes is deemed to be its fair market value.

If the rigid ground rules can be met, different values are used for certain assets. See the discussion in Chapter 5, "Special-Use Valuation of Certain Farms and Other Real Property."

A special rule applies to the basis in a beneficiary's hands of certain appreciated-value property that had been transferred to a decedent by gift within one year of his death. In the case of decedents dying after December 31, 1981, where a person inherits property that the decedent had acquired within one year of his death and the property now returns to the donor or to his spouse, the basis of this property in the beneficiary's hands is the basis in the decedent's hands immediately before his death. Such is the case whether the bequest to the donor by the decedent had been a specific bequest, a general bequest, a pecuniary bequest, or a residuary bequest. In the case of a pecuniary bequest, however, the donor will receive the benefit of the appreciated property only if its inclusion in the decedent's estate affected the amount that the donor receives under the pecuniary bequest. Here is an example:

> Assume that A transfers appreciated property with a basis of $10 and a fair market value of $100 to D within one year of D's death and that D's date of death basis was $20 and the date of death fair market value of the property was $200. If A is entitled to receive the property from the decedent, A's basis in the property is $20. If A subsequently sells the property for its fair market value of $200, he recognizes gain of $180. If, instead, the executor disposes of the property, distributing the proceeds to A, similar rules apply, and the estate recognizes a gain of $180.

This rule applies only to the extent that the donor-heir is entitled to receive the value of the appreciated property. If the heir is entitled only to a portion of the property (e.g., because the property must be used to satisfy debts or administration expenses), the rule applies on a *pro rata* basis. Thus, if in the above example, the decedent's estate consisted only of the appreciated property and the total estate liabilities were $50, the heir would be entitled to only three-fourths of the appreciated property. Accordingly, the portion of the property to which the donor-heir was not entitled (one-quarter in the example), will receive a stepped-up basis to value at date of death. In such a case, the basis of the appreciated property in the hands of the executor or the heir will be $65, i.e., one-quarter of $200 (or $50) plus three-quarters of $20 (or $15).

## LIFETIME TRANSFERS

When a person receives property by gift, it is necessary to determine (1) its adjusted basis to the donor, (2) its fair market value at the time of the gift, and (3) the amount of Federal gift tax, if any, paid by the donee.

The donor's adjusted basis is:

☐ The amount paid for the property, plus the cost of any improvements that could not be deducted for tax purposes: for instance, a new roof of a better material added to a residence he already had.

☐ *Minus* any depreciation previously deducted by the donor: for instance, when part of the residence had been used for business purposes and depreciation had been taken, or should have been taken.

If fair market value of the gift property at the time of the gift is greater than the donor's adjusted basis at that time, the donee's basis is the donor's adjusted basis at the time of the gift, increased by any gift tax the donee might have paid on this transfer. This basis cannot exceed the fair market value of the property when the gift was made.

Increase in the basis is limited to the gift tax attributable to the net appreciation in the value of the gift. Tax on the net appreciation is computed by multiplying the tax paid by the net appreciation in value and dividing the result by the amount of the gift. For this purpose, net appreciation in value is the amount by which the fair market value of the property on the date of the gift exceeds the basis to the donor immediately before the gift.

If the fair market value of the property is less than the donor's adjusted basis at the time of the gift, the donee's basis is the same as the donor's adjusted basis. Should the donee sell this property at a loss, basis is the property's fair market value at the time of the gift.

## HOLDING PERIOD

If a beneficiary acquires property subject to capital asset treatment, it is necessary to establish his holding period. Assets held by a seller for more than one year are given long-term capital asset treatment.

Sale of property inherited from a decedent is treated as long-term without reference to the time the property had been held by the estate.

For a capital asset acquired by gift, the holding period of the donee commences on the date of the gift, even though the property may be part of the decedent-donor's gross estate at the date of his death because the transfer was the kind that is considered part of the transferor's gross estate when he dies within three years of the transfer.

A remainderman's interest dates back either to the time of the decedent's death for property then owned by the decedent or to the time the property was bought by the fiduciary.

## BENEFICIARY TAXATION ON TRUST INCOME

A *simple trust* is one required by the terms of its governing instrument to distribute all of its income currently. Any other trust is a *complex* or *accumulation trust.* Thus, where trustees are given absolute and complete discretion to accumulate or to distribute the trust's income, this *discretionary trust* is a complex trust.

Simple trusts pay no Federal income tax where all income is distributed currently to the beneficiaries. The income is taxable to the beneficiaries.

In the case of complex trusts, beneficiaries are taxed if they receive distributions of income that the trust had gotten that year. In this case, the trust is not taxed on that portion of its income. When the trust accumulates taxable income, the trust pays income tax on that portion of its income.

### THE THROWBACK RULE

If beneficiaries receive distributions in one year that could have been made to them in a previous year, each beneficiary is taxed *as though* the income had been received by him when it was available, despite the fact that he pays taxes in the year of actual receipt. This so-called "throwback" treatment eliminates any inclination on the part of a friendly trustee to make the payments at a time when it is more advantageous tax-wise for a beneficiary to receive the money.

Under this rule, when the trustee makes a distribution to a beneficiary that could have been made in an earlier year (an "accumulation distribution"), the average accumulation distribution is thrown back to the beneficiary's five preceding taxable years. But with respect to these five preceding years, the year with the highest taxable income and the year with the lowest are not considered. In effect, the computation is based on a three-year average basis. The average amount for the three years then is added to the beneficiary's taxable income for these years. The additional tax is determined on the basis of the number of years during which the accumulated income was earned.

The tax may be *offset* by a credit for any taxes previously paid by the trust on this income. No refunds or credits are available, however, to any beneficiary or trust as a result of an accumulation distribution.

A special rule applies to multiple trusts where a beneficiary receives an accumulation distribution from more than two trusts in the same year. In addition, the throwback rule does not apply to any distribution of income accumulated for a beneficiary while he is a minor, that is, before the birth of the beneficiary or before he reaches age twenty-one. This exception for minors, however, does not apply in the case of distributions covered under the multiple trust rule.

## CAPITAL GAINS

The regular throwback procedure does not apply to capital gains. But a special rule covers the possibility that the grantor will place in trust property that has unrealized appreciation in order to shift the burden of the tax on the appreciation to the trust at its lowest progressive tax rates.

Under this rule, where the fair market value of the property placed in trust exceeds the price paid (if any) for the property by the trust, there is a "built-in" gain. If the trust sells this property within two years of the time it is transferred to the trust, the "built-in" gain is taxed to the trust at the grantor's tax rates. In essence, such gains are treated as if the grantor had realized the gain and then transferred to the trust the net proceeds from the sale after the tax.

## HOW TAXES ARE CALCULATED

In the case of an accumulation distribution, the trust is taxed when income is earned but not distributed promptly to beneficiaries. When the income subsequently is distributed to a beneficiary, he will be able to claim credits for the taxes previously paid by the trust.

For the purpose of computing the beneficiary's income tax on accumulation distributions, the income is treated as having come from the income of the earliest year in which the trust had had income sufficient to make the distribution.

Form 4970, "Tax on Accumulation Distribution of Trusts," is filed by a beneficiary with his own Federal income tax return. This shows the tax adjustments attributable to an accumulation made by a trust in the current year.

The tax imposed on a beneficiary with respect to an accumulation distribution is adjusted to take into account the estate tax or generation-skipping tax attributable to the accumulated income.

A distribution by an executor is not taxable to a beneficiary until this distribution properly is made under state law. For example, if the distribution is subject to recovery by the executor, the beneficiary usually is not taxed.

## GRANTOR TRUSTS

Income that is subject to a person's complete command and that he is free to enjoy at his own choice may be taxed to him as income, whether he sees fit to exercise this choice or not. Accordingly, the grantor of a trust is taxed on its income if he has retained a reversionary interest in either the trust principal or income, and his interest reasonably may be expected to take effect within ten years.

This rule does not apply, however, where he has a right to the return of trust principal only after the death of the income beneficiary of the trust.

An individual is taxed on the income of a trust to the extent that this income is used to support his legal dependents. If state law required him to support and to maintain them in a manner "suitable to his circumstances," he is taxed on trust income that is used to provide them with goods or services that are not, strictly speaking, necessary to the dependents and do not constitute support items that he legally is obliged to furnish.

Included in the father-grantor's income in one such case were amounts used to buy an automobile, musical instruments, and music lessons for minor children.

## WHEN A BENEFICIARY IS NOT TAXED ON TRUST INCOME HE RECEIVES

Income distributed by a trust retains the same character that it had in the hands of the trust. Thus, when a trust's income is from tax-exempt state or municipal bonds, this income is tax-exempt when it is distributed by the fiduciary to the beneficiary.

## DEATH BENEFIT EXCLUSION

Amounts of up to $5,000 per employee that are paid to the beneficiaries of the estate of an employee or former employee, by or on behalf of an employer and by reason of the death of the employee, are excluded from gross income of the recipient. This exclusion applies whether payment is made to the estate of the employee or to any beneficiary, whether it is made directly or in trust, whether or not it is made under a contractual obligation of the employer, and whether the payment is made in a single sum or otherwise.

The exclusion does not apply to amounts that constitute income payable to the employee during his lifetime as compensation for services, such as bonuses or payments for unused leave or uncollected salary, nor to certain other amounts that the deceased employee possessed, as a nonforfeitable right, at the time of his death.

A recipient does not have any choice as to the year in which to exclude the $5,000 death benefit.

## PAYMENT OF INSURANCE PROCEEDS TO SURVIVING SPOUSE AFTER DEATH

Life insurance proceeds payable upon the death of an insured person can be held by the insurance company under an agreement to pay interest to the beneficiary. These interest payments ordinarily are included in the beneficiary's gross income. But if the beneficiary is a surviving spouse, she may exclude payment of up to $1,000 where an election has been made to receive the proceeds in installment payments rather than as a lump sum.

## INCOME IN RESPECT OF A DECEDENT

When a person dies, all of the income to which he was entitled under the accounting system he had been using at the time of his death is included in gross income for his financial year. Almost all individuals report on the cash basis, which means that gross income includes all payments actually received or which would have been available without substantial limitation had he asked for the money, such as savings bank interest.

Where an individual had reported on the accrual basis, gross income includes all amounts to which he was entitled, regardless of when payment took place, such as the income of a lawyer who had performed services and sent out his bill, which had not been paid as yet.

All items of income and deductions that properly would have appeared on a decedent's final income tax return, except for the method of accounting he used, must be shown on the income tax returns of the person or persons who actually receive the payments as *income in respect of a decedent;* there is equivalent treatment for deductions and credits. Income in respect of a decedent includes payment received after his death because of activities he had performed, such as personal services.

The test of taxability of income as income in respect of a decedent is whether the payments after his death are in fact due to the services or economic activities he performed. *If the decedent did the work or performed the services,* the payments are taxed to the recipient in the way that they would have been taxed to the decedent. The most common examples of this are:

☐ Salaries, commissions, and bonuses to which the decedent was entitled because he had earned the money;

☐ Deferred compensation arrangements, where the pay-outs are to be made over a period of years;

☐ Investment income that was increasing prior to the decedent's death, although he may not have been entitled to receive any payment before he died;

☐ Bonuses awarded to a decedent before his death, which were payable after the date on which he died;

☐ Bonuses awarded after his death is recognition of services performed before his death.

The value of retirement payments receivable by a surviving spouse as successor to her deceased husband's right to receive such income for a specified period of time is includible in the husband's estate. The payments are includible in her gross income as income in respect of a decedent. Post-death payments to an employee's widow are treated as income in respect of a decedent despite the fact that under the terms of the employment contract, the employee never would be entitled to actual receipt of the income.

A decedent was a stockholder in a corporation, which had made a contract to sell its assets (subject to approval of a governmental regulatory agency) before his death. Approval was received after he died, and the sale was consummated. Resulting income was income in respect of a decedent because all the significant economic activity in connection with the sale of corporate assets had been accomplished prior to his death.

Income to which the decedent had a contingent claim at the time of his death is income in respect of a decedent.

Income in respect of a decedent also includes the amount of all items of gross income in respect of a prior decedent, if:

1. The right to receive these amounts was acquired by the decedent by reason of the death of the prior decedent or by bequest or inheritance from the prior decedent, and if:

2. The amount of gross income in respect of the prior decedent was not properly includible in computing the decedent's taxable income for the taxable year.

A widow, for example, may have the right to receive life insurance renewal commissions on policies that her husband had sold prior to his death. When she died, their son received the renewal commissions on the policies his father had sold, solely because the person entitled to receive income in respect of a decedent (his mother) had passed the right to receive the father's income to him. What the son received was income in respect of a prior decedent.

Income in respect of a decedent is included in the taxable year of receipt in the gross income of the following:

1. The estate of the decedent, if the right to receive the amount is acquired by the decedent's estate from the decedent.

2. The person who, by reason of the death of the decedent, acquires the right to receive the amount, if this right is not acquired by the decedent's estate from the decedent.

3. The person who acquires from the decedent the right to receive the amount by bequest of inheritance, if the amount is received after a distribution of this right by the decedent's estate.

These amounts are included in the income of the estate or of the persons who receive them whether or not these recipients report income on the cash method.

## DEDUCTIONS OF A DECEDENT

Expenses, interest, and taxes for which the decedent (or a prior decedent) was liable, that were not properly allowable as a deduction by the decedent in his last taxable year or any prior taxable year, are allowed when paid:

1. As a deduction by the estate, or

2. If the estate was not liable to pay the obligation, as a deduction by the person who, by bequest or inheritance from the decedent or by reason of the death of the decedent, acquires an interest in property of the decedent or of a prior decedent subject to the obligation.

For purposes of computing the long-term capital gains deduction (or the amount of gain for purposes of the long-term capital gains alternative tax and any net capital losses), the amount of the gain is to be reduced (but not below zero) by the amount of any applicable deduction for estate taxes attributable to a gain treated as income in respect of a decedent.

For example, if a long-term capital gain of $100 is treated as income in respect of a decedent and the estate tax attributable to that gain is $30, the amount of the recipient's long-term capital gain that is subject to the alternative tax is $70 ($100 minus $30). In addition, the amount of the long-term capital gain deduction is $42 (60 percent of $70) for all purposes, including the minimum tax. In either case, no additional deduction is allowed for the estate taxes attributable to that gain.

## DEDUCTION FOR ESTATE TAX

A person who must include any income in respect of a decedent in gross income for the taxable year may deduct in the same taxable year that portion of the Federal estate tax on the decedent's estate that is attributable to the inclusion in the estate of the right to receive that amount. State estate taxes are added to the Federal estate tax for this purpose.

In order to determine the allowable deduction, it is necessary first to compute the net value of the items that are to be treated as income in respect of a decedent. This *net value* is the value in the gross estate of all items in respect of a decedent, less the claims deductible for Federal estate tax purposes that represent allowable deductions and credits in respect of a decedent.

The estate tax attributable to that net value is an amount equal to the excess of the estate tax over the estate tax computed without including that net value in the gross estate. To arrive at that figure in recomputing the estate tax, it is necessary to exclude from the value of the gross estate the net value of all items of income in respect of a decedent.

The difference between the estate tax and the estate tax as recomputed is the total difference allowed.

In computing the estate tax without including in the gross estate the net value of the items in respect of a decedent, any estate tax deductions that may be based on the gross estate or adjusted gross estate must be recomputed to take into account the exclusion of that value from the gross estate.

The deduction of a decedent is computed by multiplying the amount of combined Federal and state estate taxes by a fraction, the numerator of which is the net amount of income in respect of a decedent and the denominator of which is the value of the gross estate.

Sometimes, each of several persons receives income in respect of a decedent in the same taxable year. Each of these persons, then, may deduct a prorated portion of the Federal estate tax paid by the estate by reason of the inclusion in the estate of the value of the right to receive the income. This proration is on the basis of the proportion of the income in respect of a decedent received by each of the persons getting the income. The actual computation of the estate tax allocated to each person is very involved. If you are one of several persons who receive income of this type in any one year, you or your accountant should look at the explanatory computation contained in Revenue Ruling 67-242, 1967-2 CB 227.

## ESTATE AS RECIPIENT OF INCOME IN RESPECT OF A DECEDENT

If income in respect of a decedent is received by an estate, the estate is the taxpayer for Federal income tax purposes. Unlike an individual taxpayer using the customary cash basis, however, a deduction is allowed the estate if, within a year of receipt, the income is distributed to beneficiaries.

## INCENTIVE STOCK OPTIONS

An incentive stock option, as created by the Economic Recovery Tax Act of 1981, is treated in a manner similar to that which had been accorded in past years to restricted and qualified stock options. An employee is not taxed when the option is granted or exercised, and he is taxed at capital gains rates when the stock received upon exercise of the option is sold. But he cannot dispose of the stock within two years after the option is granted and must hold the stock itself for at least one year. The option is transferable only at the employee's death.

## SUBCHAPTER S CORPORATIONS

A Subchapter S corporation is a corporation that, if the ground rules are met, is not subject to Federal income tax at the corporate level. The shareholders are taxed directly on their *pro rata* shares of the earnings. In addition, each shareholder deducts his share of corporate losses, up to the adjusted basis of his stock plus the adjusted basis of any debts owed to him by the corporation. Election to be taxed as a Subchapter S corporation must be made by specified times. No shareholder may be a nonresident alien, there may not be more than one class of stock, and not more than 20 percent of the corporation's gross receipts may be from passive or inactive sources.

Individuals and estates may be shareholders, as well as certain types of trust, namely:

1. Grantor trusts, that is, trusts where the grantor is deemed to be the owner.

2. Voting trusts.

3. Certain testamentary trusts.

4. Trusts that are treated as owned by a person other than the grantor. Such a trust continues to be eligible to be a shareholder for sixty days after the person's death.

5. The sole beneficiary of a trust that distributes all of its income currently can elect to be treated as the owner. The income beneficiary must be a citizen and resident of the United States and must be the beneficiary for his life, unless the trust principal is to be distributed to the income beneficiary upon termination of the trust.

For taxable years after December 31, 1981, the maximum number of shareholders is twenty-five.

Formerly, if stock passed to a beneficiary who did not file a timely election to be a Subchapter S corporation stockholder, this special treatment was lost to *all* shareholders. Now the election is not lost unless a new shareholder actually refused to become an electing shareholder within sixty days of acquiring his stock.

## DISALLOWED LOSSES IN FIDUCIARY TRANSACTIONS

For Federal income tax purposes, losses are disallowed in the case of transactions between certain defined related parties. Included are these forms of transaction betweeen fiduciaries and other parties:

☐ A grantor and a fiduciary (e.g., the trustee) of any trust.

☐ A fiduciary of one trust and a fiduciary of another trust, if the same person is the grantor of both trusts.

☐ A fiduciary of a trust and a beneficiary of that trust.

☐ A fiduciary of one trust and a beneficiary of another trust if the same person is a grantor of both trusts.

☐ A fiduciary of a trust and a corporation more than 50 percent of the stock of which is owned, directly or indirectly, by or for the trust or by or for a grantor of the trust.

Losses on transactions between an estate and an individual are *not* automatically disallowed, as they would be in the five situations just mentioned.

## SALES OR EXCHANGES OF LIFE ESTATES

A life estate enables the designated "life tenant" to receive income from specific property for as long as he lives. For example, the grantor of a trust may have provided that a designated person would receive the trust's income for the balance of his life, with a remainderman to get the property after the death of the life tenant.

If a life tenant sells or otherwise disposes of his life interest, the entire amount he receives is taxable income, without any allowance for the value or basis of the right when he received it.

But this rule does not apply when the *entire interest* is sold or otherwise transferred to another person or to two or more other persons jointly. Here, any gain is measured by the excess of proceeds received over the seller's basis. For example, if a life tenant and a remainderman hold all the interests in a property and they sell them all at the same time in a single transaction, the gain realized by the life tenant is measured by the excess of the proceeds received on the sale over his basis in the life estate.

## EXPENSES OF A WILL CONTEST

An individual became engaged in a lawsuit to uphold the validity of his uncle's will, under which the nephew was named to inherit the entire estate. He won. But inasmuch as property acquired by inheritance is not included in gross income, the tax ruling was that expenditures in connection with the acquisition similarly were nondeductible.

An attorney was not permitted to deduct legal expenses to contest his father's will, which stated that it was not the decedent's wish that his son, the attorney, take over the decedent's law practice. It was ruled that the expenses were not for the conservation or maintenance of property that he owned.

## INTEREST ON ESTATE DEFICIENCY PAID BY BENEFICIARY

Where the sole beneficiary of a decedent's estate is obliged to pay a Federal estate tax deficiency because the executor no longer has funds to pay it, the beneficiary can deduct on his own income tax return the interest applicable to the tax deficiency *after* he received the estate's assets. Interest applicable to the deficiency prior to the distribution of the estate's assets is not deductible.

## INNOCENT SPOUSE

If a husband and wife file a joint Federal income tax return, *each* person can be held fully liable for any tax deficiency, including interest and penalty thereon. But one party can be held not to be responsible in the case of unreported income where:

☐ Omission from gross income amounted to more than 25 percent of gross income on the tax return.

☐ The "innocent spouse" did not know of the omitted income and had no reason to know of it.

☐ The "innocent spouse" had not benefitted significantly from the omission.

But a wife was held personally liable even where she had not known of income unreported by her husband where, upon his death, she inherited his wealth, including the unreported income about which she had known nothing.

# 20

PROVIDING FOR THE ESTATE
TAX RETURN AND PAYMENT

## A PERSON'S RESPONSIBILITY FOR
## WHAT HAPPENS AFTER HE DIES

A decedent-to-be may believe that the filing of his estate tax return and the payment of tax are the concerns of *other people* after his death. But his estate planning should consider that the effectuation of his wishes will be impeded by interest and by penalties that may have to be paid personally by the executor, who could be a close friend or relative, where the estate tax return is not filed with promptness and completeness, or where funds are not available for tax payments. Lack of necessary tax funds can mean that estate assets will have to be sold at the wrong time, at unfavorable prices. The executor may have to devote too much of his time to scrounging for cash, to the detriment of his other duties.

As will be shown in Chapter 21, "Making It Easier for Your Executor," an individual has the responsibility of providing the fiduciary with what is necessary to accomplish his duties. Consider what the executor has to do.

## RESPONSIBILITIES OF THE EXECUTOR

The Internal Revenue Code places on the executor the responsibility for filing Federal income tax returns of the estate when due and for paying the tax determined, up to the date of discharge from his duties. If, before his discharge and the distribution of the estate's assets, he has notice of the tax liability or fails to discharge due diligence in finding out whether any tax is owing, the liability for Federal taxes may follow him *personally* after his discharge.

Even though an executor may not be required to file a Federal income tax return for the estate, he may be obliged to file Form 1087, "Nominee's Information Return." This form must be filed by any person who receives dividends or interest as a nominee for another person and makes payments to that other person totalling $10 or more during a calendar year. This occurs, of course, when an executor receives dividends on stock that is willed to a beneficiary. These forms, together with the transmittal Form 1096, must be filed with the Internal Revenue Service not later than the last day of February following the end of the calendar year during which payments are made.

Executors do not meet the required standard of care merely by employing an attorney or accountant to represent them. They must assume at least the minimum responsibility of seeing to it that the professional party they engage acts with diligence. An executor who is aware that an estate tax must be paid is required to learn the time when the return and the tax are due. This is also called for by ordinary prudence.

## POWERS OF THE EXECUTOR

An executor may exercise the rights, powers, duties, and privileges of the party for whom he acts. For example, he may elect to have appreciation on a decedent's Series EE Treasury Bonds reported each year as income instead of reporting the full appreciation when the bonds mature. Incentive stock options can be exercised during his lifetime only by the corporate employee to whom they are issued; but after his death, his executor can use this power.

An important tax election available to an executor is to renounce retroactively any recent Federal income tax returns that had been filed jointly by the decedent and his spouse. The executor has the power to disaffirm or renounce such returns for all years not yet closed by the statute of limitations, three years in most instances. A joint return usually means the payment of a lower tax than if separate returns were filed, especially after the mitigation of the "marriage penalty" by the Economic Recovery Tax Act of 1981. But a joint return also creates "joint and several tax liability." This means that each spouse can be held responsible personally not only for his or her share of the joint tax liability, but for the entire tax, including penalties and interest.

By disaffirming joint returns where permitted, an executor can make certain that the party he represents (the decedent's estate) is not held responsible for any taxes for which the other spouse really is responsible but were improperly reported. Many executors feel that the saving achieved by filing a joint return should be forfeited in preference to running the extra risk of tax, penalties, and interest by reason of the other spouse's tax-reporting error.

A spouse who has been innocent of wrongdoing will not be assessed for the tax shortcomings of the other if all three of these conditions can be proven to exist:

1. A joint return has been filed and the omission from gross income (attributable to one spouse) amounts to more than 25 percent of the gross income stated on the return.

2. The innocent spouse establishes that in signing the return, he or she did not know of, and had no reason to know of, the omission from income.

3. The innocent spouse did not significantly benefit from the items omitted from gross income.

When these conditions exist, it is inequitable to hold the spouse in question liable for the deficiency in tax. (Where the so-called innocent spouse received unusual or lavish gifts or transfers of property, or where the family's style of life suddenly became far more elaborate, it is difficult to argue that either spouse really was ignorant about what was going on.)

In view of this "innocent spouse rule," some executors feel that there is no reason to disaffirm joint income tax returns. But other executors believe that upon the death of either spouse, records are apt to be moved or otherwise become unavailable, and additional income tax deficiencies may be imposed by the Internal Revenue Service because of lack of taxpayer substantiation.

## ALTERNATE DATES OF VALUATION

Ordinarily, assets are valued as of the date of the decedent's death. But the executor may elect to have the assets valued as of the date six months after death. This can be a valuable privilege where asset values have *declined* since the date the decedent died.

Where the alternate valuation date is used, it extends to all property in gross estate, including property thrown into the estate as a result of a tax audit, such as transactions within three years of death or assets where transfers had been incomplete technically.

The election can be made only by checking a box provided for this purpose on a Federal estate tax return that is *filed on time.* The election cannot be revoked after the last day set for the filing of the return.

If the value of the gross estate is less than the unified credit, the election cannot be made.

Where the executor makes this election, the property in gross estate is valued according to these guidelines:

□ Any property distributed, sold, exchanged, or otherwise disposed of within six months after the date of death is valued as of the date on which it was distributed.

□ Property not so distributed within six months of death is valued as of the date six months after the day of the decedent's death.

□ Property such as Series EE United States Treasury Bonds, where the value is affected by the lapse of time rather than by the market, will be valued the same on the date of the decedent's death as it would be on the alternate date. When the estate includes an insurance policy, no attention is paid to an increase in its value, if this increase comes from the payment of premiums or interest earned during the six months.

## ESTATE TAX RETURN FILING REQUIREMENTS

Whether a Federal estate tax return must be filed can be seen on the following chart:

| For decedents dying in: | A return must be filed where gross estate exceeds: |
|---|---|
| 1982 | $225,000 |
| 1983 | 275,000 |
| 1984 | 325,000 |
| 1985 | 400,000 |
| 1986 | 500,000 |
| 1987 and thereafter | 600,000 |

## WHEN THE ESTATE TAX RETURN MUST BE FILED

The Federal estate tax return, Form 706, must be filed in the Internal Revenue Service Center that covers the area in which the decedent had resided within nine months after death.

If an executor believes that he will not be able to file the return on time, he should send to the Internal Revenue Service Form 4768, "Application for Extension of Time to File U.S. Estate Tax Return and/or Pay Estate Tax."

Where an executor is unable to complete the return on time, he is required to supply all of the information he has. Then it may be up to a court to determine whether sufficient data have been supplied to constitute substantial compliance with the requirement that the return be filed on time. The filing of an admittedly incomplete and estimated return does not relieve a tardy taxpayer of liability for a penalty.

If a return is not filed on time, there is a mandatory penalty, unless it can be shown that failure to file was due to reasonable cause. The penalty is one-half of 1 percent per month, up to a maximum of 25 percent for failure to pay estate tax when due or for failure to pay a tax deficiency within ten days of the date when the Internal Revenue Service makes a formal demand. The penalty for negligence, such as ignorance or carelessness, is 5 percent of the amount of the tax. Nonfiling that is the result of a willful attempt to evade tax known to be due constitutes fraud, and there is a 50 percent penalty plus various criminal penalties.

The executor has the duty of vigilance and promptness in filing an estate tax return. Failure to file a return on time can be costly to the estate he represents and to beneficiaries entitled to assets. It is his responsibility to conserve the estate assets. Employing an attorney or accountant, or both, to "do what is necessary," does not relieve the executor of responsibility for seeing that the return gets filed on time. Being "too busy" is not regarded as an excuse. Nor is a court overly sympathetic to an argument that delay had been necessitated by the complexity of the tax or other problems involved.

## WHEN THE ESTATE TAX MUST BE PAID

The Federal estate tax must be paid when the return is filed, that is, nine months after the decedent's death.

### EXTENSIONS

If the value of an interest in a closely-held business that is included in the gross estate of a decedent who was, at the time of his death, a citizen or resident of the United States exceeds 35 percent of his adjusted gross estate, the executor may elect to defer the estate tax attributable to that interest for up to fourteen years. The executor has up to five years to tender the first installment, with each subsequent installment due one year later.

The interest in a closely-held business includes for this purpose:

☐ An interest as a proprietor in a trade or business carried on as a proprietorship.

☐ Stock in a corporation carrying on a trade or business if (1) 20 percent or more in value of the voting stock of the corporation is included in determining the gross estate of the decedent or (2) the corporation had fifteen or fewer shareholders. Interests in two or more closely-held businesses with respect to each of which there is included in gross estate more than 20 percent of the total value of each such business is treated as an interest in a single closely-held business.

☐ An interest as a partner in a partnership engaged in a trade or business.

In order for the stock of a corporation to qualify as an interest in a closely-held business, it is necessary that the corporation be engaged in carrying on a trade or business at the time of the decedent's death. But it is not necessary that all the assets of the corporation be utilized in the carrying on of the trade or business. In the case of a trade or business carried on as a proprietorship, the interest in the closely-held business includes only those assets of the decedent that actually were used by him in the trade or business.

This extension provision applies to a business such as manufacturing, or a mercantile or service enterprise, as distinguished from the management of investment assets. The mere leasing of rental property normally does not include activities sufficient to be considered the conduct of a business.

Where an estate qualifies for this extended period for the payment of tax, a special 4 percent interest rate is allowed on the tax attributable to the first $1,000,000 of farm or other closely-held business property. Interest on amounts in excess of this figure are at the regular rate.

ACCELERATION OF DEFERRED PAYMENT

Under certain circumstances, any unpaid portions of taxes deferred in the manner just described will be accelerated, for the extension of time for payment will cease to exist. The unpaid installments will become due if:

1. More than a specified portion of the closely-held business is sold, exchanged, or otherwise disposed of, or

2. Money or other property attributable to that interest is withdrawn from the business, and

3. The aggregate of these distributions, sales, exchanges, or other dispositions and withdrawals exceeds 50 percent of the value of the interest.

But in applying these rules in the case of decedents dying after December 31, 1981, the apparent severity of these guidelines has been mitigated somewhat in certain instances although they have been tightened in others.

1. Dispositions and withdrawals are aggregated to determine applicability of the acceleration rules. Thus, if an estate withdraws amounts equal to 30 percent of the decedent's interest in all closely-held businesses for which deferred payment is elected and separately disposes of 20 percent or more of the decedent's interest in these businesses, the remaining unpaid tax balances will be accelerated.

2. The transfer of an interest in a closely-held business upon the death of the original decedent's heir, or the death of any subsequent transferee receiving the interest as a result of the prior transferor's death, will not be considered a disposition that accelerates payment of the original decedent's unpaid estate taxes provided that each subsequent transferee is a family member of the transferor from whom the property was received. For this purpose, "family member" means a person's spouse, brothers and sisters, ancestors, and lineal descendants.

3. Acceleration will be triggered by a delinquent payment of interest as well as a delinquent payment of tax. In consequence, an estate may not avoid payment of interest during the initial five-year period without accelerating payment of the remaining tax balance. But if the full amount of the delinquent payment (principal and all accrued interest) is paid within six months of its original due date, the remaining tax balance will not be accelerated. Instead, the payment loses eligibility for the special 4 percent interest rate and a penalty is imposed, equal to 5 percent per month, based on the amount of the payment.

## BOND FOR PAYMENT OF DEFERRED TAXES

Where there is an extended time for payment of estate taxes, the Internal Revenue Service, if it deems necessary, may require the executor to furnish a bond for the payment of the tax in an amount not more than double the amount of the tax for which the extension is granted. In addition, the executor is *personally liable* for the payment of tax unless he is discharged on payment of the tax due and on furnishing any bond that may be required for the tax that is not presently due because of an extension of time for payment.

By posting an appropriate bond, executors may postpone for six months the payment of that portion of the Federal estate tax attributable to the inclusion of a reversionary or remainder interest in the estate. For example, a decedent may have transferred property in trust for the benefit of his mother. The trust is to be terminated and the principal returned to him or *to his estate* upon her death. If the possibility of getting back this property was great enough according to actuarial assumptions of life expectancies so that its value would be includible in his gross estate, his estate will have to pay tax on a figure that includes the value of this reversionary interest, even though the estate does not yet have the money or other property representing this interest. After this six-month postponement, a further three-year moratorium may be granted, upon a showing of reasonable cause.

## LIEN TO ASSURE PAYMENT OF DEFERRED TAXES

A special lien for payment of the deferred taxes applies to real property and other assets of a farm or other closely-held business. Where this lien procedure is followed and a party is designated to make estate tax payments and to receive and to transmit notices from the Internal Revenue Service, the executor is discharged from personal liability.

The maximum amount of property which must be subjected to a lien if the executor elects to be discharged from liability cannot be greater than the sum of the deferred amount of the unpaid estate tax liability plus the aggregate amount of interest that would be payable over the first five years of the period over which the tax liability is deferred.

## PAYING THE FEDERAL ESTATE TAX WITH BONDS

The Federal estate tax can be paid only in legal tender, checks, money orders, or "flower bonds." Other forms of payment, such as the conveyance of real property, cannot be used.

Flower bonds are specially designated United States Treasuries that must be accepted by the Government at par for payment of the Federal estate tax even though, because of the low interest rates on these bonds, they are selling well below par value. They are known as flower bonds because, in the picturesque words of one court, they are "ready to 'bloom' upon the owner's death." To be acceptable at face value, the bonds must have been included in the decedent's gross estate.

Although flower bonds have not been issued for some years, vast quantities still are available on the market. They are quoted in the financial press: The *New York Times,* for example, lists them under "Government and Agency Bonds." Here are bonds currently eligible:

**Series**

| | |
|---|---|
| 3¼s | 1978-83 |
| 3¼s | 1985 |
| 4¼s | 1975-85 |
| 3½s | 1990 |
| 4¼s | 1987-92 |
| 4s | 1988-93 |
| 4⅛s | 1989-94 |
| 3s | 1995 |
| 3½s | 1998 |

A person who realizes that his estate will have tax to pay might purchase such bonds when he is elderly or in very poor health. Or an arrangement could be set up in which a person or persons are designated by a power of appointment to purchase flower bonds for a person who has been disabled by a stroke, accident, or the like, and who is unable to act for himself. Sometimes the holder of such a power also has authority to sell other property in order to finance the acquisition. At times, a trust company or other holder of discretionary power over a trading account or other money may act upon its own initiative to purchase such bonds for a person whose estate seems likely to have need for the Treasuries very soon. The requirement for use of the bonds merely is that they be part of his estate when he dies, even if he did not himself purchase them and did not know that he had them.

If an estate includes flower bonds in excess of what is required to pay the estate tax on the return as filed, an executor should not be too hasty about selling the remainder of these low-interest bonds. Conceivably there will be an estate tax deficiency at a later date, and the bonds could have been used to pay this. The remainderman may well claim that he had been shortchanged by the executor because of the use of dollars instead of deep discount bonds to discourage estate indebtedness.

An executor who does not understand the use of flower bonds owned by the estate also may find himself in difficulties. He may sell the bonds because of their low interest return. Then the estate's assets are wasted when estate tax is paid in cash instead of the bonds. Inasmuch as the bonds could have been realized on at par in payment of the estate tax, they will be valued at par on the estate tax return.

## LIABILITY OF A BENEFICIARY

A person should understand that one or more of his beneficiaries may be obliged to pay any unpaid portion of a decedent's Federal estate tax up to the value of the property each receives. This understanding should prompt the person to name an executor who is able to discharge his responsibilities properly. The executor also must be furnished with sufficient information concerning assets and liabilities so that beneficiaries will not be called upon to pay taxes.

This *transferee liability* is imposed if the estate was insolvent at the time the property was transferred to a beneficiary, or if the estate was made insolvent by the transfer. For example, if the executor distributes all of the estate's assets to beneficiaries and to the remainderman, but there is further Federal tax liability as a result of an audit that has not taken place by the time of the distributions, the estate is technically insolvent; liabilities (the unknown tax claims) are in excess of assets (all or virtually all of which have gone to the beneficiaries).

This can work out very unfortunately for a beneficiary. He can be required to pay the entire unpaid tax of the estate, up to the value of the property he received. One of several beneficiaries may be obliged to pay the entire tax liability of the estate, *even though other parties also received property,* if his property amounted to the total of the unpaid taxes. The Internal Revenue Service does not even have to send a notice of tax deficiency to the estate first, nor prove that the estate was insolvent.

All the Service must do is show that a beneficiary received property of a certain value. He then becomes liable for unpaid taxes of the estate up to that amount. If the Service made a mistake, even a mathematical error, in computing the estate's tax, this will stand up as though it were correct *unless the beneficiary can prove that the Government was in error.* This can be an impossible undertaking, because no one (including a beneficiary) is entitled to see the tax return of another party, such as the estate.

This dangerous prospect is one of the many reasons why a reliable executor or executors should be named, with good substitute or successor executors in case anything happens to the fiduciary originally named. With that protection, a state court will not be able to appoint an administrator whose interest and qualifications may be very low.

# 21

## MAKING IT EASIER FOR YOUR EXECUTOR

A person may give little if any thought to the problems of his executor or executors. If the executor named is a relative or friend, the incidental chores of the designation may be regarded simply as an obligation of kinship or friendship. You would have done as much for him. In the case of a professional fiduciary, such as a trust company, payment will be made for the responsibilities and troubles involved.

But one's executor-to-be must be briefed as fully as possible on what he must know of the future decedent's affairs if he is to do the best possible job.

Here are the advantages of informing an executor of everything he needs to know when he steps into the decedent's shoes:

☐ Nothing is apt to be overlooked in the gathering of estate assets, such as numbered Swiss bank accounts or properties held in other names.

☐ The executor's time and endeavors can be shortened and made more efficient if he knows where everything is and what claims, contingent liabilities, and trouble spots have to be provided for.

☐ An individual who has been named as executor may refuse to serve when the decedent dies because the individual feels that he does not know enough to fulfill his duties. If the decedent's chosen executor declines to serve, a court, in the absence of a contingent executor's having been named, may fill the vacuum by selecting an administrator with highly questionable ability and interest.

## WHAT TO TELL THE EXECUTOR-TO-BE

An individual wants his executor to do as good a job as possible when the time comes. That means that the executor must be as fully informed of every detail of the decedent's financial affairs and property interests as the decedent himself. On the Federal estate tax return, the fiduciary will have to say that he has made "a diligent and careful search for property of every kind left by the decedent for whose estate this return is filed." The decedent-to-be can best make certain that his executor will know what he should and *must* know if he writes a full letter to his executor with all relevant information. This letter should be kept up to date by revisions or postscripts. In order to preserve privacy, the letter may be kept in a sealed envelope, for example, as an attachment to the will, to be delivered to the executor when the time comes for him to serve.

Here is a checklist of essential information that should be in the executor's possession as the generally unascertainable time when he undertakes his fiduciary responsibilities:

1. *Location of the will.* If what is readily available is a copy, who has the original? The original should not be kept in the decedent's safe deposit box in a bank, for customarily the bank will seal this box at the time of death, to be reopened only in the presence of a representative of the Internal Revenue Service or of the state tax commission. The will, meanwhile, is unavailable.

2. *The cemetery plot identification and ownership certificate.*

3. *Instructions as to guardianship of minor children should they be orphaned by the death of the decedent.*

4. *Location of all bank accounts, with identifying serial numbers.* Which are joint accounts, and which have withdrawal powers vested in signatories? Unless the executor acts promptly to prevent this, persons with withdrawal authorization could take money out of the decedent's accounts if these parties learn of the decedent's death before the bank does.

5. *Location of safe deposit boxes, with identifying numbers.* Who has a key or knows the combination? The executor should act quickly to prevent withdrawals from the box, perhaps by having the contents transferred in the presence of a credible witness to another box to which no one else has access. The executor should be given a description of anything in this box that actually belongs to a relative or to anyone else. The source of cash contained there should be identified.

6. *Names and account numbers of all credit cards.* The executor should have these accounts closed at once.

7. *Inventory of properties owned.* Investments, with serial numbers. Names of brokers and custody accounts. Identification of properties that are not in obvious places where the executor is likely to find them: e.g., items that had been lent to a friend or to a museum or library; items that had been sent elsewhere on consignment.

8. *Location of assets.* Where are the actual securities' certificates, mortgages, evidences of borrowing by other parties? Have any properties been pledged as collateral for loans?

9. *What life insurance is there?* Physical location of the policies.

Who is the owner of each policy? Does the decedent possess any significant interest in policies on his life that are owned by other persons, such as the right to change the name of a beneficiary? Names of insurance brokers.

10. *The location of Federal income and other tax return copies.* It is highly important that the location of the workpapers used in preparing these returns should be specified, including back-up material such as vouchers and paid bills. Identify the names of the decedent's accountants and lawyers. Is there any correspondence with the Internal Revenue Service or other taxing authorities? Are there any tax refund claims pending? Where were gift tax returns filed and under what names?

11. *The location of cancelled checks, as well as current and old checkbooks.*

12. *Vital statistics concerning the decedent, including documents.* A birth certificate can be useful in establishing entitlements to annuities and to Social Security payments. A marriage license or a divorce decree can be helpful in proof of the marital deduction.

13. *Records of loans that had been made by the decedent.* This includes notes or letters referring to the loans, such as understandings about what happens to indebtedness if the lender or the borrower dies. Is any property in the decedent's possession actually collateral for a loan he had made? Was there any cancellation or forgiveness of indebtedness?

14. *Proof that property had been given away so that it is now not a part of the decedent's gross estate.* Documentation to show that assets had been given away validly, such as the recording of realty transfers, acknowledgment by donees, receipts from charitable organizations. Keep copies of correspondence notifying stock transfer agents to record new owners for securities. Have duplicates of notification to insurance companies to effect transfer of policy ownership. Keep documentation on disclaimers.

15. *Have full identification of physicians the decedent had consulted.* It may be necessary to establish that the decedent had been of sound mind when he had prepared his will or when he had performed a certain act. A disappointed heir may try to break the will.

16. *Identify all previous employers, including the United States Armed Forces.* There may be employee death benefits or other rights that are payable, not only by the decedent's most recent employer, but by companies or organizations for which he had not worked for many years. Under the Employee Retirement Income Security Act of 1974, an individual may possess vested rights, including survivorship rights where a spouse once had worked for a particular corporation even though the present decedent had not.

17. *Indicate the location* of each of the following, if applicable, as it must be filed with the Federal estate tax return and the executor is certain to require it:

(a) Copies of all real estate appraisals, if applicable.

(b) Balance sheets and profit and loss statements of closely-held corporations or individually-owned businesses.

(c) Copies of trust instruments. This includes trusts the decedent ever had created or in which he had any rights as income or other beneficiary, contingent beneficiary, remainderman, etc. Identify the name and address of the trustee(s).

(d) Copies of partnership agreements.

(e) If the decedent at any time had possessed a power of appointment, have available a certified or verified copy of the instrument granting the power and any instruments by which the power was exercised or released.

(f) Copy of any employer benefit plan that covered the decedent. Corporations subject to the Employee Retirement Income Security Act are required to provide an explanation of such a plan to each covered employee, with a statement as to his contributions, if any.

(g) Copy of the will of any person from whom the decedent had inherited property in the past ten years. If that previous decedent had been subject to the Federal estate tax, there now is available a credit for tax on prior transfers. Only if he is provided with information about this can an executor make use of this credit.

(h) Cancelled checks or receipts for property tax payments.

*Proper filing of estate and gift tax returns lessens the chances of an audit by the Internal Revenue Service.*

18. *Where property had been owned jointly, identify the names, addresses, and interests of the co-owners.* Where a co-owner of property dies, the Internal Revenue Service predictably will include the full value of the property in his gross estate, unless the executor can prove the extent to which the property had been purchased with funds furnished by other persons. Often the executor cannot do this without help from the decedent-to-be. In the case of persons dying after December 31, 1981, however, where property is held by spouses in joint tenancy with a right of survivorship, the estate of the first spouse to die will include one-half of the value of the property regardless of which spouse furnished the consideration for acquisition of the property.

19. *Guaranties and endorsements that could create liability.*

20. *What is the best possible market for shares in a closely-held corporation, collections, or specialized type of property that one owns?* Often the best market is not one that an executor is likely to know about. The value of an estate can depend to some measure upon the special market to which the executor is directed.

One major coin dealer printed in its literature this letter from a customer: "I received your brochure on selling coins through your auctions ('How to Sell Your Coins for the Best Price'). I found it to be very informative. It answered many questions I had on the subject. In fact, I had my wife read it so she could be aware of what to do with my collection should anything happen to me. We placed it in our safe deposit box with my collection so it will always be in a safe place."

21. *Have data available so that claims against the estate can be resisted by the executor.* This includes evidence that a loan had been repaid or compromised, so that nothing is owed despite the original indebtedness; that jewelry or equipment in the possession of someone else actually is the decedent's; that an original document subsequently had been modified. Evidence of the sound business purpose of a transaction may be used to satisfy a demand by the Internal Revenue Service.

22. *Preserve any kind of documentation that would lessen the value of the decedent's property.* The executor or the estate lawyer might have no knowledge of this.

In one case, this involved exceptions from a new building code that covered old structures only for as long as the existing business was conducted there.

Stock may be valued at less than its fair market value per share if subject to sale at a lower value because of a buy-sell agreement with other shareholders or the issuing corporation, or if subject to an investment letter or other restrictions. Such restrictions may or may not be printed or rubber-stamped on the stock certificates. Without the notation, the executor may overvalue the asset.

23. *Prior favorable rulings from the Internal Revenue Service.* Are there any helpful rulings from the Service as to the tax effect of transactions, tax basis, or anything else that could minimize unfavorable tax treatment? Does a prior *closing agreement* prevent the I.R.S. from taking unwelcome action?

## EFFORTS TO EASE THE EXECUTOR'S BURDENS

An individual might seek in his will to relieve an inexperienced relative or friend who is to serve as executor of personal liability for any financial shortcomings as fiduciary. But the laws of some states prohibit such relief. For example, in New York, the law declares void any provision in a will that exonerates a person acting in a fiduciary capacity from liability for failure to exercise reasonable care, diligence, and prudence.

If a person is selected as executor and he consents to serve out of a sense of obligation, he should protect himself against the consequences of his own lack of experience. This can be done by taking out an errors and omissions insurance policy to indemnify himself against claims from services rendered to the estate. If he gets paid for his services as an executor, the insurance premium is regarded as an expense in connection with the production of income, and the premium can be deducted on his income tax return, provided it is reasonable in terms of the anticipated executor's fee.

The decedent-to-be may name his spouse or some other relative or friend who is without experience in estate administration and, seeking to be helpful, may leave letters of instruction or other guidelines. But such a procedure can lead to tax troubles.

> One person wrote a letter to the person who would be his executor, requesting that a certain stock he owned be held as long as possible because, he stated, "it has a higher potential value than the ordinary market quotations would indicate." An Internal Revenue Agent happened to see this letter and sought to have the shares valued for estate tax purposes at a far higher value than the current market quotations, which ordinarily are the basis of tax valuations. It was difficult to argue that the stock was worth no more than the market quotations, considering the written opinion of the decedent, who presumably had a greater knowledge about his company's prospects than anyone else possessed.

The problems of an inexperienced executor may be eased by the designation of an experienced co-executor, discounting the possibility of a clash of personalities.

# 22

# MAKING IT EASIER
# FOR YOUR BENEFICIARIES

A person's beneficence to his beneficiaries may consist of giving or leaving property to them. But estate planning can go far beyond that. His planning can ensure that as much of his wealth as possible will be available to the parties of his choice, with minimum shrinkage because of external factors or carelessness. His wealth can be transmitted in the form that is most appropriate for each recipient, taking into consideration each beneficiary's own income tax situation and interpersonal relationships.

A thoughtful person will provide his beneficiaries with far more than a mathematical distribution of property if he is aware of the pitfalls. He will make available the proper persons to deal with his problems, and the information and substantiation necessary to take care of the estate's distribution and tax affairs. He will provide a distribution plan that considers the beneficiaries as well as the estate and its executor, that is flexible enough to cope with unpredictable circumstances, and that takes into account an understanding of the psychology of his beneficiaries.

☐ Have one or more competent executors, with contingent or successor executors, named by you. Consider carefully whether you should name your spouse or another close relative. He or she may be too involved emotionally at the time of your death to do a good job and may not be tough enough to collect debts or loaned property from other friends or relatives, to the detriment of the estate and its beneficiaries.

☐ Provide the executor with all information that he will need concerning what you own and where it is. (See Chapter 21, "Making It Easier for Your Executor.")

☐ Do not let your records and their paper trail to assets die with you. Let your executor-to-be know where all your property is located, with any identifying serial numbers or other identification. For example, property may be kept out of state or even out of the country in order to avoid attachment by creditors or a disenchanted spouse.

☐ Review your estate plan regularly to see that no one is overlooked or overprovided for. Take into account new additions to the family, marriages, divorces, deaths.

☐ Check to see whether your dispositions are stated in clear, unambiguous language so that there can be no uncertainty as to who is going to get what, and when.

☐ Make provision for contingencies, so that property will be distributed according to your alternative wishes in case a beneficiary dies before you do or if he renounces an inheritance.

☐ Give or leave property to a beneficiary in the form in which he best can handle it. This may mean outright transfers. But depending upon each beneficiary's age, experience, financial sophistication, and personal inclinations, consider the use of trusts, custodianships, and other forms of management, as well as income interests without the problems of property ownership or management.

☐ Your beneficiaries may lack your financial sophistication and your willingness to assume risks that could involve controversies with the Internal Revenue Service as well as litigation. Tax shelters may be an undesirable form of property to transfer to beneficiaries.

☐ Transfer of undivided fractional interests in property can lead to difficulties where the beneficiaries have different ideas as to the management or selling price of the property. Unified control of operations or disposition details can be effected through a mechanism such as transfer of the property to a corporation, varying numbers of shares of which go to each beneficiary. Decisions then can be made by majority vote or by an experienced executive. A voting trust can assure that no one person sells his interest to the detriment of the other beneficiaries where the whole is worth more than the sum of its parts.

☐ Avoid transmittal of property in joint ownership where one of the beneficiaries is likely to be completely dominated by another co-owner.

☐ Take steps to see that the wealth you desire to have pass to your beneficiaries is not lost to them because of what might happen to you. Protect your estate—and thus your beneficiaries—through insurance on yourself, including major medical, malpractice, liability.

☐ Make certain that premiums on your life insurance are kept up, even during a long illness, so that your beneficiaries are not deprived of the benefits.

☐ If specifically bequeathed property is disposed of or materially changed during the decedent's lifetime, the named beneficiary has nothing to receive. For example, an automobile may have been sold, or driven to the point of worthlessness, or destroyed at the moment of the decedent's death. Or jewelry may have been stolen. Take out property insurance; provide that the named beneficiary is to get the cash equivalent of any property that cannot be transmitted to him.

☐ Prevent having your estate impaired unnecessarily by Internal Revenue Service deficiencies assessed against your Federal income tax returns for past years. Perhaps you really can explain everything that was done satisfactorily. But unless well-documented and clear workpapers can be shown and explained to the I.R.S. by a knowledgeable person familiar with the facts, there are apt to be disallowances because of lack of substantiation. Remember that it is standard operating procedure for the Service to examine the Federal income tax returns of a decedent for the three years prior to his death. *Can your returns be explained satisfactorily by someone else when you are not available?*

☐ Seek to protect your beneficiaries by safeguarding them from *transferee liability*. The liability occurs when an estate distributes assets to beneficiaries without leaving enough to pay Federal taxes. If the executor suspects that there will be additional tax liability, he should not distribute assets without leaving enough to pay the liability. Where there is transferee liability, each beneficiary can be required to pay it up to the value of the property that he has received. Unfortunately, the Internal Revenue Service does not have to collect this tax on a *pro rata* basis from all beneficiaries. The decedent's most important and favorite beneficiaries, such as his wife or daughter, may have to pay out all or a substantial portion of what she had received, without any contribution by less-favored persons. Mitigate this risk by keeping good tax records so as to avoid the imposition of additional taxes and by having an executor who realizes the danger of making distributions to beneficiaries when there is reason to believe there may be additional taxes owing. "Reason to believe" is not confined to situations where the I.R.S. formally had stated that there would be additional tax liability.

☐ There may be Social Security benefits due you, or survivor benefits of some kind to which other parties are entitled. Beneficiaries will be short-changed if the amount of earnings that have been credited to your account is too low because of computer or other error. Check the balance regularly by sending Form SSA-7004 PC to the Social Security Administration, P.O. Box 57, Baltimore, Maryland 21203. You can obtain this card from the nearest office of the U.S. Department of Health and Human Services.

☐ Act to ensure that money in inactive bank accounts will be available for your beneficiaries. In many states, a bank account that has been dormant for a specified period will go to the state by *escheat*. Accordingly, all bank accounts should be churned regularly.

☐ Obtain periodically from each charitable organization to which you intend leaving a bequest an affirmative statement that the organization is *not* practicing discrimination. Your estate will be reduced by the loss of a charitable bequest, which will occur where there is discrimination.

☐ Make plans so that your estate will have sufficient liquidity at the generally unpredictable time of your death so that the executor will not have to jettison assets at the wrong time in order to raise cash for taxes or for compelling beneficiary needs. Life insurance payable to the estate would provide this cash. The proceeds would be includible in gross estate and would be taxable if the estate is sufficiently large. But even that usually would be better than sale of estate assets at sacrifice prices, to the detriment of beneficiaries.

☐ Have your will and other documents of property disposition checked by a lawyer *familiar with the laws of the state where you now live.* Even for Federal tax purposes, varying state laws determine such matters as the ownership of property. Where you move to a different state, have local counsel check whether your original plans and dispositions still are effective. When a person, during the course of his lifetime, has lived in several states because of the nature of his employment, health, or personal preferences, each of these states may claim death taxes simultaneously on the ground that under the law of its state, the decedent still was a resident subject to tax. Check with local counsel what you can do to avoid the deterioration of your estate, to the detriment of your beneficiaries.

> In one case, virtually none of the estate of a multimillionaire went to his beneficiaries because each of two states in which he had a home successfully argued in the United States Supreme Court that he was a resident, subject to state death taxes when he died.

Local counsel may recommend such steps as discontinuance of property ownership, bank and brokerage accounts, church affiliation, and medical visits to a state that person no longer considers to be his home. The validity of your will may depend upon the law of the state where you live at the time of your death. If the document does not have the minimum number of witnesses required by state law, for example, the will is not valid. Then the testamentary dispositions made by you will not be effective, and your property may not go to the beneficiaries selected by you but to your next of kin according to the state's law.

☐ Make provision in your will for how your property will be transmitted should you and your spouse die in a common disaster where it is not possible to establish the sequence of deaths. A simultaneous death clause can provide how jointly owned property, insurance proceeds, and other assets will go to beneficiaries without the need for acrimony or litigation.

☐ Where you have made lifetime gifts of property, each beneficiary's basis for determining gain or loss for Federal income tax purposes when ultimately he sells the property is the difference between realization and tax cost. His tax cost is what the donor had paid for the property. If the donor fails to make available to the donee the figures for the cost of the property, the donee's basis when he sells the assets may be regarded as *zero* by the Internal Revenue Service. The consequence is that the full price realized is taxable, without offset for basis. In order to protect the beneficiary from this, arrange to let him know what you had paid for the property. But you should also ask yourself the question: Is it more important to you to keep the price confidential or to let the beneficiary save some income taxes?

☐ Consideration of a beneficiary's Federal income tax consequences when he sells property acquired from you may determine how the property should be transferred to him. Inasmuch as the beneficiary's basis will be the donor's cost in the case of a gift, while fair market value at the time of death (or six months later if the executor elects the alternate valuation date) is the basis for inherited property, the beneficiary generally will fare better in inflationary times if he can use the higher basis at time of death.

☐ Unless the decedent directs otherwise in his will, if any part of the gross estate on which tax has been paid consists of the proceeds of life insurance policies on the life of the decedent receivable by a beneficiary other than the executor, the executor will be entitled to recover from that beneficiary such portion of the total tax paid as the proceeds of these policies bear to the taxable estate. If there is more than one beneficiary, the executor will be entitled to recover from these beneficiaries in the same ratio. In the case of such proceeds receivable by the decedent's surviving spouse for which a marital deduction is allowed, this provision does not apply to those proceeds except as to the amount in excess of the marital deductions allowed.

☐ There is a similar rule if any part of the gross estate on which the tax has been paid consists of property over which the decedent had a power of appointment. Unless the decedent directs otherwise in his will, the executor will be entitled to recover from the person receiving such property by reason of his expertise, nonexercise, or release of a power of appointment that portion of the total tax paid as the value of the property bears to the taxable estate. There are rules comparable to those of the preceding paragraph in the case of plural recipients and the marital deduction.

☐ In inflationary times, a person's preferred beneficiaries may lose out when bequests are made in the customary form of *dollar amounts*. When the decedent dies, the estate may be worth far more than he had thought it would be, so that bequests to the most favored beneficiaries could be too small while the remainderman would receive more than the decedent had anticipated. This could be avoided by bequeathing *percentages* of the estate rather than dollar amounts. What would go to the favored beneficiaries then would self-adjust to the changing size of any estate.

☐ Beneficiaries are apt to be injured financially if their expectancies are imperilled by litigation, as where a disappointed heir seeks to have a will declared invalid on the ground that the testator had not been of sound mind when he had signed the document, or had been under unreasonable influence at the time, or some such reason. Or the beneficiaries may sacrifice some part of what the will had provided for them in order to placate the dissident by a reallocation of distributions. To forestall this, an individual may have a provision in his will that if any beneficiary challenges the testament, that beneficiary's share is to be forfeited.

# 23

## *POST MORTEM* ESTATE PLANNING

Estate planning most frequently is thought of as planning to provide for what is to happen after a person's death, and includes property dispositions, the creation of trusts, the forgiveness of indebtedness. As discussed in this book, estate planning also includes affirmative steps to reduce *present* income taxes through methods such as transferring income-producing properties to a trust with a life of more than ten years so that the property *and* its income will return to the transferor after he has retired or has become less productive and will be in a lower tax bracket.

Far less frequently considered as part of estate planning are procedures by which a decedent-to-be makes plans for the distributions of property and income *after* his death in the light of circumstances and figures unknown to him when he dies. Additionally, it is possible for beneficiaries to modify a decedent's estate plan after his death, conceivably to reflect what he would have done had he been here to adjust his planning in response to later developments.

## HOW A DECEDENT CAN APPORTION HIS PROPERTY FROM THE GRAVE

An individual has worked, one way or another, for his wealth, and he should be the one to decide how it is to be distributed. That is what estate planning is all about. But at the moment of his death, all of the factors that should shape his decision may not be known. What will be the needs, objectives, and "fitness" of each beneficiary? What will be the health and earning power of each? What other income or assets does each beneficiary have? How is each one measuring up to the ideals and prejudices of the decedent-to-be? What are the Dow Jones averages at the time when distributions or allocations are to be made?

Inasmuch as the individual is not likely to know the answers to these and to other questions when he formulates his estate plan, he would like to be in position to make distributions and allocations from the grave in the light of circumstances then prevailing. With careful plans, he will be able to do this to a considerable extent. In this chapter we shall discuss the various alternatives available to the decedent-to-be.

## POWERS OF APPOINTMENT

If the proper person can be found, the bestowal of a power of appointment can be a good solution to the problem. See Chapter 12, "Powers of Appointment and Powers of Attorney."

Under a power of appointment, an individual places his property, or in most instances a designated portion of it, subject to the disposition of another person. That person must be a trusted individual who knows very well what the creator of the power would have done with his property or its income, had he been alive. Options such as financing a son's venture into a new enterprise, a daughter's purchase of a house, a brother's reimbursement for major medical expenses, the contribution of money to a certain hospital's building fund, and the like will be selected in the manner that he believes the decedent would have chosen were he alive. For this purpose, the person would take into account the decedent's point of view; his hopes, ambitions, and dislikes; the life style and character of each beneficiary or potential beneficiary; the order of priorities the decedent probably would have selected. If the individual given the power of appointment is reliable, understanding of the decedent's thinking and sympathetic to it, and endowed with the powers and means to implement this thinking, the decedent effectively is having his objectives carried out and modified according to changing circumstances, even though he is now in the grave.

## DISCRETIONARY TRUSTS

An individual may have his objectives carried out after his death through the mechanism of a trust, where the trustee has sufficient guidelines and discretionary power to use principal and/or income in the light of ever-changing circumstances. (See Chapter 7, "The Trust: The Most Versatile

Tool of All.'') If the fiduciary is a trust company, it is unlikely that the personal quirks and foibles of the decedent and of his beneficiary will be taken into account to the same degree as where a close relative or friend, long familiar with the decedent's thinking, makes the decisions. But a greater amount of permanency and, in most instances, of professionalism will be achieved.

Provision may be made in the implementing instrument that a trust for the benefit of a life tenant will be terminated in favor of the remainderman, or that income will be diverted to others, if the life tenant performs in a manner contrary to the grantor's specifications. For example, if the decedent's spouse remarries; if a son does not remain with the family business; if a daughter marries outside of her religion.

A trust may be used to provide its income to a named party for the remainder of her life, principal then passing to designated persons or organizations. But the trustee may be empowered to use principal for the life tenant's benefit in the case of extraordinary medical expenses, failure of her investments, or inability to maintain her present standard of living. Here the grantor has made provision for the diversion of funds from the remainderman to the life tenant in accordance with circumstances not in existence at the time of the grantor's death. He is controlling the channeling of funds from the grave to reflect circumstances that have changed since his death.

In states where it is not prohibited, a person may use a spendthrift trust. Here the trustee will parcel out money in such a manner that the beneficiary's creditors (other than the Internal Revenue Service) will be unable to erode the beneficiary's inheritance. The trust instrument may provide the trustee with discretion as to how much to make available to the beneficiary each year and with authority to lift the restrictions if the beneficiary no longer appears to be in need of this protection.

## LONG-TERM TRUSTS

An individual may control the use of his wealth from the grave in substantial measure through the mechanism of a long-term trust. (See Chapter 7.) A trust for the benefit of one's children usually is thought of as an arrangement that will terminate when the children, or the youngest child, reach age twenty-one or thereabouts. A person who wants principal or income of more than a stated amount to be protected against his children's immaturity, poor judgment, inexperience, or creditors until sufficient "maturity" develops may provide for continuance of the trust arrangement until each "child" is, say, age fifty-five.

## KEEPING YOUR BUSINESS IN BUSINESS

A person may be concerned that, when he dies, his executor will sell or liquidate the family business in order to relieve himself of the problems of administration. The person can ensure that the executor's reluctance to assume management will not result in having his family lose the business by providing that a trust will take over the business when he dies, the trustees named being experienced executives with a mandate to continue operations of the enterprise, at least for a stipulated period. Here the decedent-to-be has provided for continuance of the business despite the executor's preferences, and even the management of the venture after his death has been arranged by the decedent. From the grave, he is permitting the business to be carried on until, for example, his children will be able to take over the management. (See Chapter 7 and Chapter 16, "Problems When a Major Stockholder Dies.")

## CHARITABLE BEQUESTS THAT COULD PROVIDE FOR ONE'S OWN FAMILY

A testamentary trust may be set up to provide funds for the decedent's children to go to college or to graduate school, even though, without such an arrangement, his ambitions in this direction might have been frustrated because the executor considered that other priorities were higher.

An individual wishes to provide the opportunity for a college or vocational school education for any of his relatives who otherwise would be unable to afford it. His wish may be effectuated after he dies, even though at the time of his death he does not know who the parties to be benefitted may be; perhaps they have not been born. His desire may be effectuated by setting up an educational trust for the benefit of persons who meet certain standards such as the size of income of the immediate family, or small earning power, with preference to be given to members of the grantor's family who qualify. See Chapter 18, "Charitable Distributions and Bequests." A similar arrangement can be made where the educational trust provides for preference to be given to employees of the decedent's corporation, or children of employees, who qualify. Through an instrumentality he had created, children will be given the opportunity for higher education after he dies. (See Chapter 7.)

## PROVISIONS FOR CONTINGENCIES

After one's death, his estate plan to make distributions to persons of his own choice can be frustrated all too frequently by something that happens when he no longer can make other dispositions. This problem, which can take any of several forms, may be avoided by planning for contingencies that can occur.

For example, one's carefully selected executor may die before his work is done, or he may decline to serve, or he may become disqualified. Unless a contingent or successor executor has been named in the will, the missing executor will be superseded by a court-named administrator not of his own choosing. An individual virtually can be assured of having his own nominee serve as executor if there is provision in the will for a second, third, etc., person, who automatically will become successor executor if the first choice is not able to serve or to continue serving. The decedent is able to name the successor from the grave if, in fact, he already had made provision for this contingency.

Similar provision can be made in the case of one or more trustees. One can name successor trustees of his own choice to replace anyone who dies or resigns. Or he can make provisions concerning how the remaining trustees can fill a vacancy themselves.

Contingent persons also should be specified as beneficiaries, including life tenants and remaindermen. If the person or persons who had been named by the decedent dies, makes a disclaimer, or becomes incompetent, in effect, the decedent from his grave can cause another party of his choice to be named, provided that this had been recognized as a possibility during the formulation of the estate plan. One's own selection(s) still will receive the specified property or income of the estate, even if his first choice does not.

If one or more beneficiaries die before receiving the specified entitlement, there can be triggered a contingency arrangement in the will that his children or other surviving beneficiaries will divide what is available because of this event.

## SIMULTANEOUS DEATHS OF SPOUSES

Where a person provides a substantial sum for his surviving spouse, but there is no surviving spouse because of simultaneous deaths or of her dying at an earlier time, the amount that otherwise would have gone to her may be designated instead to go to other chosen or ascertainable parties.

## JOINT OR MUTUAL WILLS

If a person leaves all or a substantial part of his estate to his spouse should she survive him, he has no assurance that, upon her ultimate death, any part of his property that remains will go to his own relatives and friends. She is apt to have the same misgivings about property she leaves to her husband. (See Chapter 6, "The Tools of Estate Planning.")

In a joint will, each spouse leaves property to the other, with a prearranged allocation schedule for the division of any assets that remain after the death of the second spouse. The schedule includes relatives or other nominees of *each* spouse. So each spouse has arranged how property remaining after the death of the second spouse is to be apportioned. These distributions may be made long after a person's death in accordance with plans he had made while alive.

Mutual wills are testaments prepared by each spouse at the same time, with comparable distribution or apportionment schedules to take effect at the death of the second spouse.

## INSURANCE SETTLEMENT OPTIONS

An individual may carry insurance on his life for the benefit of designated persons. He does not know, however, the form in which the pay-out of the proceeds will be most appropriate for his beneficiary or beneficiaries. His policy can provide that appropriate settlement options made available by the insurance company are to be exercised by the beneficiaries when the policy is matured by his death. Alternatively, the policy may be payable to an insurance trust that he had set up, with the trustee to have the authority to select the settlement option that appeared most beneficial at that time. If the trustee is familiar with what the decedent would have wanted, and is responsive to those desires, the result amounts to the decedent's making a plan after his death.

## "SUGGESTIONS" TO EXECUTOR-TO-BE

An individual may write a letter to the person who will serve as his executor, including a request that certain assets not be disposed of because their value increment possibility is far greater than other people have reason to believe. If the executor sees fit to heed this advice, the decedent has been able to prevent disposition of these assets prematurely on the basis of something that still has to happen or to be understood. He may be able to ensure that his assets will be sold for the maximum possible price by informing his executor of the best market as learned from vast experience, or of someone who had expressed deep interest in buying these properties if ever they should be offered for sale. In effect, the decedent is supervising the sale of the assets from the grave. See Chapter 21, "Making It Easier for Your Executor," for further discussion.

## PERCENTAGE BEQUESTS

An individual is likely to be quite unaware of what the amount of his wealth will be on that unknown date of his death. A great risk is that because of inflation, his specific bequests will be too small in terms of the dollar values that will prevail when he dies, so that his most favored beneficiaries will receive too little, while the remainderman, who will receive whatever is left, will get more than he had intended.

Bequests in terms of specified percentages of the estate rather than specified dollar amounts will enable the favored beneficiaries to retain their status as such.

## REWRITING OF DECEDENT'S ESTATE PLAN BY HIS BENEFICIARIES

*Post mortem* planning of a decedent's estate may be arranged by his beneficiaries. For example, an individual's will may leave his assets in equal portions to his widow, his daughter, and his son. The children are concerned lest their mother lack sufficient wealth to meet her needs of her desired standard of living. So the children renounce their inheritances, which go to their mother as next of kin. That is not what the decedent had intended; at least, it was not what he had arranged to take place. But the beneficiaries are better satisfied by this arrangement, and perhaps the decedent would have been more pleased by this arrangement, had he known about it.

Or the decedent's widow, to whom all or a substantial part of his estate had been left, may not want the responsibilities and nuisance of additional wealth when she already has enough. She may be conscious of the fact that she is quite elderly or in very poor health. So she renounces the inheritance, which goes to her children.

If there is a valid disclaimer, the property will not be includible in the estate of the party who renounces the inheritance. Nor will he be subjected to gift tax because he "let" other persons get the property, for it never was his to give away. On the other hand, if a person does not receive property by inheritance but by action of law, he cannot refuse to accept it because the law says that it is his. This occurs where a person dies without a will that is valid under state law, and his property goes to his next of kin under the state's intestacy law.

A transfer of a person's entire interest in property to the person or persons who otherwise would have received the property is treated as a valid disclaimer for Federal estate and gift tax purposes, provided the transfer is made within the permissible time and the person making the disclaimer has not accepted any of the interest being disclaimed or any of its benefits.

> An individual who had been given a general power of appointment by his wife's will announced that he was using property subject to this power only for the purpose of paying estate and other death taxes on behalf of his wife. He could not disclaim the property subject to the power because this usage of property amounted to an acceptance prior to his disclaimer.

The disclaimer must be made in writing within nine months of the transfer creating the interest (or within nine months of the date the person making the disclaimer attains age twenty-one). A transfer will not be considered the necessary transfer of one's entire interest if some of the property will return to him or if he retains any control over it.

In the case of disclaimers after December 31, 1981, there no longer is a need that for Federal tax purposes, the disclaimer meet requirements of any state law.

Generally, an executor is empowered to disclaim on behalf of a decedent.

# INDEX